Mastering JavaScript

A Complete Programming Guide Including jQuery, AJAX, Web Design, Scripting, and Mobile Application Development

Published by Newstone Publishing

978-1-989726-02-0 (Paperback)

Table of Contents

Introduction

Thank you for downloading this guide. My aim is to teach you the JavaScript programming language and what you can do with it. JavaScript is a fundamental language in web design, along with jQuery and AJAX. This guide aims to teach you the language and responsive web design.

We start by meeting the JavaScript language head-on. This will take up about half of the book as we go through the fundamentals of the language with full coding examples to help you understand what it's all about. This includes practical examples for you to follow and a quick look at JSON and client-side APIs. Next, we will look at jQuery and AJAX and how they work together. You'll see exactly what they can do by using many examples.

In the third part of the guide, a walkthrough of responsive web design using jQuery and AJAX will be provided and you will learn how to build a website that works seamlessly on all platforms with a minimum of fuss – the whole idea behind responsive web design – before we move on to JavaScript scripting and User Experience, or UX as it is fondly known.

This in-depth guide is designed for beginners and for those who want to brush up on their skills. Take your time with it and make sure you understand each section before you move on to the next one.

Ready to master JavaScript? Let's dive in.

Part 1: Mastering JavaScript

What is JavaScript?

JavaScript is an object-oriented cross-platform scripting language that is commonly used for making a webpage interactive, with animations, popup menus, clickable buttons, and so on. There are other versions of the language, such as Node.js, which is a server-side version that gives you the tools to add even more functionality to a website rather than just downloading a few files, like those providing real-time collaboration between two or more computers. Within a host environment, such as a web browser, you can use JavaScript to connect to environment objects to give you more control over them.

In JavaScript, you will find a standard library containing objects like Date, Array, Math, etc., along with a core set of elements for the language, like control structures, operators, statements, etc. You can extend JavaScript for multiple purposes by adding extra objects, for example:

- Client-side JS – this will provide objects to help you control the browser and its DOM or Document Object Model. For example, some of the client-side extensions can be used to provide an application with the ability to add elements to an HTML form, and others will provide a response to user events – input on a form, mouse clicks, page navigation, and so on.

- Server-Side JS – this will supply certain objects that are relevant to JavaScript being run on a server. For example, some of these extensions will help communication between an application and a database, ensure continuity when information is moving between application invocations, and carry out manipulation of files on the server.

What all this means is when you use JavaScript in a browser, it can change how a webpage looks.

JavaScript vs. Java

While JavaScript is similar to Java in some ways, there are some fundamental differences between them. In terms of language, JavaScript is similar to Java but it doesn't have the strong type checking and the static typing Java has. It also follows much of the same syntax for expressions, the naming conventions, and fundamental constructs for control flow; the main reason why the name was changed to JavaScript from LiveScript.

Where Java has a compile-time system of using declarations to build classes, JavaScript has a runtime system that is based on fewer data types that represent string values, Boolean values, and numeric values. The JavaScript object model is prototype-based rather than class-based, which provides for a system of dynamic inheritance – what can and can't be inherited is different for each individual object. JavaScript also supports functions that have or need special requirements in terms of the declaration, and functions may also object properties and can be executed as loose-typed methods.

In contrast to Java, JavaScript is a free-form type of language, which means there is no need for all methods, variables, and classes to be declared; you don't need to worry whether the methods are protected, private or public, and there is no need for interfaces to be implemented. On top of that, there is no need for explicit typing of parameters, variables, and return types for functions.

Java is a programming language based on classes and is designed primarily for type safety and fast execution. An example of type safety is a Java integer could not be cast to an object reference, nor could it corrupt any byte codes to access the private memory. In this kind of class-based model, the programs contain only classes and related methods. The one thing that makes Java far more complex than JavaScript is that its inheritance rules and strong typing require object hierarchies that are tightly coupled.

By contrast, JavaScript is descended from several dynamically typed languages including dBase and HyperTalk. These languages provide a much wider audience with programming tools because they are significantly easier in syntax, contain built-in functionality that is specialized and has few requirements for creating objects.

The ECMAScript Specification

JavaScript was standardized to deliver an international programming language that is based on JS at ECMA International. This is the European Computer Manufacturers Association and is designed to ensure that information and communication systems are standardized. This new version of JavaScript was called ECMAScript and it works the same way in every application that includes support for the standard. This open language can be used by any company to develop its own JavaScript implementation and it can be found fully documented in the specification titled ECMA-262.

This standard has also been fully approved by the International Organization for Standardization, otherwise known as ISO-16262. The specification does not go into details of the DOM, which is standardized by W3C (World Wide Web Consortium) and/or WHATWG, otherwise called the Web Hypertext Application Technology Working Group. The DOM is used to specify how HTML objects are exposed in a script.

Getting Started

All you really need to get started with JavaScript is an up-to-date modern web browser. We'll be using Firefox and will go over some JS features that can only be found in Mozilla Firefox. There are two tools in particular included in Firefox that are very useful for getting to grips with JavaScript:

Web Console

The Web Console is very useful as it can show current information about a web page that is loaded and also has a command line for the execution of JS expressions on the web page.

Opening the console is easy. On Windows or Linux systems, just press CTRL+SHIFT+I and on Mac, press CMD+OPTION+K and then choose the Tools menu in Firefox. Click on Developer Menu, and then on the Web Console that is at the bottom of the Firefox window. Along the bottom of the Console, you will see the command line where you input the JS commands and the output shows in the panel above.

The way the console works is that the last expression entered is the one returned. To keep things simple, whenever anything is input into the console, it is surrounded by console.log and around eval, like this:

function greetMe(yourName) {

* alert('Hello ' + yourName);*

}

greetMe("Your name");

console.log(eval('4 + 4'));

Scratchpad

While the Console is great when you want to execute one line of JavaScript code; it gets insipid for several lines. You also cannot save any of your code samples in the Console so the best option is Scratchpad.

To open Scratchpad, follow the steps above and when you click on Developer menu, click on Scratchpad. A new window will open, which is actually an editor. In this you can write code and execute it in the Firefox browser, you can also save and load scripts to and from disk.

Our First Program

The easiest way to get started is to write the Hello World script; open Scratchpad and input the following code:

```
(function(){

  "use strict";

  /* Start of the code */

  function greetMe(yourName) {

    alert('Hello ' + yourName);

  }


  greetMe('World');

  /* End of the code */

})();
```

Highlight the code and press CTRL+R and you will see it all in your browser.

Throughout this code, we will look at the syntax and features of the JavaScript language giving you the tools you need to write more complex applications. For now, it is important that you remember to add (function(){"use strict"; at the start of every new code and })() at the end. You will understand what these mean shortly; for now, consider they do the following:

- Improve the performance significantly
- Prevent the dumb explanations that tend to trip beginners in JavaScript
- Stop the snippet of code executed inside the console from merging, i.e. something created in one execution gets used for a different one.

The rest of this section will examine the basic grammar, data types, variable declarations, and literals in JavaScript.

The Basics

Much of the syntax in JavaScript comes from Java but is also, in a small way, influenced by Python, Perl, and Awk programming languages.

The first thing to realize is that the JavaScript language is case sensitive and it makes use of a character set called Unicode. For example, a word like *First* may be used as the name of a variable, like this:

JavaScript is **case-sensitive** and uses the **Unicode** character set. For example, the word "*First*" (which means "early" in German) could be used as a variable name.

var First = "foobar";

However, if you called it "*first*" instead, it would not be the same. Because one starts with an uppercase letter and the other with a lowercase letter, they would be two different variables.

A statement is a list of JavaScript instructions with each one being separated by a semicolon. The exception to this is when you have a single statement on one line. This doesn't need a semicolon, but if you have multiple statements on the line, they do. However, best practice dictates that a statement is followed by a semicolon even if it isn't really needed. This will cut down on the risk of bugs in the code.

JavaScript source text is always read from left to right and is then converted to an input element sequence consisting of:

- **Tokens**
- **Control characters**
- **Line terminators**
- **Comments**
- **Whitespace**

Or a combination thereof. Tabs, spaces, and newlines characters come under the heading of whitespace.

Reserved Keywords

Like all programming languages, JavaScript has a set of reserved keywords; these cannot be used in any other way, especially not in naming identifiers or variables. The reserved words are:

- **abstract**
- **boolean**
- **break**
- **byte**

- case
- catch
- char
- class
- const
- continue
- debugger
- default
- do
- else
- enum
- export
- extends
- false
- final
- finally
- float
- for
- function
- goto
- if
- implements
- import
- in
- instanceof
- int
- interface
- let

- long
- native
- new
- null
- package
- private
- protected
- public
- return
- short
- super
- switch
- synchronized
- this
- throws
- transient
- true
- try
- typeof
- var
- void
- volatile
- while
- with

Comments

Comments in your code are purely to tell anyone who looks at your code what is happening. Provided you do them correctly, they will not be read and will not be considered part of the code. The syntax used is much the same as it is in most programming languages:

// this is a single-line comment, denoted by two forward slashes

/* this is much longer,

 * a multi-line comment starting with a forward slash and asterisk and end with an
asterisk and a backslash

 */

/* However, it is not possible for: /* comments to be nested */ SyntaxError */

Declarations

In the JavaScript language, there are three different declaration types:

- *var* - used to declare variables with the option of initializing the variable to a value

- *let* – used for declaring local values with a block scope and the option of initializing the variable to a value

- *const* – used to declare read-only named constants with block scope.

Variables

Variables are used to provide values with names. The variable names are also called identifiers and must follow specific naming conventions:

The name must begin with a letter, an underscore (_) or a $ (dollar sign).

Any subsequent characters may also be digits from 0 to 9.

The characters will include both uppercase (A to Z) and lowercase (a to z) letters.

Some examples include:

- Number_clock

- temp88

- $name

- _name

Variable Declaration

Variables can be declared in two ways:

- Using the *var* keyword. An example would be var x = 25. You can use this syntax to declare both local variables and global variables depending on the context of the execution.

- Using the *let* or *const* keyword. An example would be let y = 9. You can use this syntax to declare local variables that are block-scoped.

You can also assign a variable with a value, as in x = 25. This format will create a global variable that is undeclared and it will also generate a strict warning. An undeclared variable can lead to strange behavior and, as such, you are not encouraged to use them.

Variable Evaluation

If you declare a variable using either the *let* or *var* statements but don't assign a value to it, it will have a value of 'undefined'. If you try accessing an undeclared variable you will see the ReferenceError exception:

var a;

console.log('The value of a is ' + a); // The value of a is undefined

console.log('The value of b is ' + b); // The value of b is undefined

var b;

// (Until you have read the section on Variable Hoisting this might be confusing)

console.log('The value of c is ' + c); // An Uncaught ReferenceError: c is not defined

let x;

console.log('The value of x is ' + x); // The value of x is undefined

console.log('The value of y is ' + y); // An Uncaught ReferenceError: y is not defined

let y;

'Undefined' may also be used to see whether a value has been assigned to a variable. In the next example, we have not assigned any value to the variable called input and, as a result, the "*if*" statement will be true.

var input;

if (input === undefined) {

  doThis();

} else {

  doThat();

}

When you use an undefined value in a Boolean context, it will behave as false. For example, the next code will execute a function called myFunction because the element called myArray is undefined:

```
var myArray = [];

if (!myArray[0]) myFunction();
```

However, when it gets used in a numeric context, the value will convert to a NaN:

```
var a;

a + 2;  // Evaluates to NaN
```

When a null variable is calculated, in a numeric context the null value will behave as 0 and, in a Boolean context, as false. See the next example:

```
var n = null;

console.log(n * 34); // Will log 0 to the console
```

Variable Scope

When a variable is declared outside of a function, it is called a global variable. This is because the variable is available to all code in the current code document. If it is declared inside a function, it is called a local variable because it is only available from within the function.

Before ECMAScript 2015, JavaScript did not have block statement scope. Instead, a variable declared inside a block would be local to the specific function that the block is enclosed in. In the following example, the log will be 6 because x has a scope which is the global context or, if this code is part of a function, the scope will be the function; the scope will NOT be the "*if*" statement block:

```
if (true) {

  var x = 6;

}

console.log(x);  // x is 6
```

If you were to use the *let* declaration that ECMAScript 2015 introduced, things would be different:

```
if (true) {
```

```
    let y = 6;

}

console.log(y);  // ReferenceError: y is not defined
```

Variable Hoisting

There is something else unusual about the JavaScript variables; a variable that you declare later may be referenced without an exception being thrown. This is called variable hoisting and it means that, in a way, the variables are lifted or hoisted to the top of the statement or function. However, a hoisted variable will return an 'undefined' value, even if you declare the variable and initialize it after you refer to it, it will still return the 'undefined' value:

```
/**
 * First example
 */
console.log(x === undefined); // true

var x = 4;


/**
 * Second example
 */
// a value of undefined is returned
var myvar = 'my value';


(function() {
  console.log(myvar); // undefined
  var myvar = 'local value';
})();
```

These two examples are interpreted exactly the same as:

```
/**
 * First example
 */
var x;
console.log(x === undefined); // true
x = 4;


/**
 * Second example
 */
var myvar = 'my value';

(function() {
  var myvar;
  console.log(myvar); // undefined
  myvar = 'local value';
})();
```

Hoisting dictates that all the *var* statements inside a function must be placed near the top of the function to increase code clarity.

In ECMAScript 2015, the *let* (*const*) declaration doesn't hoist variables to the top. If you reference any variable inside a block before the variable is declared, you will get a Reference Error. This is because the variable is inside what is called a "temporal dead zone" from when the block starts to when the variable declaration has been processed:

```
console.log(x); // ReferenceError
let x = 4;
```

Function Hoisting

With a function, it will only be the declaration that is hoisted, not the actual function expression.

/ Function declaration */*

foo(); // "bar"

function foo() {

* console.log('bar');*

}

/ Function expression */*

baz(); // TypeError: baz isn't a function

var baz = function() {

* console.log('bar2');*

};

Global Variables

A global variable is a property of a global object. In a web page, a global object is a window so the syntax, window.variable is used to set global variables and access them. As a result, when you declare a global variable in one frame or window, you can access it from another simply by specifying the name of the frame or window. For example, if you had a variable named phoneNumber that you declared in one document, you would reference it from an iFrame using parent.phoneNumber.

Constants

Using the *const* keyword, you can create named constants that are read-only. The syntax is the same as it is for the variable identifier – it must have a letter, dollar sign, or underscore at the beginning and it may also contain numbers, letters, and underscores. For example:

const PI = 3.14;

Constants are not able to change values through an assignment and they cannot be declared again while a script runs. They must also be initialized to values. In terms of scope, the rules are the same as the *let* block variables; if you leave the *const* keyword out, the identifier will be seen as a variable.

Constants cannot be declared with a name already given to a variable or function within the same scope. For example:

// This would raise an error

function f() {};

const f = 8;

// So will this

function f() {

  const g = 8;

  var g;

  //statements

}

That said, the properties for any object assigned to a constant are not classed as protected. This means the following example statement would go through without any errors:

const MY_OBJECT = {'key': 'value'};

MY_OBJECT.key = 'otherValue';

The array contents are not protected either so this statement would also execute properly:

```
const MY_ARRAY = ['HTML','CSS'];

MY_ARRAY.push('JAVASCRIPT');

console.log(MY_ARRAY); //logs ['HTML','CSS','JAVASCRIPT'];
```

Data Structures and Types

At last count, the ECMAScript standard has seven data types defined, six of which are primitive data types:

1. **Boolean** – evaluates true or false

2. **null** – a special type of keyword that denotes a null value. As JS is a case-sensitive language, null, Null, NULL all mean different things

3. **undefined** – a property (top-level) with an undefined value

4. **Number** – floating-point (i.e. 2.1987) or integer (i.e. 79)

5. **String** – character sequence representing a text value (i.e. "Hello")

6. **Symbol** – brand new to ECMAScript 2015, this is a data type with unique instances that are immutable

7. **Object**

Although there are not many data types, they can all be used to perform some incredibly useful roles within your applications. Functions and objects are the other two basic elements to the language; an object can be thought of as a container (named) to hold values, while functions are the procedures performed by the application.

Converting Data Types

Because the JavaScript language is dynamically typed, you do not need to specify what data type a variable is when it is declared. The data types are automatically converted into what is required when the script is executed. For example, a variable could be defined as:

var answer = 79;

Later on, that variable could be assigned with a string value like:

answer = 'Thanks for all the gifts…';

The fact that JS is dynamically typed means there won't be any error messages arising from the assignment.

When an expression has both string values and numeric values using the + operator, the numbers will be converted to strings. For example:

x = 'The answer is ' + 79 // "The answer is 79"

y = 79 + ' is the answer' // "79 is the answer"

Where other operators have been used, the numeric values will not be converted:

'47' - 7 // 40

'47' + 7 // "477"

Converting a String to a Number

When your value is representing a number and it has been stored as a string in memory, there are two methods to convert them:

- **parseInt()**
- **parseFloat()**

The first one, parseInt() will return only whole numbers; it isn't suitable for decimals or floating numbers. Best practice says that when you use parseInt(), the radix parameter should be included to specify the numerical system in use.

An alternative way of getting a number from a string is to use the unary =+ (+) operator:

'2.2' + '2.2' // '2.22.2'

(+'2.2') + (+'2.2') // 4.4

// Note: I have included parentheses ONLY to make things clear; they are not a requirement.

Literals

Literals are used to represent fixed values, not variables. These fixed values are LITERALLY provided in the script and it covers the following literal types:

Array Literals

Array literals are lists of zero or more expressions. Each expression represents one array element enclosed in a set of [] square brackets. When you use an array literal to create an array, it must be initialized using specified values for the elements and the length of the array will be the number of specified arguments.

This next example will create an array called teas; it has three elements; thus it has a length of three:

var teas = [Darjeeling, 'Earl Grey', 'Oolong'];

Note - array literals are types of object initializers and array objects, both will be discussed later.

If a literal is used to create an array in a top-level script, the array will be interpreted every time the expression containing the array literal is evaluated. Moreover, literals used in functions are created every time the function gets called.

Additional Commas

There is no need to specify every element inside an array literal. When the array is created, if two commas are placed in the row, all of the unspecified elements are undefined. Look at this example that creates the big cat array:

var big cat = [Tiger, , Lion];

This has two elements that have values and one that does not (big cat[0] is Tiger, big cat[1] is undefined, and big cat[2] is Lion.

If a trailing comma is added to the end of the element list, it will be ignored. In the next example, we have an array of length three. myList[3] does not exist and the other commas are indicating additional elements.

Note - if you are using an older browser, eliminate the trailing comma as it can cause errors.

var myList = ['work', , 'home',];

In the next example, the array is a length of four and there are two missing – myList[0] and myList[2]:

var myList = [,'work', , 'home'];

And in this example, we also have an array with a length of four and two missing – myList[1] and myList[3]. The final comma is the only one ignored:

var myList = ['work', , 'home', ,];

It is important to understand how additional commas behave if you are to understand the language. Nevertheless, when it comes to writing code, explicitly declare the missing elements are undefined so your code is easier to maintain and simpler to read.

Boolean Literals

Boolean literals have two values – true and false. It is important NOT to confuse the primitive true and false Boolean values with the Boolean object true and false values. The object is a wrapper that goes around the primitive data type.

Numeric Literals

Integers may be expressed in four ways:

- **Decimal** – base 10 – decimal integer literals are a sequence of digits that do not have a leading zero (0)
- **Hexadecimal** – base 16 – a hexadecimal integer literal has a leading 0x or 0X and they can have letters a to f, A to F, and digits 0 to 9. The case of the character is irrelevant; it does not change the value.
- **Octal** – base 8 – an octal integer literal has a leading 0, 0o, or 0O and can only have the digits 0 to 7.
- **Binary** – base 2 – a binary integer literal has a leading 0b or 0B and can only have the digits 0 and 1.

A few examples:

0, 123 and -456 (decimal, base 10)

016, 0002 and -0066 (octal, base 8)

0x1123, 0x00111 and -0xF1A7 (hexadecimal, "hex" or base 16)

0b11, 0b0011 and -0b11 (binary, base 2)

Floating-point Literals

A floating-point literal is made up of these parts:

- A decimal integer preceded with a + or a -
- A decimal point
- A fraction, which is another decimal number
- An exponent

The exponent is an E or an e with an integer following. This may be preceded by a + or a -. Floating-point literals must include a minimum of one digit and an e, E or a decimal point.

The syntax looks like this:

[(+|-)][digits].[digits][(E|e)][(+|-)]digits]

An example:

3.1415926

-.123456789

-3.1E+12

.1e-23

Object Literals

Object literals are lists containing zero or more pairs, each with a property name and the associated object value. The list is contained within a set of {} curly brackets. An object literal should never be used at the start of a statement otherwise, one of two things will occur – an error will be thrown or things won't work right because the opening curly bracket will be seen as being the start of a block.

The next example is of an object literal. The first element in the object called car is defining a property called myCar. This is then assigned to a new string called Jupiter. The second element, getCarProperty, is then assigned with the result of the function called carTypes being invoked. The third element is a special property and uses a variable that already exists, sales.

var sales = 'Opel';

```
function carTypes(name) {

  if (name === 'Suzuki') {

    return name;

  } else {

    return "Sorry, we don't have any " + name + ".";

  }

}
```

```
var car = { myCar: 'Jupiter', getCar: carTypes('Suzuki'), special: sales };
```

```
console.log(car.myCar);   // Jupiter

console.log(car.getCar);  // Suzuki

console.log(car.special); // Opel
```

On top of that, a string or numeric literal can also be used as a property name or you can nest one object in another. Here are a couple of examples:

```
var car = { manyCars: {a: 'BMW', b: 'Mercedes'}, 7: 'Jaguar' };
```

```
console.log(car.manyCars.b); // Mercedes

console.log(car[7]); // Jaguar
```

The name of an object property can be any type of string, including an empty one. Conversely, if the name is not a valid number or identifier, it must be contained inside a set of quotes. Not valid identifiers also can't be opened as dot properties but can be both accessed and set using [], the notation similar to an array.

```
var unusualPropertyNames = {

  ": This is an empty string',

  '!': 'Bang!'

}
```

```
console.log(unusualPropertyNames.");   // SyntaxError: Unexpected string

console.log(unusualPropertyNames["]);  // An empty string

console.log(unusualPropertyNames.!);   // SyntaxError: Unexpected token !

console.log(unusualPropertyNames['!']); // Bang!
```

Enhanced Object Literals

In ECMAScript2015, an object literal has support to set prototypes at the time of construction, short for foo - for example, foo assignments, making super calls, defining methods, computing names of properties with expressions. These work to bring the object literal closer to the class declaration and allow for designs based on objects to gain some benefit from the same conveniences:

```
var obj = {

  // __proto__

  __proto__: theProtoObj,

  // Short for 'handler: handler'

  handler,

  // Methods

  toString() {

   // Super calls

   return 'd ' + super.toString();

  },

  // Computed (dynamic) property names

  [ 'prop_' + (() => 79)() ]: 79

};
```

Also note:

```
var foo = {b: 'beta', 3: 'three'};

console.log(foo.b);   // beta

console.log(foo[3]);   // three
```

//console.log(foo.3); // SyntaxError: missing) after the argument list

//console.log(foo[b]); // ReferenceError: b has not been defined

console.log(foo['b']); // beta

console.log(foo['3']); // three

Regex Literals

Regex literals are patterns in between slashes, as in this example:

var re = /ab+c/;

We'll discuss these in more detail later.

String Literals

String literals are made up of zero or more characters inside a set of quotations marks – double ("") or single ("). You must use the same type of quotation marks for the delimiting, for example, either a pair of double quotes or a pair of single quotes. You must not use two different types. Look at these examples:

'foo'

"bar"

'5678'

'one line \n another line'

"Bob's dog"

Any string object method can be called on the value of a string literal; JavaScript will convert the literal into temporary string object automatically, then it will call the method and discard the provisional object. The String.length property can also be used with a string literal:

console.log("Bob's dog".length)

// This will print all the symbols, including the whitespace, in the string.

//The value will be 9.

Template literals are also available in ECMAScript 2015. These are enclosed between a set of back-ticks (` `) rather than the quote marks. The template strings make string construction much easier to read. You also have the option of adding a tag to customize the string construction, avoid injection attacks, or use string contents to construct structures of a higher level.

```
// the basic creation of a literal string

`In JavaScript '\n' is a line-feed. `


// Multiline strings

`Template strings can go over multiple lines

in JavaScript but the lines inside double or single

quotes cannot. `


// String interpolation

var name = 'Bob', time = 'today';

`Hello ${name}, how are you ${time}? `


// An HTTP request prefix is constructed to interpret

the replacements and the construction

POST `http://foo.org/bar?a=${a}&b=${b}

    Content-Type: application/json

    X-Credentials: ${credentials}

    { "foo": ${foo},

      "bar": ${bar}} `(myOnReadyStateChangeHandler);
```

Unless you need to use a string object for a specific reason, try to use string literals.

Special Characters

Along with standard characters, there are also some special ones to use in strings, for example:

'one line \n another line'

These are the special characters, along with their meaning, which can be used in a JS string:

Character	Meaning
\'	Single quote or apostrophe
\"	Double quote
\\	Backslash
\0	Null Byte
\b	Backspace
\f	Form feed
\n	New line
\r	Carriage return
\t	Tab
\u{XXXXX}	Point escapes (Unicode) i.e. \u{2F804} means the same as the standard Unicode escapes \uD87E\uDC04
\uXXXX	Unicode character specified by the hexadecimal digits (XXXX). i.e. \uA00A9 is the Unicode equivalent of the Copyright symbol
\v	Vertical tab
\XXX	Latin-1 encoded character specified by a maximum of three octal digits from 0 to 3777. i.e. \251 is the octal equivalent of the Copyright symbol
\xXX	Latin-1 encoded character specified by the hexadecimal digits from 00 to FF. i.e. \xA9 is hexadecimal equivalent of the Copyright symbol

Escaping Characters

To use a quotation mark in your string, always precede it with a backslash; this is called "escaping" the quote mark. For example:

var quote = "She read \"Moby Dick\" by Herman Melville.";

console.log(quote);

And the result would be:

She read "Moby Dick" by Herman Melville

If you want a literal backslash in the string, the backslash character must be escaped. For example, to assign a string with the file path c:\temp, you would do this:

var home = 'c:\\temp';

Line breaks can also be escaped by using a backslash to precede them. Both the backslash and the line break will be removed from the string value:

*var str = 'the string *

*is broken down *

*over multiple *

lines.'

console.log(str);   // the string is broken down over multiple lines.

JavaScript does not have support for the "*heredoc*" syntax used in PHP large blocks of text with the quote mark delimiters. You can get close by including both a line break escape and the escaped line break at the end of every line, like this:

var poem =

'Strawberries are red,\n

Blueberries are blue.\n

Honey is sweet,\n

and so is foo.'

With ECMAScript 2015, we saw the introduction of another literal, the template literal. These provide loads of extra features, including the multiline string:

var poem =

'Strawberries are red,

Blueberries are blue.

Honey is sweet,

and so is foo.'

Control Flow and Statements

JavaScript provides support for a neat set of statements, especially those under the heading of control flow statements. These statements are useful to add interactivity to an application. Before we move on to the different types of statement, there are two things to recognize:

- Statements must be separated with a semicolon

- JS expressions are also classed as statements – more about expressions later.

Block Statement

The block statement is a basic one used for grouping statements together. It must be enclosed by a set of curly brackets {}. For example:

{

  statement_1;

  statement_2;

  .

  .

  .

  statement_n;

}

Use a block statement with a control flow statement, i.e. *if, while, for*:

while (x < 15) {

  x++;

}

The block statement here is {x++;)

Important Note

Before ECMAScript 2015, JavaScript did not have support for block statements. Instead, any variable introduced inside a block was scoped to the script or function that contains it. The effects of setting that variable to continue outside the block. In simple terms, it means the block statement would not define the scope. The result of a standalone block is not the same as Java or C would produce. For example:

```
var x = 2;

{

  var x = 4;

}
```

```
console.log(x); // outputs 4
```

The *var x* statement inside the block is within the same scope as the *var x* block before the statement, which is why the output is 4. In Java or C, the output would have been 2.

With ECMAScript 2015, the *const* and *let* variable declarations became block-scoped.

Conditional Statements

Conditional statements are sets of executable commands only if a given condition evaluates true. There are two conditional statements supported in JavaScript – *if-else* and *switch*.

if...else

The *if* statement is used to execute a statement provided a logical condition evaluates true. The else clause is optional and is used if the logical condition evaluates false. An *if* statement would look something like this:

```
if (condition) {

  statement_1;

} else {

  statement_2;

}
```

The condition may be a statement or expression to evaluate either true or false. If the condition is true, statement_1 is implemented. If it is false, statement_2 is executed. Both statements may be any statement, including nested *if* statements.

Statements can also be compounded and several conditions can be tested in order using *else if*:

```
if (condition_1) {
```

```
  statement_1;
} else if (condition_2) {
  statement_2;
} else if (condition_n) {
  statement_n;
} else {
  statement_last;
}
```

When you have several conditions, the only executed is the first that evaluates as true. If you want all the statements executed, they must be grouped in a block statement inside {{...}}. Block statements are the best practice, especially if you have nested *if* statements:

```
if (condition) {
  statement_1_executes_if_condition_is_true;
  statement_2_executes_if_condition_is_true;
} else {
  statement_3_executes_if_condition_is_false;
  statement_4_executes_if_condition_is_false;
}
```

Try not to use simple statement in conditional expressions; assignment and equality may be confused if the code is glimpsed at. An example of what not to do is:

```
if (x = y) {
  /* statements go here */
}
```

If an assignment is needed in a conditional expression, it is better to add another set of parentheses around it, like this:

```
if ((x = y)) {
  /* statements go here */
```

}

Falsy Values

These are the values that will evaluate to false. These are termed "Falsy values":

- 0
- empty string ("")
- false
- NaN
- null
- undefined

When it gets passed to a conditional statement, any other value will evaluate true – and that includes objects.

It is important not to be confused by the primitive true and false Boolean values and the Boolean object true and false values. For example:

var b = new Boolean(false);

if (b) // the condition will evaluate to true

if (b == true) // the condition will evaluate to false

In the next example, we have a function called checkData. Provided the number of the characters within a Text object is four, it will evaluate true. If not, an alert is displayed and false is returned:

function checkData() {

  if (document.form1.fourChar.value.length == 4) {

    return true;

  } else {

    alert('Enter four characters exactly. ' +

    document.form1.fourChar.value + ' is not valid.');

    return false;

  }

}

Switch Statements

We use *switch* statements so that an expression can be evaluated; an attempt is then made to match the value of the expression with a case label. If there is a match, the associated statement is executed. A *switch* statement looks like this:

switch (expression) {

   case label_1:

    statements_1

    [break;]

   case label_2:

    statements_2

    [break;]

    ...

   default:

    statements_def

    [break;]

}

First, the program will look for a case clause that has a case label that matches the expression value. Control is then transferred to the clause and the associated statement is executed. If a matching case label is not found, the program will continue looking for a default clause (this is optional). If it finds a default clause, control is transferred to it and the associated statements are executed. If the program does not find a default clause, execution will move to the statement immediately following the switch. Convention says the last clause is the default clause but this is not necessarily a fact.

The *break* statement, also optional, may be associated with each of the case clauses to make sure the *switch* is broken out of as soon as a matched statement is found and executed; execution moves to the statement proximately following the *switch*. If there is no *break* clause, execution continues with the next statement inside the switch.

In the next example, if vegtype evaluates to "Peppers", the value is matched with the case called "Peppers" and the associated statement is executed. If the program encounters a *break* clause, the *switch* statement is terminated and control will move to the first statement following the switch. If the break clause were left out, the statement associated with the case "Potatoes" would be executed as well:

var vegtype = 'Peppers';

```
switch (vegtype) {
    case 'Peas':
        console.log('Peas are $0.49 a pound.');
        break;
    case 'Beans':
        console.log('Beans are $0.22 a pound.');
        break;
    case 'Peppers':
        console.log('Peppers are $0.58 a pound.');
        break;
    case 'Potatoes':
        console.log('Potatoes are $3.50 a pound.');
        break;
    case 'Celery':
        console.log('Celery is $0.58 a pound.');
        break;
    case 'Onions':
        console.log('Celery and Onions are $3.85 a pound.');
        break;
    default:
        console.log('Sorry, we don't have any ' + vegtype + '.');
}
console.log("Would you like anything else?");
```

Exception Handling Statements

A *throw* statement is used to throw an exception while a *try...catch* statement is used to handle them.

Exception Types

Any object may be thrown but not all of the thrown objects will be equal. Numbers and strings are commonly thrown as errors, but a more effective way is to use a specially created exception type.

The *throw* Statement

When an exception is thrown, the expression with the value being thrown must be specified:

throw expression;

Any expression may be thrown; it does not have to be specific. The next example shows multiple exceptions being thrown, each a different type:

throw 'Error3';   // String type

throw 42;   // Number type

throw false;   // Boolean type

throw {toString: function() { return "I am an object!"; } };

Objects may be specified when an exception is thrown and the object properties may then be referenced in the *catch* block:

// Create the object type UserException

function UserException(message) {

  this.message = message;

  this.name = 'UserException';

}

// The exception should convert to a string when it is used as a string

// (i.e. by the error console)

UserException.prototype.toString = function() {

  return this.name + ': "' + this.message + '"';

}

// Create one instance of the object type and then throw it

throw new UserException('the value is too high');

The try...catch Statement

This statement is used to mark a specific statement block to be tried. At least one response should be specified in the case of an exception being thrown. The *try...catch* statement will catch any thrown exception.

The *try...catch* statement has a try block, with at least one statement in it, and a catch block that has the statements specifying the action should be an exception thrown in the try block. The idea is to have the *try* block be successful; if not, control should be passed to the *catch* block. If an exception is thrown by any statement in the *try* block or by any function called from the *try* block, control will move to the *catch* block immediately. If an exception does not get thrown, the *catch* block is missed out. Once the *try and catch* blocks have been executed, the *finally* block will execute – this happens BEFORE the statements coming after the *try...catch* block is executed.

In the next example, a function is being called to retrieve the name of a month from an array; the name retrieved is based on the value passed to that function. If there is no month number (1 to 12) corresponding to the value, an exception gets thrown with an "InvalidMonthNo" value and all the statements inside the catch block will set the variable called monthName as unknown.

function getMonthName(mo) {

  mo = mo - 1; // Change the month number for the array index (1 = Jan, 12 = Dec)

  var months = ['Jan', 'Feb', 'Mar', 'Apr', 'May', 'Jun', 'Jul',

      'Aug', 'Sep', 'Oct', 'Nov', 'Dec'];

 if (months[mo]) {

   return months[mo];

 } else {

   throw 'InvalidMonthNo'; //we use the throw keyword here

 }

}

try { // these are the statements being tried

  monthName = getMonthName(myMonth); // the function may throw an exception

```
}
catch (e) {

  monthName = 'unknown';

  logMyErrors(e); // the exception object is passed to the error handler -> your function

}
```

The catch Block

Catch blocks can handle any or all of the exceptions the try block may generate:

```
catch (catchID) {

  statements

}
```

An identifier is specified in the **catch** block (catchID in the above syntax), which hold the value specified by the *throw* statement. This identifier may be used to obtain some info about the thrown exception. The identifier is created by JavaScript at the time the *catch* block is first entered and it only lasts as long as the *catch* block. Once execution of the **catch** block has completed, the identifier will become unavailable.

In the next example, an exception is thrown and, when this happens, control is moved directly to the *catch* block:

```
try {

  throw 'myException'; // an exception is generated

}
catch (e) {

  // these statements will handle any exception

  logMyErrors(e); // the exception object is passed to the error handler

}
```

The finally Block

In the *finally* block are statements that execute once the *try and catch* blocks are finished but before the statements following *catch...try*. This block will be executed regardless of whether an exception gets thrown; if there is an exception, the finally statements will be executed whether the exception is handled by the *catch* block or not.

The *finally* block is often used to make a script fail with grace when exceptions are thrown. For example, your script may be tying up a specific resource and you need it released.

In this example, a file is opened, and the statements about needing to use the file are executed. Should an exception be thrown at the time the file is open, that file will be closed by the *finally* block before the script can fail, thus freeing those resources:

openMyFile();

try {

  writeMyFile(theData); //an error may be thrown

} catch(e) {

  handleError(e); // we handle any errors we get

} finally {

  closeMyFile(); // the resource must always be closed

}

If a value is returned by the *finally* block, it will become the value for the entire *try...catch ...finally* procedure, no matter what the return statements are inside the *try* block and *catch* block:

function f() {

  try {

  console.log(0);

  throw 'fictitious';

  } catch(e) {

  console.log(1);

  return true; // the return statement gets suspended

      // until the finally block has finished

  console.log(2); // not reachable

```
  } finally {

    console.log(3);

    return false; // the previous "return" is overwritten

    console.log(4); // not reachable

  }

  // "return false" now gets executed

  console.log(5); // not reachable

}

f(); // console 0, 1, 3; returns false
```

Where the *finally* block overwrites the return value, it is also applicable to any exception the *catch* block throws or re-throws:

```
function f() {

  try {

    throw 'fictitious';

  } catch(e) {

    console.log('caught inner "fictitious"');

    throw e; // the throw statement gets suspended until

           // the finally block has finished

  } finally {

    return false; // the previous "throw" gets overwritten

  }

  // "return false" is now executed

}


try {

  f();
```

```
} catch(e) {

  // this cannot be reached because the throw in

  // the catch block has been overwritten

  // by the return in the finally block

  console.log('caught outer "fictitious"');

}
```

```
// OUTPUT

// caught inner "fictitious"
```

Nested try...catch Statements

It is possible to nest one or more try...catch statements inside another. If the inner nested statement has no catch block, it must have a finally block and a match is checked for in the outer try...catch block.

Using Error Objects

Depending on what the error type is, a more refined error message can be made by using two object properties – 'message' and 'name'. The latter will give a generalized error class, such as 'Error' or 'DOMException', while the former will give you a clearer message than converting the object into a string.

To use these properties while throwing your own exceptions, for example, if the *catch* block doesn't separate system exceptions from your exceptions, you would make use of the Error constructor, as in this example:

```
function doSomethingThatCausesErrors() {

  if (ourProgramHasMadeAMistake()) {

    throw (new Error('The message'));

  } else {

    doSomethingThatThrowsAJavaScriptError();

  }

}
```

....

```
try {

  doSomethingThatCausesAnError();

} catch (e) {

  console.log(e.name); // logs 'Error'

  console.log(e.message); // logs 'The message' or a JavaScript error message)

}
```

Promises

Something else was introduced with ECMAScript 2015- the support for Promise objects. These allow you to take control of the flow of asynchronous and deferred operations.

A *Promise* must be in one of the following states:

- **Pending** – the initial state; the object has not been fulfilled, nor has it been rejected

- **Fulfilled** – the operation has been successful

- **Rejected** – the operation has failed

- **Settled** – the *Promise* has been fulfilled or rejected but is not in the pending state

The example below gives you an idea of how the *Promise* flows to load an image to a website using XMLHTTPRequest:

```
function imgLoad(url) {

  return new Promise(function(resolve, reject) {

    var request = new XMLHttpRequest();

    request.open('GET', url);

    request.responseType = 'blob';

    request.onload = function() {

      if (request.status === 200) {

        resolve(request.response);
```

```
    } else {
      reject(Error('Image didn\'t load successfully; error code:'
            + request.statusText));
    }
  };
  request.onerror = function() {
    reject(Error('There was a network error.'));
  };
  request.send();
});
}
```

Loops and Iteration

Loops provide programmers with an easy way to do something repetitively. Have you ever played a game where one person tells another to take so many steps in X direction and then so many steps in Y direction? You can think of a loop as a computer version of that game. For example, you could express the idea of walking six steps to the west with this loop:

var step;

for (step = 0; step < 6; step++) {

   // Runs 6 times, with values of steps 0 through 5.

   console.log('Walking west one step');

}

There are quite a few types of loops but they all do the same thing – repeat a given action a specified number of times (even zero). The loop structures offer a different method to determine where a loop will start and where it ends. Some situations are best served by one type of loop more than another.

JavaScript provides the following statements for the loops:

The *for* Statement

The *for* loops will repeat until a given condition has evaluated to false. The syntax for a *for* loop statement looks like this:

for ([initialExpression]; [condition]; [incrementExpression])

   statement

Upon execution of a *for* loop, this is what happens:

- If there is an initializing expression (initialExpression in our syntax), it is executed first. This is included to initialize at least one loop counter, but you can have more complex expressions if you wish. The initializing expression may also declare one or more variables.

- Next, the condition expression will be executed. If the value is true, the associated statements are executed, but if the value is false, the for loop is terminated. If you leave the condition expression out, it will be assumed the condition is true.

- The statement will execute. For multiple statements to be executed, you must group the statements using the block statement – {...}.

- If an updateExpression (incrementExpression) is used, it will be executed.

- Control goes back to the condition expression.

In the following example, we have a function with a *for* statement; the *for* statement is counting selected options in a list that scrolls. We use a <select> element to enable a multiple selection. The variable named i is declared and initialized to zero. The function will check to see if the variable is less than the number of options contained in the <select> part; the ensuing *if* statement is performed and i is incremented by 1 after each loop pass:

```
<!DOCTYPE html>

<html>

<head>

  <meta charset="utf-8">

  <title>jQuery Click Handler Demo</title>

  <link rel="stylesheet" type="text/css" href="css/style.css">

  <script src="js/jquery-3.3.1.min.js"></script>

  <script type="text/javascript">

    function howMany(selectObject) {

      var numberSelected = 0;

      for (var i = 0; i < selectObject.options.length; i++) {

      if (selectObject.options[i].selected) {

        numberSelected++;

      }

      }

      return numberSelected;

    }
```

```
        </script>
    </head>
    <body>
        <form name="selectForm">
            <p>
                <label for="musicTypes">Choose a few types of music and click the button
below:</label>
                <select id="musicTypes" name="musicTypes" multiple="multiple">
                    <option selected="selected">Heavy Metal</option>
                    <option>Rock</option>
                    <option>Soul</option>
                    <option>Big Band</option>
                    <option>Folk</option>
                    <option>Country & Western</option>
                </select>
            </p>
            <p><button id="btn" type="button" onclick="alert('Number of options selected: ' +
howMany(document.selectForm.musicTypes));">How many have been
selected?</button>
        </form>
    </body>
</html>
```

The *do...while* Statement

The *do...while* loop will repeat until a given condition has evaluated to false. The syntax is:

```
do
    statement
```

while (condition);

Before the condition is checked, the statement will continue to execute until false is returned by the *while* condition. Again, for the execution of multiple statements, group them using the block statement. If the condition evaluates true, the statement execution is repeated. Once each execution has finished, the condition will be checked again. When the condition evaluates to false, no more executions take place and control is passed to the first statement after the *do...while* loop.

In the next example, our *do loop* will iterate a minimum of one time and will continue to iterate until i is equal to or more than 6:

var i = 0;

do {

  i += 1;

  console.log(i);

} while (i < 6);

The *while* Statement

The statements in a *while* loop will continue to execute until the specified condition evaluates to false. The syntax is:

while (condition)

 statement

As soon as the condition evaluates false, the loop statement will no longer be executed and the control will pass to the first statement after the loop. The condition is checked before the loop execution; if the value true is returned, a further check is made on the condition. If it is false, no further checks happen and control will go to the first statement after the *while* loop.

Once more, block statements should be used to execute multiple statements.

In the first example, the *while* loop will continue to iterate for as long as n is less than four:

var n = 0;

var x = 0;

while (n < 4) {

```
  n++;

  x += n;

}
```

With every iteration, n is incremented by the loop and the resulting value added to x. As such, x and n will have these values:

- After pass one, n = 1, x = 1

- After pass two, n = 2, x = 3

- After pass three, n = 3, x = 6

- After pass four, n = 4, x = 10

Once pass four has finished, the condition of n < 4 is not true anymore and the loop will terminate.

In the second example, you can see the effect of an infinite loop and why you should never use them. A loop condition must, at some point, evaluate false, otherwise, you run the risk of a loop not terminating – ever. The statements below do just that because the condition can never evaluate to false:

```
while (true) {

  console.log('Hello, everyone!');

}
```

The *labeled* Statement

Labels are identifiers in a statement, allowing you to reference them somewhere else in the code. For example, a *label* can be used to identify a loop, and then you can make use of continue or break statements to indicate if a program continues with the execution or breaks out of the loop.

The syntax looks like this:

label :

   statement

The *label* value can be any identifier in JavaScript provided it is not one of the reserved keywords. The statement identified with the *label* can be any statement. On the next example, a *label* of markLoop is used to identify a *while* loop:

markLoop:

while (theMark == true) {

  doSomething();

}

The *break* Statement

A *break* statement is used to terminate a loop, a *switch* statement or together with a *labeled* statement:

- When the *break* is used with no label, the inner enclosing *do...while, while, for,* or *switch* statement is terminated with immediate effect and the control is transferred to the next available statement.

- When the break is used with a *label*, the labeled statement specified is terminated.

The syntax looks like:

break [label];

The first part (break) will end the inner enclosing switch or loop while the second part (label) will end the specified labeled statement,

With the first example below, we iterate through an array until the index for an element with a *theValue* value is found:

for (var i = 0; i < a.length; i++) {

  if (a[i] == theValue) {

    break;

  }

}

In the second example, we use the *break* statement to break to a *label*:

var x = 0;

var z = 0;

labelCancelLoops: while (true) {

  console.log('Outer loops: ' + x);

```
    x += 1;

    z = 1;

    while (true) {

      console.log('Inner loops: ' + z);

      z += 1;

      if (z === 12 && x === 12) {

        break labelCancelLoops;

      } else if (z === 12) {

        break;

      }

    }

}
```

The *continue* Statement

The *continue* statement is used to restart *do...while, while,* or *label* statements:

- When a continue statement is used without a label, the ongoing iteration of the inner enclosing statement (*do, do...while, for*) is terminated and the loop execution moves to the next iteration. Unlike the *break* statement, the *continue* statement won't terminate the loop altogether. In *while* loops, it will go to the condition; in *for* loops, it goes to the increment expression.

- When a *continue* statement is used with a *label*, the statement applies to the loop statement the *label* identifies.

The syntax looks like:

continue [label];

In the first example below, we have a continue statement used with a while loop; the statement will execute when i is a value of three. As such, n will have the values of one, three, seven, twelve:

```
var i = 0;

var n = 0;
```

```javascript
while (i < 5) {

  i++;

  if (i == 3) {

    continue;

  }

  n += i;

  console.log(n);

}
//1,3,7,12
```

```javascript
var i = 0;

var n = 0;

while (i < 5) {

  i++;

  if (i == 3) {

    // continue;

  }

  n += i;

  console.log(n);

}
// 1,3,6,10,15
```

In the second example, we have a statement with a label of checkiandj. In that statement there is another one with a label of checkj. If the continue statement is detected, the current iteration of checkj is terminated and the next one begins. This will continue for as long as the condition returns true. When it returns false, the rest of the checkiandj statement will complete and the continue to iterate until the condition returns the value false. When this happens, the program control will go to the statement immediately after checkiandj.

If the *continue* statement contained a checkiandj label, the program control would move to the top of the statement after the checkiandj:

```
var i = 0;

var j = 10;

checkiandj:
 while (i < 4) {
   console.log(i);

   i += 1;

   checkj:
    while (j > 4) {
      console.log(j);

      j -= 1;

      if ((j % 2) == 0) {

        continue checkj;

      }
      console.log(j + ' is odd.');

    }
    console.log('i = ' + i);

    console.log('j = ' + j);

 }
```

The *for...in* Statement

A *for...in* statement will iterate a given variable over the enumerable properties of a specified object. For every unmistakable property, the specified statements will be executed. The syntax looks like:

```
for (variable in object) {
```

statements

}

In this example, we have a function that takes an object and the object name as an argument. It will iterate over every property in the object and the result will be a string listing the names and values of each property:

function dump_props(obj, obj_name) {

  var result = '';

  for (var i in obj) {

    result += obj_name + '.' + i + ' = ' + obj[i] + '<br>';

  }

  result += '<hr>';

  return result;

}

For an object called car with two properties, make and model, the result could be:

car.make = BMW

car.model = X7

You might be tempted to use a *for...in* statement to iterate over the elements in an array, but what you get, as well as the numeric indexes, are the names of the user-defined properties. As such, traditional loops with numeric indexes are better for array iterations; they don't iterate over user-defined properties as the *for...in* statement does if array objects are modified in any way.

The *for...of* Statement

A *for...of* statement will create a loop that iterates over all the iterable objects, such as arguments, Array, Set, Map, and so on. This will result in a custom iteration hook being invoked and statements will be executed for each property value:

for (variable of object) {

  statement

}

In the following example, you can see the difference between a *for...in* and a *for...of* loop. The *for...in* loop will iterate over the names of the properties, the *for...of* loop will iterate over the values.

```
var arr = [3, 5, 7];

arr.foo = 'hello';


for (var i in arr) {

    console.log(i); // logs "0", "1", "2", "foo"

}


for (var i of arr) {

    console.log(i); // logs 3, 5, 7

}
```

Functions

Functions are a basic JavaScript building block; they are procedures, or sets of statements either calculating values or carrying out a task. Before using a function, it must be defined within the scope it will be called from.

Defining or Declaring Functions

Function definitions are also known as function statements or function declarations. They are made up of the keyword and:

- The function name

- The parameters that go with the function. These must be separated by a comma and enclosed in a set of parentheses

- The statements used for defining it, inside a set of curly brackets {}.

As an example, this code defines a function called circle:

function circle(number) {

*return number * number;*

}

This function has one parameter, which is called number. It has a single statement stating the function parameter -number in our case- is to be multiplied by itself and returned. The statement called *return* is specifying the value the function should return:

return number * number;

Primitive parameters, like numbers, are passed by value to a function. Although the value is returned, and if the function changes the parameter values, it will not be globally reflected, nor will it be reflected in the function that calls it.

If an object is passed, a non-primitive value like an array, as the parameter, and the object properties are changed by the function, the change can be seen externally to the function, as you can see in the next example:

function myFunc(theObject) {

theObject.make = 'BMW';

}

```
var mycar = {make: 'Opel', model: 'Astra', year: 1999};

var x, y;


x = mycar.make; // x will get the value "Opel"

console.log(x);


myFunc(mycar);

y = mycar.make; // y will get the value "BMW"

        // (the function changed the property called make)

console.log(y);
```

Function Expressions

The function declaration that was used in the above example is, in syntactical terms, a statement. We can also use a function expression to create a function. These can be anonymous functions, i.e. they don't need to be named. For example, we could have defined a function called square like this:

```
var square = function(number) { return number * number; };

var x = square(4); // x gets the value 16
```

That said, functions created by function expressions do not need to be anonymous; you can provide a name and the name may be used within the function as a reference to itself or in a debugger as a way of identifying that specific function in a stack trace:

```
var factorial = function fac(n) { return n < 2 ? 1 : n * fac(n - 1); };


console.log(factorial(3));
```

A function expression can be convenient to pass one function to another as an argument. In the next example, you can see a map function; the first argument should be a function and the second argument should be an array:

```
function map(f, a) {
```

```
var result = [],i; // A new array is created

 for (i = 0; i != a.length; i++)

   result[i] = f(a[i]);

  return result;

}
```

In the next code example, the function has received another function defined using a function expression; the function is executed for each element of the second argument array:

```
function map(f, a) {

  var result = []; // A new array is created

  var i; // Declare variable

  for (i = 0; i != a.length; i++)

   result[i] = f(a[i]);

  return result;

}

var f = function(x) {

  return x * x * x;

}

var numbers = [0, 1, 2, 5, 10];

var cube = map(f,numbers);

console.log(cube);
```

The function will return [0, 1, 8, 125, 1000].

We can also use a condition to define a function. The next example shows a function definition to outline myFunc if num is equal to 0:

```
var myFunc;

if (num === 0) {
```

```
myFunc = function(theObject) {

  theObject.make = 'BMW';

  }

}
```

Calling a Function

When you define a function, you are not executing it. You have only given the function a name and specified what happens upon calling it. The actions specified with the given parameters will only be performed when the function is called. For example, if a function called square is defined, it could be called like this:

square(5);

This statement is calling the function with 5 as an argument. When the function statements are executed, a value of 25 will be returned.

A function cannot be called if it is not in scope; however, the declaration may be hoisted so it appears underneath the call in your code:

console.log(square(5));

/ ... */*

*function square(n) { return n * n; }*

The scope is the function in which a function has been declared or, if it gets declared as a top-level function, the scope will be the whole program.

Note

This can only work if the above syntax is used to define the function (i.e.. funcName(){}/ The following code example won't work; hoisting will only work with declaration and not function expression:

console.log(square); // square is hoisted with an undefined initial value

console.log(square(5)); // TypeError: square is not a function

var square = function(n) {

  *return n * n;*

}

You are not limited to using numbers and strings for function arguments. Whole objects may be passed as well. One example is a function called *show_props*, taking an object as one of the arguments.

Functions can also call themselves. In the next example, we have a function to recursively compute factorials:

function factorial(n) {

  if ((n === 0) || (n === 1))

    return 1;

  else

    *return (n * factorial(n - 1));*

}

The factorials one to five could then be computed like this:

var a, b, c, d, e;

a = factorial(1); // a will get the value of 1

b = factorial(2); // b will get the value of 2

c = factorial(3); // c will get the value of 6

d = factorial(4); // d will get the value of 24

e = factorial(5); // e will get the value of 120

You can call functions in other ways too. Sometimes you may need to dynamically call a function, have varying function arguments, or the function call context must be set to a given object determined at runtime. As it happens, a function is actually an object itself and each will have methods. The apply() method is one of those.

Function Scope

When a variable is defined in a function, it may not be accessed from outside the function – the variable is only defined within the function scope. Nonetheless, a function can have access to all the functions and variables defined in the same scope as the function. In simpler terms, if you define a function in the global scope, it will access every variable defined in the global scope. If you define a function within a function, it will access the defined variable within the parent or enclosing function, along with all other variables that the parent function has access to.

```javascript
// These are the variables defined in the global scope
var num1 = 25,
    num2 = 5,
    name = 'Choudhury';


// This function has also been defined in global scope
function multiply() {
  return num1 * num2;
}


multiply(); // Returns 125


// An example of a nested function
function getScore(name) {
  var num1 = 3,
      num2 = 4;


  function add() {
    return name + ' scored ' + (num1 + num2);
  }


  return add();
}


getScore("Choudhury"); // Returns "Choudhury scored 7"
```

Scope and the Function Stack

Functions can both refer to themselves and call themselves. They can refer to themselves in three ways:

- Using the function name

- Using arguments.callee

- Using a variable in scope to refer to it

Look at this function definition:

var foo = function bar() {

* // the statements go here*

};

In the body of the function, these are all equivalent:

- bar()

- arguments.callee()

- foo()

A function calling itself is termed a recursive function. Think of recursion as a loop because both will execute a piece of code several times and both need a condition to avoid an infinite loop or infinite recursion.

Look at this loop:

var x = 0;

while (x < 12) { // "x < 12" is the condition for the loop

* // do something*

* x++;*

}

We can convert this to a recursive function and add a call to the function:

function loop(x) {

* if (x >= 12) // "x >= 12" is the exit condition (which is the equivalent of "!(x < 12)")*

```
    return;

  // do something

  loop(x + 1); // this is the recursive call

}

loop(0);
```

Some algorithms cannot be converted into an iterative loop, not a simple one anyway. Take a tree structure like the DOM; getting the nodes is better suited to recursion:

```
function walkTree(node) {

  if (node == null) //

    return;

  // do something with the node

  for (var i = 0; i < node.childNodes.length; i++) {

    walkTree(node.childNodes[i]);

  }

}
```

Comparing it to a function loop, each of the recursive calls makes its own multiple recursive calls.

Recursive algorithms can be converted into non-recursive ones, but the logic tends to be complex requiring a stack to help out. Recursion makes use of the function stack.

In the next example you can see how stacks behave:

```
function foo(i) {

  if (i < 0)

    return;

  console.log('start: ' + i);

  foo(i - 1);

  console.log('finish: ' + i);
```

```
}
foo(3);
```

```
// Output:

// start: 3
// start: 2
// start: 1
// start: 0
// finish: 0
// finish: 1
// finish: 2
// finish: 3
```

Nested Functions and Closures

Functions can be nested inside one another and the inner function (the nested one) is private to the outer function. It will also form a closure, which is an expression, commonly a function with free variables in an environment that binds or closes the expression.

Because a nested function is classed as a closure, it can inherit all the variables and arguments from the outer or containing function. In simple terms, the inner function has the scope of the outer one.

In summary:

Inner functions can only be accessed from a statement in the outer or enclosing function.

Inner functions form closures and may use variables and arguments from the enclosing function; the enclosing function may NOT use variables and arguments from inner functions.

The following are some examples of nested functions:

```
function addSquares(a, b) {
```

```
function square(x) {

  return x * x;

}

  return square(a) + square(b);

}

a = addSquares(2, 3); // returns 13

b = addSquares(3, 4); // returns 25

c = addSquares(4, 5); // returns 41
```

Because the inner function has formed a closure, the outer function can be called and arguments specified for both the inner and outer functions:

```
function outside(x) {

  function inside(y) {

    return x + y;

  }

  return inside;

}

fn_inside = outside(3); // Think of it as asking for a function that will add 3 to
whatever is given

              // it

result = fn_inside(5); // returns 8


result1 = outside(3)(5); // returns 8
```

Preserving Variables

Have you noticed when the inside is returned, x is preserved? Closures must preserve the variables and the arguments in all the scopes that it references. Because each call can potentially provide one or more new arguments, new closures are created for every call to the outside. Memory can be freed up only when the returned inside can no longer be accessed.

This isn't different from the way other objects store references, but it isn't obvious because the references are not directly set and cannot be inspected.

Multiply-Nested Functions

We can also have multiply-nested functions; these are functions containing a function that comprises a function. For example, a function called A contains a function called B. B also contains a function called C. Both B and C functions will form closures so B can have access to A and C can have access to B. Because C has access to B which, in turn, can access A, C also has access to A.

Still with me?

What this means is the closures may have several scopes; recursively, they will contain the scope from the functions containing it. We call this scope chaining and we'll look into that later. For now, look at this example:

function A(x) {

  function B(y) {

   function C(z) {

    console.log(x + y + z);

   }

   C(3);

  }

  B(2);

}

A(1); // logs 6 (1 + 2 + 3)

What we have here is C accessing y from B and x from A. It is possible for these reasons:

- B has formed a closure that includes A. This means B has access to the variables and arguments in A.

- C has formed a closure including B.

- Because the B closure includes A, the C closure also includes A. C has access to the variables and arguments in B and A. Simply put, C will chain the scopes of B and A – in that specific order.

However, we cannot reverse this. A does not have access to C because A has no access to the variables and arguments in B and C is a variable of B. As such, C is private to B.

Name Conflicts

When you have two variables or arguments within all the scopes of a closure and they share a name, a name conflict will arise. Innermost scopes tend to take priority while the outermost scope is low in precedence. This is what we call the scope chain. The first link in the chain is the innermost scope while the last one is the farthest.

For example:

```
function outside() {

  var x = 5;

  function inside(x) {

    return x * 2;

  }

  return inside;

}


outside()(10); // this will return 20, not 10
```

In this example, the conflict arises with the statement called return x and is between the inside x parameter and the outside x variable. The scope chain is {inner, outer, global object}. As such, the inner x will take precedence over the outer x and 20, which is the inner x is returned rather than 10, the outer x.

Closures

Let's go in-depth for one of the most powerful of all JavaScript features – the closure. You already know we can nest functions and the inner function has full access to the arguments to the variables in the outer function, along with any other variable or argument that the outer function has access to. You also know this doesn't work in reverse – the outer function cannot access any variables or arguments in the inner function and this gives the inner function variables an encapsulation of sorts. In addition, because the inner function accesses the outer function variables and arguments, it will have a longer life than the actual execution of the outer function provided the inner function lives longer. Closures are created when inner functions are made available in some way to any scope outside of the outer function.

var pet = function(name) {   // The outer function defines a variable with the name of "name"

var getName = function() {

return name;   // The inner function can access the variable called "name" in the outer function

//function

}

return getName;   // the inner function is returned which exposes it to the outer scopes.

}

myPet = pet('Tessa');

myPet();   // Returns "Tessa"

It can get more complex than this piece of code though; we can also return an object that has methods to manipulate the inner variables of the outer function:

var createPet = function(name) {

var sex;

```javascript
  return {
    setName: function(newName) {
      name = newName;
    },

    getName: function() {
      return name;
    },

    getSex: function() {
      return sex;
    },

    setSex: function(newSex) {
      if(typeof newSex === 'string' && (newSex.toLowerCase() === 'male' ||
        newSex.toLowerCase() === 'female')) {
        sex = newSex;
      }
    }
  }
}

var pet = createPet('Tessa');
pet.getName();            // Tessa
```

pet.setName('Eddie');

pet.setSex('male');

pet.getSex();   // male

pet.getName();   // Eddie

In this code, the inner functions can access the outer function's name variable but the inner variables can only be accessed via the inner functions. The inner variables for the inner functions create safe places for the outer variables and arguments, storing compressed and persistent data that the inner functions can work with. The functions do not need to have a name or a variable assigned to them.

var getCode = (function() {

  var apiCode = 'o]Eal(eh&2';   // We don't want any outsiders to be able to modify this code...

  return function() {

   return apiCode;

  };

})();

getCode();   // Returns the apiCode

When using closures there are a few drawbacks to watch for. If a variable is defined by an enclosed function and has the same name as a variable in outer scope, the variable can never be referenced in the outer scope again.

var createPet = function(name) { // The outer function is defining a variable with a name of "name".

  return {

   setName: function(name) {   // The enclosed function has also defined a variable called "name".

    name = name;   // How are we going to access "name" that the outer function defined?

```
        }
      }
    }
```

The Arguments Object

Function arguments are maintained in an object similar to an array. Arguments passed to a function can be addressed like this:

arguments[i]

The argument's ordinal number is represented by i beginning at zero. The first argument passed to a function is arguments[0] and arguments.length indicates the number of arguments.

The arguments object can be used to call functions containing more arguments than the function is supposed to accept as per its formal declaration. This is quite useful when you have no advance idea of the number of arguments being passed to a function. The arguments.length can be used to determine how many arguments are passed and then the arguments object accesses each of those arguments.

The following is an example that concatenates multiple strings. The function has only one formal argument; the string specifying the characters separating the concatenated items. The function definition is:

function myConcat(separator) {

var result = ''; // initialize list

var i;

// iterate through the arguments

for (i = 1; i < arguments.length; i++) {

result += arguments[i] + separator;

}

return result;

}

Any number of functions could be passed to the function and each one will be concatenated into a string called "list".

// returns "purple, yellow, green, "

myConcat(', ', 'purple', 'yellow', 'green');

// returns "rhinoceros; buffalo; tiger; puma; "

myConcat('; ', 'rhinoceros', 'buffalo', 'tiger', 'puma');

// returns "mint. rosemary. thyme. pepper. cilantro. "

myConcat('. ', 'mint', 'rosemary', 'thyme', 'pepper', 'cilantro');

Note

The arguments variable may be "array-like" but it isn't an array. It indeed contains a numbered index and it also has a property called length. What it doesn't encompass are the manipulation methods that an array has.

Function Parameters

From ECMAScript 2015, there are two new parameter types – default and rest.

Default

In JavaScript, function parameters automatically default to undefined. Still, there are situations where it can be useful to set a different value. This is where the default parameters come into play.

Previously, the strategy for default settings was to test the values of the parameters in the function body and then assign a value if they weren't defined. If in the next example, we didn't provide a value for b in the function call, the value would default to undefined when a*b is evaluated, and the multiply call would return NaN. However, the second line of the code catches that:

function multiply(a, b) {

  b = typeof b !== 'undefined' ? b : 1;

  *return a * b;*

}

multiply(5); // 5

When using default parameters, you no longer add the check into the function body, all you need is to put the default value of b as 1 in the function head:

function multiply(a, b = 1) {

* return a * b;*

}

multiply(5); // 5

Rest

The syntax for the rest parameter lets us use an array to represent an indefinite argument number. In our example, the rest parameter will collect the arguments, starting at the second one and going to the end. These are then multiplied by the first argument.

We use an arrow function here - these will be discussed next:

function multiply(multiplier, ...theArgs) {

* return theArgs.map(x => multiplier * x);*

}

var arr = multiply(2, 1, 2, 3);

console.log(arr); // [2, 4, 6]

Arrow Functions

Arrow function expressions have a much shorter syntax than a standard function expression. They do not have their own *new.target, super, this* or *arguments* keywords. They are anonymous and were introduced as a result of two factors:

Shorter Functions:

Some functional patterns welcome the use of shorter functions. For example:

var a = [

* 'Boron',*

* 'Nitrogen',*

'Oxygen',

'Fluorine'

];

var a2 = a.map(function(s) { return s.length; });

console.log(a2); // logs [5, 8, 6, 8]

var a3 = a.map(s => s.length);

console.log(a3); // logs [5, 8, 6, 8]

No Binding of this Keyword

Until arrow functions were introduced, each new function would have to define a value for this, but with OOP or object-oriented programming it is not ideal:

function Person() {

  // The Person() constructor defines `this` as itself.

  this.age = 0;

  setInterval(function growUp() {

    // In nonstrict mode, the growUp() function defines `this`

    // as the global object, which is not the same as the `this`

    // defined by the Person() constructor.

    this.age++;

  }, 1000);

}

var p = new Person();

This was fixed in ECMAScript 2015 by assigning the *this* value to a variable which can be closed over:

function Person() {

  var self = this; // Some may choose `that` and not `self`.

       // Choose one and maintain consistency.

  self.age = 0;

  setInterval(function growUp() {

   // The callback is referring to the `self` variable of which

   // the value is the expected object.

   self.age++;

  }, 1000);

}

An alternative is to create a bound function so the correct value could be passed to the function called growUp().

Arrow functions do not have a *this* of their own; instead the value of the execution context that encloses it is used. As such, in the next example, the *this* inside the function being passed to setInterval will have an identical value to the *this* contained in the enclosing function:

function Person() {

  this.age = 0;

  setInterval(() => {

  this.age++; // |this| properly refers to the person object

  }, 1000);

}

var p = new Person();

Predefined Functions

JavaScript provides a number of built-in top-level functions:

- **eval()** – this method is used for evaluation code represented as strings

- **uneval()** – this process creates string representations of an object's source code

- **isFinite()** – this function determines if a passed value is a finite number. If necessary, it will convert the parameter to a number first. It is a global function

- **isNaN()** – this is used to determine if a value is NaN (Not a Number)

- **parseFloat()** – this method parses string arguments; a floating-point number is always returned

- **parseInt()** – this function is used for parsing string arguments; an integer of specified radix is returned. Radix is the mathematical numeral system base

- **decodeURI()** – this process decodes URIs (Uniform Resource Identifiers) created using encodeURI() or similar

- **decodeURIComponent()** – this method will decode a URI component that was created using encodeURIComponent() or similar

- **encodeURI()** – is used to encode a URI; it replaced each instance of given characters by between one and four escape sequences that represent the UTF-8 character encoding.

- **encodeURIComponent()** - this routine encodes a URI component in the same way as above – using escape sequences to replace given characters

- **escape()** – this is now a deprecated method; used for computing new strings where hexadecimal escape sequences replace given characters. encodeURI() or encodeURIComponent should be used instead

- **unescaped()** – this is another deprecated method; used for computing strings where a hexadecimal character gets replaced by the character it originally represented. Use decodeURI or decodeURIComponent() instead.

Expressions and Operators

Expressions and operators are a great part of JavaScript and we'll go over what they are and how to use them, and give examples.

Operators

JavaScript supports the use of the following operators:

- Assignment operators
- Comparison operators
- Arithmetic operators
- Bitwise operators
- Logical operators
- String operators
- Conditional (ternary) operator
- Comma operator
- Unary operators
- Relational operators

Note that JavaScript has unary and binary operators, along with a special ternary operator called the conditional operator. Binary operators need two operands; one before and one after the operator:

operand1 operator operand2

For example, 5+6 or x*y.

Unary operators need one operand and it can go before the operator or after it:

operator operand

or

operand operator

for example, x++ or ++x

Assignment Operators

Assignment operators are used to assign values to the operand on the left based on the value of the operand on the right. The basic operator is the equal sign (=) used to assign the right value to the left, i.e. x=y will assign y's value to x.

There are some compound operators as well:

Name	Shorthand Operator	Meaning
Assignment	x = y	x = y
Addition assignment	x + = y	x = x + y
Subtraction assignment	x -= y	x = x − y
Multiplication assignment	x *= y	x = x * y
Division assignment	x / = y	x = x / y
Remainder assignment	x %= y	x = x y
Exponentiation assignment	x **= y	x = x ** y
Left-shift assignment	x <<= y	x = x << y
Right-shift assignment	x >>= y	x = x >> y
Unsigned right-shift assignment	x >>>= y	x = x >>> y
Bitwise AND assignment	x &= y	x = x & Y
Bitwise XOR assignment	x ^= y	x = x ^ y
Bitwise OR assignment	x |= y	x = x | y

Destructuring

For some of the more complex assignments, you can use the destructuring assignment. This is an expression allowing you to extract data from an object or an array using syntax that mirrors the object literal or array construction:

var foo = ['one', 'two', 'three'];

// without destructuring

var one   = foo[0];

var two   = foo[1];

var three = foo[2];

// with destructuring

var [one, two, three] = foo;

Comparison Operators

Comparison operators compare their own operands and return logical values based on whether the comparison evaluates true or not. The operands may be logical, string, numerical or object values.

Most of the time, if the operands are not the same type, JS will try to convert them to a more appropriate type. In general, this will result in numerical comparisons.

There is one exception to this conversion; when the comparison includes the === operator and the !== operator. Both of these are used for strict quality and inequality comparisons and will not try converting operands before they compare.

In the following code, following this you will see a description of the comparison operators as they relate to it, along with examples that will return true:

var var1 = 3;

var var2 = 4;

Operator	Description	Examples
Equal (==)	if the operands are equal, returns true	3 == var1
		"3" == var1
		3 == '3'
Not equal (!=)	if the operands are not equal, returns true	var1 != 4
		Var2 != "3"
Strict equal (===)	if the operands are equal and the same type, returns true	3 === var1
Strict not equal (!==)	if the operands are the same type but not	var1 !== "3"

	equal or are different types	3 !== '3'
Greater than (>)	if left operand is greater than right	var2 > var1
	operand, returns true	"12" > 2
Greater than or equal to (>=)	if the left operand is greater than or equal to the right, returns true	var2 >= var1 var1 >= 3
Less than (<)	if the left operand is less than the right Operand, returns true	var1 < var2 "2" < 12
Less than or equal to (<=)	if the left operand is less than or equal to the right, returns true	var1 <= var2 var2 <= 5

Don't confuse => as being an operator; it is the arrow function notation.

Arithmetic Operators

Arithmetic operators take a numerical value, which can be a variable or a literal, as an operand and will return one numerical value. There are standard operators:

- Addition (+)
- Subtraction (-)
- Multiplication (*)
- Division (/)

These work the same way as all other programming languages when used with a floating-point number. For example:

1 / 2; // 0.5

1 / 2 == 1.0 / 2.0; // this is true

There are also other arithmetic operators described below with examples:

Operator	Description	Example
Remainder (%)	Binary. Returns an integer remainder of division between the operands.	12 % 5 returns 2
increment (++)	Unary. Adds 1 to the operand. If it is used	if x = 3, ++x will set

	as a prefix (++x), will return the operand value plus one. If it is used as a postfix (x++) will return the operand value before one is added.	x to 4; returns 4. x++ will return 3 and sets x as 4
Decrement (--)	Unary. Will subtract one from the operand and return a value analogous to the increment operator.	if x is 3, --x will set x as 2; returns 2. x—will return 3 and x is set to 2.
Unary negation (-)	Unary. Will return the negation of the return operand.	if x is 3, -x will -3
Unary plus (+)	Unary. Tries converting operand to numbers if not already converted.	+"3" will return 3 +true will return 1
Exponentiation (**)	Will calculate the base to the power of the exponent, i.e. $base^{exponent}$	2 ** 3 will return 8+ 10 ** -1 returns 0.1

Bitwise Operators

Bitwise operators treat operands as 32-bit sets, which are zeroes and ones, instead of octal, hexadecimal, or decimal. As an example, the binary representation of nine (a decimal number) is 1001. A bitwise operator will use the binary representation of a number to perform the operation but will return numerical values.

These are the JavaScript Bitwise operators:

Operator	Usage	Description
Bitwise AND	a & b	A one is returned in each of the bit positions where the corresponding bits of the operands are both ones.
Bitwise OR	a | b	A zero is returned in each of the bit positions where the corresponding operand bits are both zeros.
Bitwise XOR	a ^ b	A zero is returned in each of the bit positions where the corresponding bits are all the same

and a one is returned for the corresponding bits that are different.

Bitwise NOT	~ a	The operand bits are inverted.
Left shift	a <<	a is shifted in a binary representation to the left and right in zeros.
Sign-propagating	a >> b	a is shifted b bits left in a binary representation and the bits that are shifted off are discarded.
Zero-fill	a >>> b	a is shifted b bits right in binary representation, the bits that are shifted off are discarded and zeros are shifted in from the left.

The Bitwise Logical Operators

Theoretically, bitwise logical operators work like this:

- They convert operands into integers of 32-bits and express them using a series of zeros and ones (bits). If a number has more than 32-bits, the most significant of those bits are discarded. For example, this converted integer has more than 32 bits:

1110011011111010000000000000000110000000000001

Once converted into a 32-bit integer, it will look like this:

10100000000000000110000000000001

- The bits in the first operand are paired with the analogous bits in the other operand; i.e. first bit paired to first bit, second to second, and so on.

- The logical operator is applied to each separate pair and a bitwise result is constructed.

For example, the binary number nine representation is 1001 and, for fifteen, the representation is 1111. In the examples below, the results of the operators are being applied to those values:

Expression	Result	Binary Description
15 & 9	9	1111 & 1001 = 1001
15 | 9	15	1111 | 1001 = 1111
15 ^ 0	6	1111 ^ 1001 = 0110

| ~15 | -16 | ~00000000...00001111 = 11111111...11110000 |
| ~9 | -10 | ~00000000...00001001 = 11111111...11110110 |

Bitwise Shift Operators

Bitwise shift operators take two operands. The first one will be a quantity that needs shifting and the second will specify how many bit positions by which the first operand will be shifted. The operator controls the shift operation direction.

The operands are converted by shift operators into 32-bit integers and the result will be of the same type as that of the left operand.

These are the Bitwise shift operators:

Operator	Description	Example
Left shift (<<) is	The first operand is shifted a specified number of bits left. The excess bits that shift left get discarded and zero bits shift in from the right.	9<<2 will return 36; 1001 shifted 2 bits left and becomes 100100, or 36.
Sign propagating (>>)	The first operand is shifted a given number of bits right. The excess bits shifted right get discarded. Copies of the furthest left bit shift in from the left.	9>>2 will return 2, 1001 is shifted 2 bits right and becomes 10, or 2. Likewise, -9>>2 will return -3; the sign is a preserved one.
Zero-fill (>>>)	The first operand is shifted a given number of bits right. The excess bits shifted right get discarded and zero bits shift in from the left.	19>>>2 will return 4;10011 shifts 2 bits right and becomes 100, or 4.

Logical Operators

Logical operators are mostly used with logical values, which are Booleans, returning a value that is also Boolean. However, the value returned by the || and && operators will be of a specified operand. For that reason, when these operators are used with non-Boolean values, they can return non-Boolean values.

These are the logical operators:

Operator	Usage	Description
Logical AND (&&)	expr1 && expr2	expr1 is returned if converted to false, otherwise expr2 is returned. As such,

when this is used with a Boolean value it will return true if both left and right operand are true; otherwise false.

| Logical OR (||) | expr1 || expr2 | expr1 is returned if converted to true, otherwise expr2 is returned. As such, when this is used with a Boolean value it will return true or one of the operands is true; false is returned if both operands are false. |
| Logical NOT (!) | !expr1 | It only has one operand so, if this is converted to true, false will be returned, otherwise true is returned. |

Some of the expressions that may convert to false are expressions that evaluate to 0, null, undefined, NaN, or "", which is an empty string.

The following are some examples of the && operator:

var a1 = true && true;   // t && t returns true

var a2 = true && false;   // t && f returns false

var a3 = false && true;   // f && t returns false

var a4 = false && (3 == 4); // f && f returns false

var a5 = 'Cat' && 'Dog';   // t && t returns Dog

var a6 = false && 'Cat';   // f && t returns false

var a7 = 'Cat' && false;   // t && f returns false

These are examples of the || operator:

var o1 = true || true;   // t || t returns true

var o2 = false || true;   // f || t returns true

var o3 = true || false;   // t || f returns true

var o4 = false || (3 == 4); // f || f returns false

var o5 = 'Cat' || 'Dog';   // t || t returns Cat

var o6 = false || 'Cat';   // f || t returns Cat

var o7 = 'Cat' || false;   // t || f returns Cat

And these are the ! operator:

var n1 = !true; // !t returns false

var n2 = !false; // !f returns true

var n3 = !'Cat'; // !t returns false

String Operators

Comparison operators may be used on string values but there is also another one; the concatenation operator (+) is used to concatenate or join two string values. The value returned is a union of the two strings.

An example:

console.log('my ' + 'string'); // console logs the string "my string".

You can also use +=, which is the shorthand assignment operator, to do the same job:

var mystring = 'alpha';

mystring += 'bet'; // will evaluate to "alphabet" and the value is assigned to mystring.

The Conditional Operator – Ternary

This is the only operator in JavaScript that can take three operands; there are two possible it can have and it will have one, based on a given condition. The syntax used is:

condition ? val1 : val2

If the condition evaluates true, the operator will have the value val1; if not, it will have val2. The conditional operator can be used wherever a standard operator is used:

var status = (age >= 18) ? 'adult' : 'minor';

In this statement, the value of "adult: is assigned to the variable if the age is 18 or over, otherwise, it is "minor".

The Comma Operator

The *comma* operator evaluates both operands; the value assigned to the last operand is returned. This is mostly used for loops and allows for the update of multiple variables on each loop iteration.

For example, if you have a 2-dimensional array with 10 elements on one side, the comma operators can be used to update two variables simultaneously. In this example, the values printed will be the diagonal array elements:

var x = [0,1,2,3,4,5,6,7,8,9]

var a = [x, x, x, x, x];

for (var i = 0, j = 9; i <= j; i++, j--)

  console.log('a[' + i + '][' + j + ']= ' + a[i][j]);

Unary Operators

Unary operations only have one operand.

The delete Operator

The *delete* operator is used to delete objects, object properties, or elements at given array indexes. The syntax used is:

delete objectName;

delete objectName.property;

delete objectName[index];

delete property; // only legal in a with statement

In this, objectName will be the name of the object, property will be a property that already exists, and index will be an integer representing an element location in an array. The last one in the example can only legally be used in a *with* statement and is used to delete properties from objects.

The *delete* operator can also be used to remove an implicitly declared variable but not variables declared using the *var* statement.

If the *delete* operator is successful, the element or property affected will be set as undefined. If this can be accomplished, the operator will return true, and false if it isn't possible:

x = 44;

var y = 45;

myobj = new Number();

myobj.h = 4;   // create a property called h

delete x;   // will return true (can delete if it was implicitly declared)

delete y;   // will return false (cannot delete if it was declared using var)

delete Math.PI; // will return false (cannot delete properties that are predefined)

delete myobj.h; // will return true (can delete properties that are user-defined)

delete myobj;   // will return true (can delete if it was implicitly declared)

Deleting Elements from Arrays

When an array element is deleted it will not affect the length of the array. For example, if you were to delete a[4], a[5] would still be [5] and [4] would be undefined.

When an element is removed using the *delete* operator, the element is removed from the array entirely. In the next example, we use the delete operator to remove trees[3] but, because it can still be addressed, it will return undefined:

var trees = ['elm', 'ash', 'cedar', 'poplar', 'maple'];

delete trees[3];

if (3 in trees) {

* // this does not get executed*

}

If you still want the element to exist but it has an undefined value, the undefined keyword should be used rather than the delete operator. In the next example, we assign trees[3] with undefined but the element will still be there:

var trees = ['elm', 'ash', 'cedar', 'poplar', 'maple'];

trees[3] = undefined;

if (3 in trees) {

* // this will be executed*

}

The typeof Operator

You can use the *typeof* operator in two ways:

typeof operand

typeof (operand)

The operator will return a string indicating what type the unevaluated operand is. The operand may be a variable, string, object, or keyword with a type that is returned. The parentheses are not required.

Let's say we define these variables:

var myFun = new Function('5 + 2');

var shape = 'square';

var size = 1;

var foo = ['Banana', 'Pineapple', 'Papaya'];

var today = new Date();

Using the typeof operator, we would get the following results:

typeof myFun;   // will return "function"

typeof shape;   // will return "string"

typeof size;   // will return "number"

typeof foo;   // will return "object"

typeof today;   // will return "object"

typeof doesntExist; // will return "undefined"

The typeof operator will return these results for the true and null keywords:

typeof true; // will return "boolean"

typeof null; // will return "object"

When you use the *typeof* operator with a string or number, you get these results:

typeof 62;   // will return "number"

typeof 'Hello world'; // will return "string"

With property values, the result is the value type in the property:

typeof document.lastModified; // will return "string"

typeof window.length;   // will return "number"

typeof Math.LN2;   // will return "number"

The results for functions and methods are:

typeof blur;   // will return "function"

typeof eval;   // will return "function"

typeof parseInt;   // will return "function"

typeof shape.split; // will return "function"

Lastly, the *typeof* operator will return these results for predefined objects:

typeof Date;   // will return "function"

typeof Function; // will return "function"

typeof Math;   // will return "object"

typeof Option;   // will return "function"

typeof String;   // will return "function"

The void Operator

You can use the *void* operator in these two ways:

void (expression)

void expression

This operator will specify an expression that should be evaluated but without returning a value. The parentheses used in the first way are optional but it is good practice. In the second way, expression is just the JS expression to be evaluated.

The *void* operator can be used to specify expressions as hypertext links. While the expression is calculated, it will not be loaded to replace the current document.

In the following example, we create the hypertext link, but when it is clicked on, it won't do anything. Instead, when it is clicked, void(0) will evaluate it as undefined, which has no effect whatsoever in JS:

<a href="javascript:void(0)">Click here to do nothing</a>

The hypertext link in this example will submit a form when it is clicked on:

```
<a href="javascript:void(document.form.submit())">
```

Click here to submit</a>

The in Operator

The *in* operator will return a value of true if a given property is contained in a given object. The syntax used is:

propNameOrNumber in objectName

In this, propNameOrNumber is a symbol, numeric, or string expression representing a specified array index or property name, while objectName is, obviously, an object name.

These examples show the *in* operator being used:

```
// Arrays

var trees = ['elm', 'ash', 'cedar', 'poplar', 'maple'];

0 in trees;      // will return true

3 in trees;      // will return true

6 in trees;      // will return false

'ash' in trees;   // will return false (the index number must be specified,
          // not the value at the index)

'length' in trees; // will return true (length is an Array property)


// built-in objects

'PI' in Math;       // will return true

var myString = new String('coral');

'length' in myString;  // will return true


// Custom objects

var mycar = { make: 'Suzuki', model: 'Swift', year: 2010 };

'make' in mycar;  // will return true
```

'model' in mycar; // return true

The instanceof Operator

The *instanceof* operator will return true provided a certain object is of a given type. The syntax used is:

objectName instanceof objectType

In this, objectName is the name of the object being compared to objectType, the type of the object such as Array or Date.

Use the *instanceof* operator when you want an object type confirmed at runtime. For example, when exceptions are being caught, depending on what exception type is thrown, you can branch-off to different code for exception handling.

In the next example, we use the *instanceof* operator to find out if theDay is a Date object and, because it is, the statements inside the *if* statement will be executed:

var theDay = new Date(2000, 12, 17);

if (theDay instanceof Date) {

* // statements that will execute*

}

Operator Precedence

Operator precedence is the order in which operators are applied when an expression is evaluated. This precedence can be overridden with the use of parentheses.

Below is the operator precedence, from high to low:

Operator Type	Individual Operators
member	[] .
call/create instance	new ()
negation/increment	! - ~ + ++ void typeof delete
multiply/divide	* / %
addition/subtraction	+ -
bitwise shift	<< >> >>>
relational	< <= > >= in instanceof

equality	== != === !==
bitwise AND	&
bitwise XOR	^
bitwise OR		
logical AND	&&
logical OR	||
conditional	?:
assignment	= += -= *= /= %= <<= >>= >>>= &= ^= |=
comma	,

Expressions

Expressions are valid code units that will resolve into a value.

Every expression written correctly will resolve to a value but there are two different types of expressions – those assigning a variable with a value and those that evaluate.

An example of the first type is x = 7. The assignment operator (=) has been used to assign a variable called x with a value of 7 and the expression will evaluate to 7. For the second type, an example would be 4 +3. The addition operator (+) is used to add the values together but doesn't assign a result to a variable, which would again be 7.

In JavaScript, you will find these expression categories:

- **Arithmetic** – These evaluate to numbers, for example, 3.14159 and usually use arithmetic operators.

- **String** – These evaluate to character strings, for example, "123" or "book", and usually use string operators.

- **Logical** – These will evaluate to either true or false and often use the logical operators.

- **Primary expressions** – These are basic JS keywords and general JS expressions.

- **Left-hand-side expressions** – These values are the assignment destination.

Primary Expressions

The basic expressions and keywords in JavaScript are:

this

The *this* keyword is used to reference the current object. By and large, this would be the calling object in the method. The keyword is used with either the bracket or dot notation, as follows:

this['propertyName']

this.propertyName

Let's say we have a function named "validate". This function is used to validate value properties for a given object and its low and high values:

function validate(obj, lowval, hival) {

  if ((obj.value < lowval) || (obj.value > hival))

    console.log('Invalid Value!');

}

Validate could be called in the onChange event handler for each form element; the *this* keyword would pass the form element, as you can see in this example:

<p>Enter a number between 20 and 99:</p>

<input type="text" name="age" size=3 onChange="validate(this, 20, 99);">

Grouping Operator

The grouping operator is used to control precedence in evaluation expressions. For example, multiplication and division could be overridden first, followed by addition and subtraction so addition is evaluated first:

var a = 1;

var b = 2;

var c = 3;

// default precedence

*a + b * c;   // 7*

```
// evaluated by default like this
a + (b * c);  // 7
```

```
// now overriding precedence
// addition before multiplication
(a + b) * c;  // 9
```

```
// which is equivalent to
a * c + b * c; // 9
```

Left-Hand-Side Expressions

These values are the assignment destination:

new

The *new* operator is used to create instances of object types that can be user-defined or built-in. The operator should be used like this:

```
var objectName = new objectType([param1, param2, ..., paramN]);
```

super

We use the *super* keyword to call functions on the parent of an object. One valuable way it is used is with classes to call the parent constructor.

```
super([arguments]); // the parent constructor is called
```

```
super.functionOnParent([arguments]);
```

Spread Operator

The *spread* operator is used when you want to expand an expression in a place where multiple arrays literal elements or numerous function call arguments are expected.

Today, if you wanted to create an array using an existing array as part of it, using the array literal syntax would not be enough, and forces you to use imperative code, a combination of *concat, splice, concat*, etc. Using the *spread* operator negates that, making it much easier.

```
var parts = ['shoulders', 'knees'];
```

var lyrics = ['head', ...parts, 'and', 'toes'];

In much the same way, the operator can be used in function calls:

function f(x, y, z) { }

var args = [0, 1, 2];

f(...args);

Numbers and Dates

JavaScript provides several concepts, functions, and objects to use when calculating and working with numbers and dates, including those numbers written in the different bases – octal, hexadecimal, decimal, binary, etc. – along with a global Math object that lets us do all sorts of operations on those numbers.

Numbers

All numbers in JavaScript are implemented in a specific format known as "double-precision 64-bit binary format IEEE 754", for example, numbers between $-(2^{63}-1)$ and $2^{63}-1$. As well as floating-point numbers, there are also three symbolic values in the number type:

- +Infinity

- -Infinity

- NaN (not a number)

Integers in JavaScript don't have a specific data type although you can use BigInt to represent very big integers. Nevertheless, the use of BigInt comes with some caveats – BigInt and Number values cannot be used together in the same operation and the Math object also cannot be used with BigInt values.

There are four number literal types you can use:

Decimal

1234567890

42

// Caution when using leading zeros:

0888 // 888 parsed as a decimal

0777 // parsed as an octal in non-strict mode (511 in decimal)

Note

Decimal literals can begin with a zero with another decimal digit following it. On the other hand, if all digits following the leading zero are less than 8, the number is parsed as octal.

Binary Numbers

The syntax for the binary number also uses a leading zero again, this time a lower or upper-case Latin letter follows it – "B" (0B or 0b). If the digits that follow this are not a 0 or a 1, you will get a "Missing Binary Digits" syntax error.

var FLT_SIGNBIT = 0b10000000000000000000000000000000; // 2147483648

var FLT_EXPONENT = 0b01111111100000000000000000000000; // 2139095040

var FLT_MANTISSA = 0B00000000011111111111111111111111; // 8388607

Octal Numbers

The octal syntax also has the leading zero. If the following digits are not within the 0 to 7 range, the number is interpreted as decimal:

var n = 0755; // 493

var m = 0644; // 420

In ECMAScript 5, strict mode does not allow the use of the octal syntax, but it does have support in all major browsers by adding a zero to the front of the octal number, i.e. 0644 === 420 and"\045" === "%". In ECMAScript 2015, there is support for octal numbers that have a 0o prefix, for example:

var a = 0o10; // ES2015: 8

Hexadecimal Numbers

The syntax for the hexadecimal number has a leading zero with a lower or upper-case Latin letter "X" (0X or 0x). If the following digits are not within the 0123456789ABCDEF range, you will get an "Identifier Starts Immediately After Numeric Literal" syntax error:

0xFFFFFFFFFFFFFFFF // 295147905179352830000

0x123456789ABCDEF   // 81985529216486900

0XA   // 10

Exponentiation

1E3 // 1000

2e6 // 2000000

0.1e2 // 10

Number Object

The Number object built-in to JavaScript contains properties relating to numerical constraints, like NaN, maximum value, and infinity. The property values cannot be changed; they are used like this:

var biggestNum = Number.MAX_VALUE;

var smallestNum = Number.MIN_VALUE;

var infiniteNum = Number.POSITIVE_INFINITY;

var negInfiniteNum = Number.NEGATIVE_INFINITY;

var notANum = Number.NaN;

Predefined Number object properties are always referred to in the following ways, never as a property for a user-defined number object:

These are the properties for the Number object:

Property	Description
Number.MAX_VALUE	largest number that can be represented
Number.MIN_VALUE	smallest number that can be represented
Number.NaN	a special value to represent "not a number"
Number.NEGATIVE_INFINITY	a special value for negative infinite, returns on overflow
Number.POSITIVE_INFINITY	a special value for positive infinite, returns on overflow
Number.EPSILON	The difference between 1 and the smallest value larger than 1 that may be represented as a number.
Number.MIN_SAFE_INTEGER	the minimum safe JS integer
Number.MAX_SAFE_INTEGER	the maximum safe JS integer

Number Methods

Method	Description
Number.parseFloat()	will parse a string argument, returning a floating-point number. Works as the global parseFloat() function does
Number.parseInt()	will parse a string argument, returning an integer of a specified base or radix. Works as the global parseInt() function does
Number.isFinite()	will determine if the value passed is an infinite number
Number.isInteger()	will determine if the value passed is an integer
Number.isNaN()	will determine if the value passed is NaN. A much better version of the global isNaN().
Number.isSafeInteger()	will determine if the value provided is a safe integer number

Number Prototype

This provides us with methods to retrieve information from various Number object formats. These are the methods:

Method	Description
toExponential()	returns a string that uses exponential notation to represent a number
toFixed()	returns a string using fixed-point notation to represent a number
toPrecision()	returns a string using fixed-point notation to represent a number to specific precision

Math Object

The Math object built-in to JavaScript provides methods and properties for use with mathematical functions and constants. For example, the PI property has a value of pi (3.141...) and this would be used like this:

Math.PI

Math methods are standard math functions, such as logarithmic, trigonometric, exponential, etc. To use a trigonometric function of sine, you would do this:

Math.sin(1.56)

All the trigonometric methods of the object take their arguments in radians.

These are the methods in the Math object:

Method	Description
abs()	Absolute value
sin(), cos(), tan()	the standard trigonometric functions taking arguments in radians
asin(), acos(), atan(), atan2()	the inverse trigonometric functions with return values in radians
sinh(), cosh(), tanh()	the hyperbolic functions, with arguments in the hyperbolic angle
asinh(), acosh(), atanh()	the inverse hyperbolic functions with return values in the hyperbolic angle
pow(), exp(), expm1(), log10(), log1p(), log2()	the logarithmic and exponential function
floor(), ceil()	will return the smallest or largest integers less, greater, or equal to a specified argument
min(), max()	returns the min or max value of a list of arguments (numbers separated by commas)
random()	will return a random number between 0 and 1
round(), fround(), trunc(),	the truncation and rounding functions
sqrt(), cbrt(), hypot()	the square root, cube root and square root of square arguments sum
sign()	sign of number, indicates negative, positive, or zero

clz32(), imul()	indicates how many leading zero bits are in a 32-bit representation; the result of the multiplication (c-like 32-bit) of two arguments

You cannot create Math objects; always use the one that is built-in.

Date Object

There is no data type in JavaScript for a date, but a *Date* object and associated methods let you work with both date and time. There are various methods in the object to set and get dates as well as manipulate them, but it has no properties.

JavaScript is much the same as Java in the way it handles dates; both sharing many of the same techniques and storing dates – as a number of milliseconds from 1 Jan 1970 00:00:00, using a Unix Timestamp to indicate the number of seconds from 1 Jan 1970 00:00:00.

The range of the *Date* object is -100,000,000 to 100,000,000 days relative to 1 Jan 1970 UTC.

Creating a *date* object is done like this:

var dateObjectName = new Date([parameters]);

Here, dateObjectName is the name for the *Date* object you are creating. This can be a new one or a property of an object already in existence.

If you don't use the new keyword to call *Date*, you will get a string representing the current time and date.

The parameter can be any of the following:

- Nothing - the current time and date will be created, i.e. today = new Date()

- A string representing a date in "month day year hours:minutes:seconds" format, i.e. varXmas18 – new Date("December 25, 2018 14:25:34"). If you don't comprise the hours, minutes or seconds, the value is set as zero

- A set of integer values representing year, month, day. i.e. var Xmas18 = new Date(2018, 12, 25)

- A set of integer values representing year, month, day, hours, minutes, seconds, i.e. Xmas18 = new Date(2018, 11, 25, 8, 45, 26);

Date Object Methods

Date object methods come under four broad categories:

- **Set methods -** sets the date and time values

- **Get methods** – gets the date and time values

- **To methods** – for returning the string values from the Date objects

- **Parse and UTC methods** – for parsing the Date strings

The set and get methods allow you to set and get seconds, minutes, hours, days of the week, months and years. While there is a method called *getDay*, returning the day of the week, there isn't a method called *setDay* – you can't do this because the days of the week are already set. Both methods represent values using integers as follows:

- **Seconds and minutes** – from 0 to 59

- **Hours** – from 0 to 23

- **Days** – from 0 to 6 (Sunday to Saturday)

- **Date** – from 1 to 31 (days of the month)

- **Months** – from 0 to 11 (January to December)

- **Year** – starts at 1900

Let's say you wanted to define this date:

var Xmas18 = new Date('December 25, 2018');

Xmas18.getMonth() would return 11 and Xmas09.getFullYear would return 2018.

getTime() and setTime() are both useful methods for date comparisons. With getTime(), the value returned for a date object would be the number of milliseconds passed since 1 Jan 1970 00:00:00.

The code below displays how many days are left in the current year:

var today = new Date();

var endYear = new Date(2018, 11, 31, 23, 59, 59, 999); // Set day and month

endYear.setFullYear(today.getFullYear()); // Set year to this year

*var msPerDay = 24 * 60 * 60 * 1000; // Number of milliseconds per day* *var daysLeft = (endYear.getTime() - today.getTime()) / msPerDay;*

var daysLeft = Math.round(daysLeft); //returns days left in the year

A *Date* object has been created and named "Today"; it will contain the current date. A *Date* object called "endYear" is then generated and the year is set to the current year. Taking the number of milliseconds in a day, the number of days left from today to the *endYear* are computed using getTime(); the result is rounded up to a whole number.

A useful way of assigning date string values to existing *Date* objects is to use the parse method. For example, in the next code we use both parse and setTime to assign the IPOdate object with a date value:

var IPOdate = new Date();

IPOdate.setTime(Date.parse('Aug 9, 2018'));

In the next example we use the function called JSClock() to return the time in digital clock format:

function JSClock() {

  var time = new Date();

  var hour = time.getHours();

  var minute = time.getMinutes();

  var second = time.getSeconds();

  var temp = '' + ((hour > 12) ? hour - 12 : hour);

  if (hour == 0)

    temp = '12';

  temp += ((minute < 10) ? ':0' : ':') + minute;

  temp += ((second < 10) ? ':0' : ':') + second;

  temp += (hour >= 12) ? ' P.M.' : ' A.M.';

  return temp;

}

First we create a new *Date* object using the JSClock function; the object is called "time", No arguments are provided, so the current date and time are used to create time. We then call the getHours(), getMinutes(), and getSeconds() methods to assign the values of the current hour to hour, the current minute to minute and the current second to second.

The four trailing statements use time to build a string value. The first one creates a variable called "temp" and uses a conditional expression to assign a value to it; if hour – 12 (the hour is greater than 12), otherwise hour; unless hour is 0, in which it would be 12.

In the next statement, a minute value is appended to the temp variable. If the minute value is less than 10, a string is added with a preceding zero by the conditional expression. If not, a string containing a demarcating colon is added. A third statement does the same with the seconds. Lastly, a conditional expression is used to assign PM to the temp variable if the hour is 12 or greater, otherwise, AM is appended.

Strings

In JavaScript, we represent text using string data. A string is a series of 16-bit elements of all unsigned integers. Each string element has a position in the string with the first element starting at index 0. A string length is determined by the number of elements and you can create a string using string objects or string literals.

String Literals

Simple strings can be created using single quotes or double quotes; again, remember to use the same ones – either single OR double; never mix the quote marks.

'foo'

"bar"

For advanced strings, we can use the following escape sequences:

Hexadecimal

The number that follows \x is seen as a hexadecimal number

'\xA9' // "©"

Unicode

There must be at least four hexadecimal digits after \u for this escape sequence:

'\u00A9' // "©"

Unicode Code Point

The Unicode code point escape was introduced with ECMAScript 2015. They are used to escape any character using the hexadecimal numbers; this makes it possible to use them up to 0x010FFFF. Often, with the simpler Unicode escape, you need to write both sides separately to get the same result.

'\u{2F804}'

// the same with the Unicode escapes

'\uD87E\uDC04'

String Objects

A string object is a wrapper that encloses the data type of string primitive:

const foo = new String('foo'); // Creates a String object

console.log(foo); // Displays: [String: 'foo']

console.log(typeof foo); // Returns 'object'

You can use a string literal value to call the string object methods; JS converts the literal into a temporary object, calls the string object method, and then the temporary object is discarded. The String.length property can also be used with a string literal.

Unless a string object is specifically required, use string literals because the objects can often cause counterintuitive results:

const firstString = '2 + 2'; // Creates a string literal value

const secondString = new String('2 + 2'); // Creates a String object

console.log(eval(firstString)); // Returns the number 4

console.log(eval(secondString)); // Returns the string '2 + 2'

String objects have one property – length – to indicate how many UTF-16 code units the string contains. In the next example, x is assigned a value of 13 because the string, "Hello, World!" contains 13 characters. Each of these characters is represented by a single UTF-16 code unit and each unit may be accessed with an array bracket style. The individual characters cannot be changed because strings are immutable.

const hello = 'Hello, World!';

const helloLength = hello.length;

hello[0] = 'L'; // This won't do anything, because strings are immutable

console.log(hello[0]); // This returns "H"

There are several methods that go with the string object:

Method	Description
charAt, charCodeAt, codePointAt	will return the character/character code at the given string position

indexOf, lastIndexOf	will return the position or last position respectively of the given substring in the string
startsWith, endsWith, includes	will return whether a given string is at the start, end, or contained within the string
concat	will combine the test from two given strings and return one new string
fromCharCode, fromCodePoint	will construct a string from a given sequence of values (Unicode). This is a string class method, not an instance
split	the string object is separated into substrings to create an array of strings
slice	will extract a specified part of the string and return it as a new string
substring, substr	will return a given subset; either the start and end indexes are specified or the start and a length
match, matchAll, replace, search	allows string objects to work with regular expressions
toLowerCase, toUpperCase	will return the string in lower or uppercase
normalize	will return the Unicode Normalization Form of the value of the calling string
repeat	will return a string that has the object elements repeated a given number of times
trim	will trim all whitespace from the start and end of the string

Multi-Line Template Literals

A template literal is just a string literal that allows expressions to be embedded. They can be used with string interpolation and multi-line-strings. Instead of the quotation marks, backticks (` `) are used to surround a template literal. They can have place holders in them, i.e. ${expression} – the dollar sign and curly braces indicate the placeholder.

Multi-Lines

If you insert a new line character into the source, it is considered part of the template literal. With a normal string, the following syntax would be used for multi-line strings:

console.log('string text line 1\n

string text line 2');

// "string text line 1

// string text line 2"

But you can now write it like this:

console.log(`string text line 1

string text line 2`);

// "string text line 1

// string text line 2"

Embedded Expressions

To embed an expression in a normal string, you would use this syntax:

const five = 5;

const ten = 10;

*console.log('Fifteen is ' + (five + ten) + ' and not ' + (2 * five + ten) + '.');*

// "Fifteen is 15 and not 20."

With a template literal, you can make your syntax a lot sweeter to read and understand:

const five = 5;

const ten = 10;

console.log(`Fifteen is ${five + ten} and not ${2 * five + ten}.`);

// "Fifteen is 15 and not 20."

Internationalization

The ECMAScript Internationalization API provides three main features – number formatting, time and date formatting, and string comparisons that are language-sensitive. The namespace is the Intl object and the constructors for the objects called DateTimeFormat, NumberFormat, and Collator are all properties of Intl.

Formatting Data and Time

To format date and time, we use the DateTimeFormat object. The next example will format the date – note the result would be different for different time zones:

```
const msPerDay = 24 * 60 * 60 * 1000;


// July 17, 2014 00:00:00 UTC.

const july172014 = new Date(msPerDay * (44 * 365 + 11 + 197));


const options = { year: '2-digit', month: '2-digit', day: '2-digit',

        hour: '2-digit', minute: '2-digit', timeZoneName: 'short' };

const americanDateTime = new Intl.DateTimeFormat('en-US', options).format;


console.log(americanDateTime(july172014)); // 07/16/14, 9:00 PM GMT-3
```

Formatting Numbers

For number formatting, such as currencies, for example, we use the NumberFormat object:

```
const gasPrice = new Intl.NumberFormat('en-US',

        { style: 'currency', currency: 'USD',

          minimumFractionDigits: 3 });


console.log(gasPrice.format(5.259)); // $5.259
```

```javascript
const hanDecimalRMBInChina = new Intl.NumberFormat('zh-CN-u-nu-hanidec',

        { style: 'currency', currency: 'CNY' });


console.log(hanDecimalRMBInChina.format(1314.25)); // CN¥ 1,314.25
```

Collation

When we want to compare strings and sort them, we use the Collator object. For example, in the German language, there are two sort orders – dictionary and phonebook. With the latter, the sound is emphasized and letters such as "ä", and "ö", are expanded before sorting to "ae", "oe", and so on:

```javascript
const names = ['Hochberg', 'Hönigswald', 'Holzman'];


const germanPhonebook = new Intl.Collator('de-DE-u-co-phonebk');


// as if sorting ["Hochberg", "Hoenigswald", "Holzman"]:

console.log(names.sort(germanPhonebook.compare).join(', '));

// logs "Hochberg, Hönigswald, Holzman"
```

Because some of the German words are conjugated using additional umlauts, it makes sense in dictionary sort to order the words ignoring the umlaut unless the sort order requires sorting by umlaut only, for example, schon and then schön:

```javascript
const germanDictionary = new Intl.Collator('de-DE-u-co-dict');


// as if sorting ["Hochberg", "Honigswald", "Holzman"]:

console.log(names.sort(germanDictionary.compare).join(', '));

// logs "Hochberg, Holzman, Hönigswald"
```

Regular Expressions

A regular expression is a pattern used in JavaScript to find and match combinations of characters in a string. These are also objects. We use RegExp and two of its methods – exec and test – and we also use the string methods, search, split, replace, and match.

How Regular Expressions are Created

Regular expressions are constructed using a regular expression literal. This pattern is surrounded by slashes:

var re = /ab+c/;

The regular expression literal compiles the regular expression when the script is loaded. This can make an improvement to the performance provided the expression stays constant.

Another way to create a regular expression is to call the RegExp object constructor function:

var re = new RegExp('ab+c');

With the constructor function, the regular expression is compiled at runtime. This is the method to use when you discern the pattern of the regular expression is going to change, or if you are getting the pattern from another source and don't know what it is.

Writing Regular Expression Patterns

Regular expression patterns are constructed of simple characters, like /def/, or you can use a mixture of simple characters and special ones, like /de*f/ or /Title (g+)\. \g*/. The parentheses in the last example are used as memory devices, i.e. the match is remembered when it needs to be used later on.

Simple Patterns

A simple pattern is made up of characters for which you want a direct match. For example, the pattern of /def/ will match combinations of characters in a string ONLY where "def" appear in that order and together. For example, if you have a string of text reading, "this is a definite match" the pattern would match the substring "def".

Special Characters

When you need to find something that isn't a direct match, like finding whitespace, two or more d's, and so on, your pattern will need to include special characters. For example,

/de*f/ will match with any combination of characters where a single 'd' is followed by zero or more character 'e's followed by the 'd'. The * symbol indicates 0 or more occurrences of the item preceding the symbol. For example, if you had a string of "fddeeefedf", the match would be with the substring "deeef".

These are the special characters that may be used in a regular expression along with a full description of their use:

Character	Meaning
\	Matches with the following rules:

If a backslash precedes a simple (non-special) character, it indicates that the following character is a special one and is not to be literally interpreted. For example, 'b' with no \ preceding it matches a lowercase 'b' anywhere it occurs but '\b\' on its own is denoting a word boundary and doesn't match with any character.

If a backslash precedes a special character, it is indicating that the following character is non-special and should be literally interpreted. For example, the pattern /b*/ is relying on the special character of '*' to find 0 or more matches to 'b'. However, if you had a pattern of /b*/ is telling us that the '*' character is not special and that means it can match strings like 'b*'.

One thing you must not forget is that the escape (\) itself has to be escaped when you use the RegExp notation because it is an escape character in a standard string.

^   This is used to match the start of the input. If you have a multi-line flag set as true, it will also match straight after any line break character.

For example, / ^B/won't match the 'B' inside the string "a B" but it will match with the 'B' in "A Bee".

$ It is used to match the end of the input. If the multiline flag has been set as true, it will also match right before any line break character.

For example, /t$/ will not match with the 't' in "heater" but it will match in "heat".

*   This will match the expression that precedes it 0 or more times and is the equivalent of {0,}.

For example, /bo*/ will match 'boon' and it will match 'b' in "a bird sang" but it wouldn't match anything in "a cat meowed".

+   This will match the expression that precedes it 1 or more times and is the equivalent of {1,}

For example, /b+/ would match the 'b' in "banded" and it would match all the bs in "bbbbbanded" but it wouldn't match anything in "anded"

?   This will match the expression that precedes it 0 or 1 times and is the equivalent of {0,1}.

For example /e?de/ would match the 'ed' in 'banded' and the 'de' in 'ceded' and it would also match the 'e' in 'code'.

If you use it right after a quantifier - *, ?, +, or {} – it will ensure the quantifier matches the least number of characters (i.e. the quantifier will be non-greedy); the default is to match as many characters as possible (i.e. greedy). For example, if you applied /d+/ to '123abc' it would match '123' but if you applied /\d+?/ to '123'abc' it would match only the '1'.

This is also used in the lookahead assertions which will be described later under the entries of x(?!y) and x(?=y).

.   A decimal point character will match with any single character by default with the exception of the newline character.

For example, /.n/ will match with the 'an' and 'on' in the string " nay, it is an apple on the plate, not an orange" but it won't match with "nay".

If you set the s ("dotAll") flag to true, it will match the newline characters.

(x)   This will match 'x' and it will remember the match as you can see in the following examples. The parentheses, in this case, are called 'capturing parentheses'.

In the pattern of /(foo)(bar)\1\2/ the (foo) and the (bar) will match and the first two words in the "foo bar foo bar" string will be remembered. \1 and \2 are indicating the first and the second substring matches in the parentheses – foo and bar – matching with the last two words in the string.

(?x)	This will match x but the match will not be remembered. In this case, the parentheses are 'non-capturing' and they will allow you to define a subexpression that the regular operators for expressions can be used with. For example, an expression of /(?:foo){1,2}. If that expression read /foo{1,2} the match would only apply to the final 'o' in the word 'foo'. By using the non-capturing set of parentheses, {1,2} is applied to the whole word.
x(?=y)	This is called a lookahead and can only match 'x' if it is followed by 'y'.
	For example, /Tom(?=Thumb)/ will only match "Tom" if it is followed by "Thumb" whereas /Tom(?=Thumb|Tailor)/ matches "Tom" if it is followed by "Thumb" or "Tailor" but neither "Thumb" nor "Tailor" will be part of the results.
x(?!y)	This is a negated lookahead and will only match 'x' if it isn't followed by 'y'.
	For example, /\d+)?!\.)/ can only match a number if a decimal point does not follow it. /\d+(?!\.)/.exec(3.141) is a regular expression that will not match '3.141' but it will match '141'.
(?<=y)x	This is known as a look behind and will match x only if it is preceded by y.
	For example, /(?<=Tom)Thumb/ will only match "Thumb" if "Tom" precedes it. /(?<=Tom|Jack)Thumb/ will only match "Thumb" if "Tom" or "Jack" precedes it. However, "Tom" or "Jack" will not be in the results.
(?<!y)x	This is a negated look behind and only matches x if it isn't preceded with y.
	For example, /(?<!-)\d+/ will only match a number that isn't preceded by the minus symbol (-). /(?<!-)\d+/.exec('5') will match '5' but in /(?<!-)\d+/.exec('-5') will not be matched because a minus sign precedes the number.
x|y	This will match 'x' but if there is no match, it will match 'y'.
	For example, /blue|black/ will match 'blue' in "blue denim" and 'black" in "black denim" . The order of 'x' and 'y' is important; i.e. a*|b will match an empty string in "b" but if you used b|a*, it would match with a simple 'b' in the string.

{n}	This will match n occurrences exactly of the expression that precedes it. N has to be a positive integer.
	For example, /a{2} will not match the 'a' in "banded" but it will match every 'a' in "baanded" along with the first two a's in "baaanded".
{n,}	This will match at least n occurrences of the expression that precedes it and N has to be a positive integer.
	For example, /b{2,} will match "bb", "bbbb" and "bbbbb" but it will not match "b".
{n,m}	In the case of m and n being positive integers and n <= m, it will match at least n and most of the m occurrences of the expression that precedes it.
	For example, /a{1,3}/won't match anything in "bnded", the "a" in "banded", the first two a's in "banded" and the first three in "baaaaaaanded". In "baaaaaaanded" the match would be "aaa" although there are more a's in the string.
[xyz]	This is the character set pattern type and it will match any of the characters inside the square brackets and that includes any escape sequences. When used in a character set, special characters such as the asterisk (*) and the dot (.) are not treated as special and do not need to be escaped. As per the following examples, you can use a hyphen to specify a range of different characters.
	A pattern of [a-d] performs the same as [abcd] and will match 'b' in "banded" and 'c' in "candy". With the /[a-z.]+/ and the /[\w.] patterns, the whole string of "test.i.ng" is matched.
[^xyz]	This is a complemented or negated character set which means it matches anything not inside the set of brackets. A character range may be specified with the hyphen and anything that works inside a standard character set will also work in this situation.
	For example, [^abc] and [^a-c] are the same and, to start with, will match the 'r' in "bricks" and the 'h' in "change".
[\b]	This will match U+0008, a backspace but, if you want a literal backspace character matched, you must use the square brackets.

It also matches a word boundary. These match a position in between a word character and a non-word character or vice versa. They also match the start of the string and/or the end of the string. Word boundaries are characters that are not to be matched. Think of them as an anchor; not to be included. This means a matched word boundary has a length of zero.

The following examples use an input string of 'moon'. /\bm/ will match because `b` is at the start of the string. /oo\b/ - the 'b' will not match because it is preceded by a word character and followed by one too. /oon\b/ - the 'b' matches because it is at the end of the string. /\w\b\w/ - the 'b' can't match anything because it is preceded by a word character and followed by one too.

\B   This will match a non-word boundary and will match these cases:

Before the first string character

After the last string character

In between a pair of word characters

In between a pair of non-word characters

An empty string

For example, /\B.../ will match the 'oo' in 'moon' and /y\B./ will match the 'ye' in 'yesterday'.

\cX   Where X will be a character between A and Z; will match a control character somewhere in the string.

For example, /\cM/ will match the control -M (u+000D) in any string.

\d   This matches any digit character and is equivalent to [0-9].

For example, /\d or /[0-9] will match the '2' in "B2 is the room number"".

\D   This matches any non-digit number and is equivalent to [^0-9].

For example, /\D/ or /[^0-9] will match the 'B' in "B2 is the room number".

\f   This will match a form feed or U+000C.

\n	This will match a line feed or U+000A.
\r	This will match a carriage return or U+000D.
\s	This will match a whitespace character that includes a space, form feed, tab, or line feed and is the equivalent of [\f\n\r\t\v\u00a0\u1680\u2000-\u200a\u2028\u2029\u202f\u205f\u3000\ufeff].

For example, /\s\w*/ will match the word 'bar' in the string 'foo bar'. |
| \S | This will match any character that is not white space and is equivalent to [\f\n\r\t\v\u00a0\u1680\u2000-\u200a\u2028\u2029\u202f\u205f\u3000\ufeff].

For example, /\S*/ will match the word 'foo' in the string 'foo bar' |
| \t | This will match a tab or U+0009 |
| \v | This will match a vertical tab or U+000B |
| \w | This will match any of the alphanumeric characters, and that includes an underscore; it is the equivalent of [A-Za-z0-9_].

For example, /\w/ will match the 'a' in band', the '6' in $6.85 and the '2' in '2D'. |
| \W | This will match any of the non-word characters and is the equivalent of [^A-Za-z0-9_].

For example, /\W/ or /[^A-Za-z0-9_] will match the '%' in '25%' |
| \n | This is a back-reference to the last substring that matched the n parenthetical, counting the left parentheses, in the regular expression (when n is a positive integer)/

For example, /banana(,)\spineapple\1/ will match "apple, pineapple" in the string "apple, pineapple, peach, pear". |
| \0 | This will match a NULL or U+0000 character. This must not precede another digit because \0<digits> is actually an octal escape sequence. Instead, you should use \x00 |
| \xhh | This will match a character with two hexadecimal digits or an hh code |

\uhhhh	This will match a character with four hexadecimal digits or an hhhh code
\u{hhhh}	When the u flag is set, this will match a character with a Unicode value of hhhh or hexadecimal digits.

To escape user input treated as literal strings in regular expressions (normally, this would be seen as a special character) you can use a simple replacement:

function escapeRegExp(string) {

  return string.replace(/[.*+?^${}()|[\]\\]/g, '\\$&'); // $& means the whole matched string

}

The g that follows the regular expression is a flag or option that will carry out a global search; it looks in the entire string and it will return every match. This will be explained in more detail later.

Using Parentheses

When you use a set of parentheses around a part of the expression, that part will be remembered and it can then be recalled later for further use. For example, in the pattern of /Title (\d+)\.\d*/ - what you see here is a number of extra special characters and escaped characters along with an indication that the section inside the parentheses is to be remembered. More precisely, it will match the characters "Title" followed by at least one numeric character - \d indicates numeric characters and + indicates at least one time. The decimal point, a special character in its own right, follows this preceding that with \ indicates that a literal character must be looked for – the decimal point in this case – followed by a numeric character 0 or more times. The parentheses indicate that the first numeric characters matched will also be remembered.

This pattern would be found in something like "Open Title 4.5, page 7" – the '4' will be remembered. If you had a string of "Open Title 3 and 4" there would not be a match because the 3 is not followed by a decimal point.

If you want a substring matched without the matched bit being remembered, the pattern inside the parentheses should be prefixed with ?:. For example, the pattern (?:\d+) will match at least one numeric character but the matched characters will not be remembered.

Working with the Regular Expression

As you know, the RegExp methods test and exec are used with regular expressions, along with the string methods split, search, replace, and match.

These are the methods with a description:

Method	Description
exec	This RegExp method will execute the search for a specified match in the given string. One of two results is returned – a null because there isn't a match or an array containing the matched information
test	This RegExp method tests a string for a match and the return will be true if there is a match, false if not.
match	This string method will execute the search for a specified match in the given string. Either a null is returned for no match or an array of the matched information.
matchAll	This string method will return an iterator that has all matches and capturing groups included.
search	This string method will test a string for a match. The result will either be a -1 if the search is unsuccessful or, if it is, the index of the match.
replace	This string method will execute a search for a specified match in a given string. The substring that matches is replaced with a specified substring.
split	This string method will use a fixed string or a regular expression to break a string down into an array of separate substrings.

The RegExp test or String search methods should be used when you want to see if a pattern is found or not. If you want more information, the RegExp exec or String match methods should be used but the execution will be slower. If you use exec or match and a match is found, an array is returned and the properties for all the objects associated with the regular expression are updated, along with the RegExp object. If there is no match, null is returned by exec, which will coerce to false.

Look at this example where we use exec to look for a match:

var myRe = /d(b+)d/g;

var myArray = myRe.exec('cdbbdbsbz');

If you don't need access to the regular expression properties, you could create myArray in this way:

var myArray = /d(b+)d/g.exec('cdbbdbsbz');

  // similar to "cdbbdbsbz".match(/d(b+)d/g); however,

  // "cdbbdbsbz".match(/d(b+)d/g) outputs Array ["dbbd"], while

  // /d(b+)d/g.exec('cdbbdbsbz') outputs Array ['dbbd', 'bb', index: 1, input: 'cdbbdbsbz'].

If you want a regular expression constructed from the string, another way is this:

var myRe = new RegExp('d(b+)d', 'g');

var myArray = myRe.exec('cdbbdbsbz');

Using these scripts, the match is successful; an array is returned and the properties are updated.

As you can see, a regular expression that was created with an object initializer can be used without assigning it to any variable. If you do, each new occurrence will be a brand new regular expression. It is for this reason that, if you opt to do this without assigning it to the variable, you will not be able to access any of the properties of the regular expression.

For example:

var myRe = /d(b+)d/g;

var myArray = myRe.exec('cdbbdbsbz');

console.log('The value of lastIndex is ' + myRe.lastIndex);

// "The value of the lastIndex is 5"

But if you write it this way:

var myArray = /d(b+)d/g.exec('cdbbdbsbz');

console.log('The value of lastIndex is ' + /d(b+)d/g.lastIndex);

// "The value of lastIndex is 0"

Where you see /d(b+)d/g in each statement, they are two different objects and, as such, the lastIndex property will have different values. If you require access to the properties of the expression that used an object initializer to create it, it should be assigned to a variable first.

Parenthesized Substring Matches

When you add parentheses to a regular expression pattern, the submatch that corresponds to it will be remembered. For example, /a(b)c/ will match all occurrences of the characters "abc" and will remember the 'b'. Recalling parenthesized matches (substrings) should be done using the [1], ... [n] array elements.

There is no limit to the number of substrings possible and an array that is returned will hold every possible match. In the next example, we use replace() to change the words contained in the string. $1 and $2 are used by the script to indicate the first parenthesized substring match and the second one:

var re = /(\w+)\s(\w+)/;

var str = 'Bilbo Baggins';

var newstr = str.replace(re, '$2, $1');

console.log(newstr);

// "Baggins, Bilbo"

Advanced Search Using Flags

With a regular expression, you have no less than six optional flags for different functionalities, such as case-insensitive and global searching. You can use these flags together or on their own; if you choose to use them together, you can use them in any order you want so long as they are a part of the regular expression.

Flag	Description
g	Indicates a global search
i	Indicates a case-insensitive search
m	Indicates a multi-line search
s	Indicates that . (dot) can match to newline characters

u	Indicates "unicode" and that the pattern should be treated as a sequence of code points (Unicode)
y	Indicates a "sticky" search; it starts at the current point in the string that is being targeted to search for the matches.

If you want a flag included with the regular expression, this is the syntax you should use:

var re = /pattern/flags;

Or this:

var re = new RegExp('pattern', 'flags');

The flags must be an integral part of the expression and cannot be added or taken out later.

For example, re = /\w+\s/g will create a regular expression that will search for at least one (specified) character with a space after it and it will search the entire string for the match.

var re = /\w+\s/g;

var str = 'fee fi fo fum';

var myArray = str.match(re);

console.log(myArray);

// ["fee ", "fi ", "fo "]

The line below could be replaced:

var re = /\w+\s/g;

with this line:

var re = new RegExp('\\w+\\s', 'g');

and you will get the exact same result.

When you use the 'g' flag with the exec() method, it will behave differently, i.e. the "class" and the "argument" roles are reversed. With the match() method, the data type or string class will own the method, with the regular expression being an argument while, with the exec() method, the regular expression owns the method and the string is the argument. We use 'g' with exec() if we want iterative progression:

var xArray; while(xArray = re.exec(str)) console.log(xArray);

// produces:

// ["fee ", index: 0, input: "fee fi fo fum"]

// ["fi ", index: 4, input: "fee fi fo fum"]

// ["fo ", index: 7, input: "fee fi fo fum"]

We use the 'm' flag when we want a multiline input string to be treated as if it were multiple lines. With the 'm' flag, $ and ^ will match at the beginning or end of a line I the string instead of the beginning and end of the whole string.

The following are some examples of how regular expressions are used:

Changing Order in Input Strings:

In this example, a regular expression is formed and the string.replace() and string.split() methods are used. An input string with rough formatting is cleaned; the string contains names, starting the first name last, each separated with a blank, a tab, and one semicolon. Lastly, the name order is reversed to the last name first and the list is sorted:

// There are several spaces and tabs in the name string,

// and there may be several spaced between the first and last names.

var names = 'Red Trump; Fred Perry; Helen Simons; Bill Bobbins; Chris Cross ';

var output = ['---------- Original String\n', names + '\n'];

// Now two regular expression patterns are prepared along with array storage.

// The string is split into the array elements.

// pattern: possible white space followed by semicolon followed by possible white space

var pattern = /\s;\s*/;*

// The pattern above is used to split the string into pieces and

```javascript
// the pieces are stored in an array named nameList
var nameList = names.split(pattern);


// new pattern: one or more characters followed by spaces followed by characters.
// Parentheses are used to remember parts of the pattern.
// These parts can then be referred to later.
pattern = /(\w+)\s+(\w+)/;


// Here is a new array containing the names that are being processed.
var bySurnameList = [];


// The name array is displayed and the new array populated
// with name, last first, separated with commas.
//
// Using the replace() method will replace pattern matches
// with the string that was memorized - the second memorized part
// followed with a comma, space, and the first memorized part.
//
// The $1 and $2 variables refer to the memorized
// parts while matching the pattern.


output.push('---------- After Split by Regular Expression');


var i, len;
for (i = 0, len = nameList.length; i < len; i++) {
```

```
    output.push(nameList[i]);

  bySurnameList[i] = nameList[i].replace(pattern, '$2, $1');

}


// The new array is displayed

output.push('---------- Names Reversed');

for (i = 0, len = bySurnameList.length; i < len; i++) {

  output.push(bySurnameList[i]);

}


// Sorted by last name and then displayed as a sorted array.

bySurnameList.sort();

output.push('---------- Sorted');

for (i = 0, len = bySurnameList.length; i < len; i++) {

  output.push(bySurnameList[i]);

}


output.push('---------- End');


console.log(output.join('\n'));
```

Special Characters to Verify Input

In the next example, a user will be asked to input a phone number. When the "check button is pressed by the user, the script will confirm the number is valid. If it is (it will match the sequence of characters the regular expression specifies) a message is shown that authenticates the number, thanking the user. If it isn't, a message is shown telling the user that the number is invalid.

When you use the non-capturing parentheses (?:, the regular expression will look for the following:

- Three numeric characters - \d{3}, OR | a left parenthesis \ (with three digits following it \d{3}, then a closing parenthesis \) followed by the (last non-capturing parenthesis)) then a single dash, a forward slash or a decimal point.

When this is found, the character ([-\/\.]) followed with three digits \d{3}, then the memorized dash, forward slash, or decimal point match, \1, then four digits \d{4} will be remembered.

When the Enter key is pressed by the user, a Change event is activated and this will set the RegExp.input value:

<!DOCTYPE html>

<html>

<head>

<meta http-equiv="Content-Type" content="text/html; charset=ISO-8859-1">

<meta http-equiv="Content-Script-Type" content="text/javascript">

<script type="text/javascript">

var re = /(?:\d{3}|\(\d{3}\))([-\/\.])\d{3}\1\d{4}/;

function testInfo(phoneInput) {

var OK = re.exec(phoneInput.value);

if (!OK)

window.alert(phoneInput.value + ' isn\'t a phone number with area code!');

else

window.alert('Thanks, your phone number is ' + OK[0]);

}

</script>

</head>

<body>

<p>Enter your phone number (with area code) and then click "Check".

```
<br>The expected format is like ###-###-####.</p>

<form action="#">

<input id="phone"><button
onclick="testInfo(document.getElementById('phone'));">Check</button>

</form>

</body>

</html>
```

Indexed Collections

In this section, we will look at data collections that are ordered using the index value. This will include all arrays, and any array-like construct, like the TypedArray and Array objects.

Array Objects

Arrays are sets of values in a specified order that are referred to using names and indexes. For example, an array name emp that had a list of employee names with indexes of their numerical staff numbers. In this case, emp[1] is employee one, emp[2] is employee two and so on.

There are no explicit data types for arrays in JavaScript but you can use the Array object already defined, along with its methods for working with an array. The Array object comes with methods that help you manipulate your arrays in different ways, like joining them, sorting them, and reversing them. It also has a property that determines the length of the array and several other properties that can be used with a regular expression.

Creating the Array

These statements will each create an array:

var arr = new Array(element0, element1, ..., elementN);

var arr = Array(element0, element1, ..., elementN);

var arr = [element0, element1, ..., elementN];

(element1, element1, ..., element) lists the element values; when specified, the array will be initialized with those values as the elements and the length property will be set according to the number of elements or arguments.

The brackets are called array initializers or array literals and are a much shorter way of creating arrays than the other methods, thus making it the preferred way.

If you wanted to create an array that had no items and a non-zero length, you could use one of these:

var arr = new Array(arrayLength);

var arr = Array(arrayLength);

// This has exactly the same effect

var arr = [];

arr.length = arrayLength;

Note

In this code, arrayLength has to be a Number; if it isn't, an array that has just one element is created. When arr.length is called, arrayLength is returned but the array has undefined elements in it. If you ran a *for...in* loop over the array, none of the elements would be returned.

As well as the new variable shown above, you can also assign arrays as properties of new objects or those that already exist:

var obj = {};

// ...

obj.prop = [element0, element1, ... elementN];

// OR

var obj = {prop: [element0, element1, ..., elementN]};

If you want an array initialized with a single element and that element is a Number, the bracket syntax must be used. When you pass one Number value to an Array() function or constructor, it will not be interpreted as a single element; rather, it will be an arrayLength:

var arr = [42];   // Creates an array with a single element:

       // the number 49.

var arr = Array(42); // Creates an array with no elements

       // and arr.length set to 49; this is

       // equivalent to:

var arr = [];

arr.length = 49;

If you call Array(N) and N is a non-whole number with a non-zero fractional part, the result will be a RangeError. The next example is an illustration:

var arr = Array(9.3); // RangeError: Invalid array length

If arrays that have single elements with an arbitrary data type are required, use array literals or create empty arrays first and then add the element.

With ECMAScript 2015, arrays with single elements can be created using Array of the static method:

let wisenArray = Array.of(8.3); // wisenArray contains a single element 8.3

Array Population

Arrays can be populated by assigning the elements with values, like this:

var emp = [];

emp[0] = 'Davey Jones';

emp[1] = 'Phil Hammond';

emp[2] = 'Steven West';

Note

If a non-integer value is supplied to the array operator in this example, a property would be created inside the object that represents the array, rather than an array element.

var arr = [];

arr[3.4] = 'Lemons';

console.log(arr.length); // 0

console.log(arr.hasOwnProperty(3.4)); // true

Arrays can also be populated at the time they are created:

var myArray = new Array('Hello', myVar, 3.14159);

var myArray = ['Banana', 'Pineapple', 'Lemon'];

Referencing Other Elements

Other elements in the array may be referenced using their ordinal number. The following array is an example:

var myArray = ['Wind', 'Rain', 'Snow'];

The first element would be referenced as myArray[0], the second as myArray[1] and so one, remembering that indexing begins at 0.

Note

You can also use the square brackets [] which is the array operator, to access the properties of an array (the arrays are objects as well). For example:

var arr = ['four', 'five', 'six'];

console.log(arr[2]); // six

console.log(arr['length']); // 3

Understanding Array Length

At implementation, an array will store its elements as object properties and the array index is used as the name of the property. The length property is something special because it will always return the index attached to the last element plus one. In the next example, Kelly is indexed as 25, so cats.length will return 25 + 1. Remember that array indexes are 0-based, starting at 0, so the length property will always be one higher than the highest stored index:

var cats = [];

cats[30] = ['Kelly'];

console.log(cats.length); // 31

The length property may also be assigned when you write a shorter value than the number.

var cats = ['Kelly', 'Jasmine', 'Suzy'];

console.log(cats.length); // 3

cats.length = 2;

console.log(cats); // logs "Kelly, Jasmine" - Suzy has been removed

cats.length = 0;

```
console.log(cats); // logs []; the cats array is empty
```

```
cats.length = 3;
```

```
console.log(cats); // logs [ <3 empty items> ]ber of the items stored, the array will be
```
truncated while writing 0 will empty it out:

Iteration over an Array

One of the commonly used operations is iteration over array values, with each value being processed in a specified way. The easiest way to do that is like this:

```
var colors = ['purple', 'yellow', 'orange'];
```

```
for (var i = 0; i < colors.length; i++) {

  console.log(colors[i]);

}
```

If you already know that none of your array elements are going to evaluate to a Boolean false, for example, if they are all DOM nodes, there is a better way of writing the code:

```
var divs = document.getElementsByTagName('div');
```

```
for (var i = 0, div; div = divs[i]; i++) {

  /* Process div in a way */

}
```

Doing this takes away the need to check the array length and makes sure every time the loop goes around. The div variable is reassigned to the current item.

Another way of iterating over your array is to use the forEach() method:

```
var colors = ['purple', 'yellow', 'orange'];
```

```
colors.forEach(function(color) {

  console.log(color);

});
```

```
// purple
```

```
// yellow
```

// orange

Alternatively, you can use the ECMAScript 2005 arrow functions to shorten the *forEach* parameter code:

var colors = ['purple', 'yellow', 'orange'];

colors.forEach(color => console.log(color));

// purple

// yellow

// orange

The function that we pass to *forEach* will be executed one time for each separate element; the array element is passed as the function argument. In a *forEach* loop, unassigned values are ignored and will not be iterated over.

Note, on the definition of the array, the elements that are left out will not be listed when *forEach* iterates over them, but they will be listed when undefined has been assigned to the element manually:

var array = ['first', 'second', , 'fourth'];

array.forEach(function(element) {

  console.log(element);

});

// first

// second

// fourth

if (array[2] === undefined) {

  console.log('array[2] is undefined'); // true

}

array = ['first', 'second', undefined, 'fourth'];

array.forEach(function(element) {

  console.log(element);

});

// first

// second

// undefined

// fourth

Because the elements in JavaScript are saved as standard object properties, you should not use a *for...in* loop to iterate over the arrays; if you do, you will get a list of all the normal elements and the enumerable properties.

Array Methods

Array objects have these methods:

- **concat()** – this will join arrays together and return a brand-new array:

var myArray = new Array('4', '5', '6');

myArray = myArray.concat('d', 'e', 'f');

// myArray is now ["4", "5", "6", "d", "e", "f"]

- **join(delimiter = ',')** – this will join all array elements into one string:

var myArray = new Array('Wind', 'Rain', 'Snow');

var list = myArray.join(' - '); // list is "Wind - Rain - Snow"

- **push()** – this will add at least one element to the end of the array and will return the new array length:

var myArray = new Array('4', '5');

myArray.push('6'); // myArray is now ["4", "5", "6"]

- **pop()** – this will remove the last array element and return it as the value:

var myArray = new Array('4', '5', '6');

var last = myArray.pop();

// myArray is now ["4", "5"], last = "6"

- **shift()** – this will remove the first array element and return it as the value:

var myArray = new Array('4', '5', '6');

var first = myArray.shift();

// myArray is now ["5", "6"], first is "4"

- **unshift()** – this will add at least one element to the start of the array, returning the new array length:

var myArray = new Array('4', '5', '6');

myArray.unshift('7', '8');

// myArray becomes ["7", "8", "4", "5", "6"]

- **slice(start_index_upto_index)** – this will extract a specified part of the array and return it as a new array:

var myArray = new Array('a', 'b', 'c', 'd', 'e');

myArray = myArray.slice(4, 7); // starts at index 4 and extracts all the elements

  // until index 6, returning ["b", "c", "d"]

- **splice(index, count_to_remove, addElement4, addElement5, ...)** – this will remove specified elements from the array and, if required (optional), will replace them. It will return the removed items:

var myArray = new Array('4', '5', '6', '7', '8');

myArray.splice(4, 6, 'a', 'b', 'c', 'd');

// myArray is now ["4", "a", "b", "c", "d", "8"]

// The code started at index one (or where the number "5" was),

// it removed 6 elements from there, and then inserted all the consecutive

// elements in its place.

- **reverse()** – this will transpose array elements in place – the first element will become the last and vice versa; the array reference is returned:

var myArray = new Array('4', '5', '6');

myArray.reverse();

// transposes the array so that myArray = ["6", "5", "4"]

sort() – this will sort the array elements in place, returning an array reference:

var myArray = new Array('Wind', 'Rain', 'Snow');

myArray.sort();

// sorts the array so that myArray = ["Snow", "Rain", "Wind"]

The sort() method may also work out how the elements are compared by taking a callback function.

This technique and all the others that take a callback (see below) are termed iterative methods. This is because, in one way or another, they will iterate over the whole array. Each will take a second optional argument named thisObject; if it is provided, thisObject will then become the *this* keyword value within the callback function body. It isn't provided, like other cases where functions are invoked externally to the context of an explicit object; it refers to the window or global object when the arrow function is used as the callback or to undefined when normal functions are used.

Callback functions are called with two arguments, both elements of the array. In the example function below, two values are compared and one out of three different values is returned. In this case, we are sorting using the last letter in a string:

var sortFn = function(a, b) {

if (a[a.length - 1] < b[b.length - 1]) return -1;

if (a[a.length - 1] > b[b.length - 1]) return 1;

if (a[a.length - 1] == b[b.length - 1]) return 0;

}

myArray.sort(sortFn);

// sorts the array so that myArray = ["Wind","Snow","Rain"]

In this:

If the sorting system determines that a is less than b, -1 or another negative number will be returned.

If the sorting system determines that a is greater than b, 1 or another positive number will be returned.

If a and b are equivalent, 0 will be returned.

- indexOf(searchElement[.fromIndex]) – this will look for searchElement in the array and it will return the first match index:

var a = ['a', 'b', 'a', 'b', 'a'];

console.log(a.indexOf('b')); // logs 1

// Now have another go, beginning after the last match

console.log(a.indexOf('b', 2)); // logs 3

console.log(a.indexOf('z')); // logs -1, because 'z' was not found

- lastIndexOf(searchElement[.fromIndex]) – this works in a similar way to indexOf but it begins at the end, searching back through the array:

var a = ['a', 'b', 'c', 'd', 'a', 'b'];

console.log(a.lastIndexOf('b')); // logs 5

// Now have another go, beginning before the last match

console.log(a.lastIndexOf('b', 4)); // logs 1

console.log(a.lastIndexOf('z')); // logs -1

- forEach(callback{. thisObject]) – a callback is executed on every item in the array, returning undefined:

var a = ['a', 'b', 'c'];

a.forEach(function(element) { console.log(element); });

// logs each item in turn

- map(callback{, thisObject]) – this will return a new array showing the value returned from each array item having a callback executed on it:

```
var a1 = ['a', 'b', 'c'];

var a2 = a1.map(function(item) { return item.toUpperCase(); });

console.log(a2); // logs ['A', 'B', 'C']
```

- filter(callback[, thisObject]) – this will return a new array that has items where the callback returned a value of true:

```
var a1 = ['a', 5, 'b', 10, 'c', 15];

var a2 = a1.filter(function(item) { return typeof item === 'number'; });

console.log(a2); // logs [5, 10, 15]
```

- every(callback[, thisObject]) – this will return true if the callback on every single array item retunes true:

```
function isNumber(value) {

  return typeof value === 'number';

}

var a1 = [1, 2, 3];

console.log(a1.every(isNumber)); // logs true

var a2 = [1, '2', 3];

console.log(a2.every(isNumber)); // logs false
```

- some(callback[, thisObject]) – this will return true if the callback is true for one or more item array:

```
function isNumber(value) {

  return typeof value === 'number';

}

var a1 = [1, 2, 3];

console.log(a1.some(isNumber)); // logs true

var a2 = [1, '2', 3];

console.log(a2.some(isNumber)); // logs true
```

var a3 = ['1', '2', '3'];

console.log(a3.some(isNumber)); // logs false

- reduce(callback{, intialValue]) – this will apply the callback of (accumulator, currentValue[, currentIndex, array]) for every array value. It does this to reduce the list down to one item. The reduce() function will return the final value that the callback function returned. If initialValue is specified, the initial value is used as the first parameter in the callback when it is called. The second parameter value will be the value attributed to the first array item.

  On the first call, if initialValue has not been specified the two-parameter values are the first and the second array elements. On each call subsequent to this, the value of the first parameter will be the value that was returned on the previous call and the next array value will be the second parameter.

  If access is required by the callback function to the entire array or to the index of the item being operated on at the time, these will be made available as optional parameters:

var a = [5, 10, 15];

var total = a.reduce(function(accumulator, currentValue) { return accumulator + currentValue; }, 0);

console.log(total) // Prints 30

- reduceRight(callback[, initialValue]) – this works in the same way as reduce() but begins with the final element.

Both reduce() and reduceRight() are the least obvious of all iterative methods and should really be used for the algorithms where two values are recursively combined to reduce the sequence to one value.

Multi-Dimensional Arrays

It is possible to nest arrays, which means one array may contain another one as part of its elements. Using this, we can create multi-dimensional arrays. The next example is creating a two-dimensional array:

var a = new Array(4);

for (i = 0; i < 4; i++) {

 a[i] = new Array(4);

```
for (j = 0; j < 4; j++) {

  a[i][j] = '[' + i + ', ' + j + ']';

 }

}
```

This example shows an array being created with these rows:

Row 0: [0, 0] [0, 1] [0, 2] [0, 3]

Row 1: [1, 0] [1, 1] [1, 2] [1, 3]

Row 2: [2, 0] [2, 1] [2, 2] [2, 3]

Row 3: [3, 0] [3, 1] [3, 2] [3, 3]

Arrays and Regular Expressions

When a regular expression and a string are matched resulting in an array, that array will return the elements and the properties storing the information regarding the match. The returned value of RegExp.exec(), String.split), and String.match() is an array.

Working with Array-Like Objects

Some of the JavaScript objects, like the NodeList that document.getElementsByTagName() returns or arguments objects available in a function body will look and act as arrays at first, but they do not share all the array methods. For example, while the arguments object has a length attribute, it cannot implement the *forEach* method.

We can also call array prototype methods against these array-like objects, for example:

```
function printArguments() {

  Array.prototype.forEach.call(arguments, function(item) {

    console.log(item);

  });

}
```

We can use array prototype methods on strings too because they provide us with sequential access to their contained characters in much the same way as an array:

```
Array.prototype.forEach.call('a string', function(chr) {
```

```
    console.log(chr);

});
```

Typed Arrays

A typed array in JavaScript is an array-like object that provides us with the means to access data of a raw binary nature. An array object will dynamically shrink and grow and may contain any valid JS value. The JS engine can also carry out optimization so the arrays are speedy, but as web applications grow in power, and with video and audio manipulation being added all the time, it is clear that we could use JS code to manipulate the raw binary data contained in a typed array quite easily and swiftly.

Typed Array Architecture – Buffers and Views

To ensure the maximum efficiency and flexibility, typed arrays split the implementation into views and buffers. Buffers are implemented using the ArrayBuffer object and are objects that represent chunks of data. They don't have any real format and they offer no means to access their contents. You need views to gain access to the memory that a buffer contains. These provide the context in the form of data types, the starting offset and the number of elements and transform the data into typed arrays.

ArrayBuffer

This is a data type used for representing generic binary data buffers that are fixed in length. It isn't possible for direct manipulation of an ArrayBuffer's content to be done but, by creating a DataView or a typed array view, a specific format is used to represent the buffer and the contents, and used to be read and written to.

Typed Array Views

All typed array views have names that are self-descriptive and will provide views for the standard numeric types, such as Uint32, Int8, Float64 and so on. The Uint8ClampedArray is a special view used to clamp values between 0 and 255.

Below is a list of the typed array views:

- **Int8Array** – has a value range of -128 to 127, a byte size of 1 and is an 8-bit two's complement signed integer

- **Uint8Array** – has a value range of 0 to 255, a byte size of 1 and is an 8-bit unsigned integer

- **Uint8ClampedArray** – has a value range of 0 to 255, a byte size of 1 and is a clamped 8-bit unsigned integer

- **Int16Array** – has a value of -32768 to 32767, a byte size of 2 and is a 16-bit two's complement signed integer

- **Uint16Array** – has a value range of 0 to 65535, a byte size of two and is a 16-bit unsigned integer

- **Int32Array** – has a value range of -2147483648 to 2147483647, a byte size fo 4 and is a 32-bit two's complement signed integer

- **Uint32Array** – has a value range of 0 to 4294967295, a byte size of 4 and is a 32-bit unsigned integer

- **Float32Array** – has a value of $1.2x10^{-38}$ to $3.4x10^{38}$, a byte size of 4 and is a 32-bit IEEE floating-point number with 7 significant digits

- **Float64Array** – has a value range of $5.0x10^{-324}$ to $1.8z10^{308}$, a byte size of 8 and is a 64-bit IEEE floating-point number with 16 significant digits.

Keyed Collections

In this section, we will look at data collections ordered using keys. The two objects having elements that can be iterated in the order they were inserted are Map and Set.

Maps

With ECMAScript 2015, a new data structure was introduced to map values to values. The Map object is a simple map that maps keys to values and can iterate over the elements in the order they were inserted.

In the next example are some of the operations you can do with a Map; using a *for...of* loop will return an array for each iteration, showing [key, value] pairs.

var sayings = new Map();

sayings.set('mouse', 'squeak');

sayings.set('donkey', 'bray');

sayings.set('horse', 'neigh');

sayings.size; // 3

sayings.get('fox'); // undefined

sayings.has('bird'); // false

sayings.delete('mouse');

```
sayings.has('mouse'); // false

for (var [key, value] of sayings) {

  console.log(key + ' goes ' + value);

}
// "donkey goes bray"
// "horse goes neigh"


sayings.clear();

sayings.size; // 0
```

Comparing Map and Object

Traditionally, we use objects to map strings to values. An object lets us set a key to a value, retrieve the values, remove keys, and check whether a key is storing something. The Map object has several advantages making them far better maps:

- Object keys are strings; in a Map object they can be any value.

- Map objects make it easy to get a Map size whereas, with objects, you need to track the size manually.

- Maps iterate over elements in the order they are inserted.

- Objects have prototypes, which means the map has default keys, although this can be bypassed with map = Object.create(null).

How do you decide whether to use a map or an object? These tips will help you:

- If the keys are not known until runtime, use Maps. Also, use Maps when the keys are all of the same types and the values are also the same type.

- If you need to store a primitive value as a key, use Maps. Object will treat every key as an individual string regardless of whether it is a Boolean, Number, or any Primitive value.

- If there is logic that performs operations on individual elements, use Maps.

The WeakMap Object

This is a collection containing key/value pairs where the keys are only objects but the values can be any arbitrary value. The references to the objects are held in the keys weakly, and this means if there is no other reference to that object, they may be targeted by garbage collection (GC). The WeakMap and Map APIs are the same.

One of the differences between Map and WeakMap is the WeakMap keys are not enumerable; this means no method will provide you a list of keys. If the keys were enumerable, the resulting list would be dependent on the garbage collection state.

WeakMap objects can be used to store private data for objects or to hide details of implementation. In the next example, the methods and the private data belong in the object and have been stored in the WeakMap objects called privates. Everything that is exposed on the prototype and the instance is public while nothing else can be accessed from external sources because the privates WeakMap has not been exported out of the module:

```
const privates = new WeakMap();


function Public() {

  const me = {

    // The private data goes here

  };

  privates.set(this, me);

}


Public.prototype.method = function() {

  const me = privates.get(this);

  // Do something with the private data in `me`...

};


module.exports = Public;
```

Sets

A Set object is another collection, this time it is of values. The elements can be iterated over in the order they were inserted and -an important note- a value held in a Set may only have one occurrence, making it unique to the collection.

The example below shows some of the operations that can be done with a Set:

```
var mySet = new Set();

mySet.add(1);

mySet.add('some text');

mySet.add('foo');


mySet.has(1); // true

mySet.delete('foo');

mySet.size; // 2


for (let item of mySet) console.log(item);

// 1

// "some text"
```

Conversion between Arrays and Sets

Arrays can be created from Sets using either the spread operator or *Array.from*. The Set constructor can also take arrays to convert in the opposite direction. Don't forget that the Set object stores unique values, so if there are any duplicate elements when the conversion happens, they will be deleted.

```
Array.from(mySet);

[...mySet2];


mySet2 = new Set([1, 2, 3, 4]);
```

Comparing Arrays and Sets

Traditionally in JavaScript, sets of elements are stored inside arrays but, with the Set object, there are several other advantages:

- It is faster to check if elements are in collections than using *indexOf* for the array.

- A Set object will let you use values to delete elements whereas, with the array, you would need to splice based on the index of the element.

- You cannot find a NaN value using *indexOf* in the array.

- Unique values are stored in the Set object so you don't need to track duplicates.

The WeakSet Object

A WeakSet object is a collection containing objects which may only occur on one occasion; they are unique to the collection and are also not enumerable.

The key differences between the Set and the WeakSet are:

- Whereas a Set contains objects and values, the WeakSet only has objects.

- A WeakSet is weak; object references are held weakly and if there is no reference anywhere else, they are subject to garbage collection.

- WeakSets are not enumerable and there is no list of objects currently stored within the collection.

Uses of the WeakSet objects are limited. Because they do not leak memory, DOM elements can be used as keys and marked for the purpose of tracking.

Map and Set Key/Value Equality

Both the Map object key equality and the Set object value equality are based on a "same value zero algorithm":

- Equality works in the same way as the identity comparison operator ===

- -0 and +0 are seen as equal

- NaN is seen as equal to itself, contrary to ===

Working with Objects

The JavaScript language was designed as a simple model based on objects. Objects are property collections and the properties are a combination of a key (name) and the associated value. If the value of a property is a function, the property becomes known as a method. There are predefined objects in the browser but you can also define your own.

In this section, we will look at how objects, functions, properties, and methods are used and how you can create objects.

Objects

As it is in most programming languages, a JavaScript object is comparable to a real-world object and the concept is best understood using tangible, real-world objects.

JavaScript objects are standalone and they have types and properties. Think of a cup and its properties – material, design, color, size, etc. In the same way, a JavaScript object has properties which are used to define the object characteristics.

Objects and Properties

The properties associated with a JavaScript object are easily explained as being variables attached to the object. The properties define the object's characteristics and you can access these properties using simple dot notation:

objectName.propertyName

Like all variables in JavaScript the name of the object, which can be a standard variable, and the names of the properties are all case-sensitive. To define a property, you assign a value to it. For example, in the code below, we create an object called myCar and we provide it with three properties called make, model, and year:

var myCar = new Object();

myCar.make = 'Opel;

myCar.model = 'Vectra';

myCar.year = 2008;

If an object property has not been assigned, it is undefined. It does not automatically evaluate as a null:

myCar.color; // undefined

Object properties can be set or accessed with a bracket notation and the objects are sometimes known as associative arrays; this is because every property is associated with the string value to access the property. For example, accessing the myCar object properties would be like this:

myCar['make'] = 'Opel';

myCar['model'] = 'Vectra';

myCar['year'] = 2008;

The name of an object property may be any JavaScript string so long as it is valid, or it can be anything that may be converted into a string, including empty strings. However if the property name is not a valid identifier, such as a name that has a hyphen, space, or starts with a number, it can only be accessed with the square bracket notation. The square bracket notation [] is also useful for dynamic determination of property names, i.e. it is runtime before the name is determined.

Here are some examples:

// we create four variables and assign them all at once,

// using commas to separate each one.

var myObj = new Object(),

  str = 'myString',

  rand = Math.random(),

  obj = new Object();

myObj.type   = 'Dot syntax';

myObj['date created'] = 'String with a space';

myObj[str]   = 'String value';

myObj[rand]   = 'Random Number';

myObj[obj]   = 'Object';

myObj['']   = 'An empty string';

console.log(myObj);

Note

All the keys within the [] notation will be converted into strings unless they are Symbols. A property name in JavaScript must be a string or a symbol. In the above code, when we add the key obj to myObj, the obj.stString() method is called and the resulting string is the key.

Properties can also be accessed using a string value stored within a variable:

var myCar = new Object();

var propertyName = 'make';

myCar[propertyName] = 'Opel';

propertyName = 'model';

myCar[propertyName] = 'Vectra';

propertyName = 'year';

myCar[propertyName] = '2008';

The bracket notation can also be used with a *for...in* loop so the enumerable object properties can be iterated over. The following example shows how this works – the function will display all the object properties when the object and its name are passed to the function as arguments:

function showProps(obj, objName) {

  var result = '';

 for (var i in obj) {

   // obj.hasOwnProperty() is used for filtering properties out of the prototype chain for the object.

  if (obj.hasOwnProperty(i)) {

    result += objName + '.' + i + ' = ' + obj[i] + '\n';

```
    }

}

    return result;

}
```

So if a function call of *showProps(myCar, 'myCar')* was made it would return this:

myCar.make = Opel

myCar.model = Vectra

myCar.year = 2008

Enumeration of Object Properties

From ECMAScript 2015, there are now three ways of traversing or listing object properties:

- A *for...in* Loop – This will traverse all the enumerable properties in an object and the object's prototype chain.

- Object.keys(o) – This will return an array containing the enumerable property names of an object called 'o' – it will not return the names from the prototype chain.

- Object.getOwnPropertynames(o) – This will return an array containing the property names from an object called 'o', whether they are enumerable or not; it will not return the names from the prototype chain.

Before ECMAScript 5, the only way to list the object properties was by using the function shown in the example below, as there were no native methods to list them:

```
function listAllProperties(o) {

        var objectToInspect;

        var result = [];


        for(objectToInspect = o; objectToInspect !== null;

        objectToInspect = Object.getPrototypeOf(objectToInspect)) {

        result = result.concat(
```

```
        Object.getOwnPropertyNames(objectToInspect)

    );

  }


      return result;

}
```

This is a useful way of showing any hidden properties, i.e. those in the prototype chain that cannot be accessed via the object because there is another property in the chain with the same name. To list all the accessible properties, you would simply delete the duplicates from the array.

Creating a New Object

In JavaScript, there are several objects already predefined but you can also create an object of your own by using an object initializer. Another way of doing it is to create a construction function first and then invoke the function through object instantiation with the new operator.

Using an Object Initializer

Yet another way is to use an object initializer, sometimes called using literal notation to create the object.

The syntax used for this is:

var obj = { property_1: value_1, // property_# may be an identifier...

      2:   value_2, // or a number...

      // ...,

      'property n': value_n }; // or a string

In this, obj is the new object's name, each {property_} is an identifier which could be a string literal, a number or a name and each value_ is an expression with a value that has been assigned to {property_}. Both the obj and the assignment are optional; there is no need to refer to the object anywhere else, it doesn't need to be assigned to a variable. Note, if the object shows up where a statement is expected to appear, the object literal must be enclosed in parentheses so it doesn't get mixed up with a block statement.

An object initializer is an expression and each one will result in the creation of a new object whenever the statement it is in is executed. If you have identical object initializers, they will create distinct objects that do not compare as equal to one another. An object gets created as if new Object() had been called, i.e. an object that is created from a literal expression will be an object instance.

In the next statement, we create an object and assign it to a variable called x only if the expression called *cond* evaluates true:

if (cond) var x = {greeting: 'hello there'};

In the next example, myBMW is created with three properties. Note that the property called engine is an object as well and it has its own set of properties:

var myBMW = {color: 'black', wheels: 4, engine: {cylinders: 6, size: 2.5}};

Object initializers can also be used to create arrays.

Using a Constructor Function

Alternatively, try these two steps to create the object:

1. Write the constructor function to define the object type. Use an uppercase letter as the initial letter, as per convention.

2. Use new to create an object instance.

Defining the object type is done by creating a function for the type; the function will specify the name, the properties, and the methods. For example, if you wanted a new object type for cars, you would call it Car and the properties would be make, model, and year. This is the function you would write:

function Car(make, model, year) {

  this.make = make;

  this.model = model;

  this.year = year;

}

This keyword for assigning the properties with values based on those that were passed into the function.

Now an object can be created, called mycar:

var mycar = new Car('Mercedes', 'Compressor', 2000);

In the statement, we created the object called mycar and then assigned the values to the properties. The value if mycar.make will be a string of Mercedes, mycar.year would be an integer of 2000, and so on.

By using a call to new you can create as many Car objects as you want, for example:

var mickscar = new Car('BMW', 'X5', 2005);

var samscar = new Car('Audi', 'A4', 2007);

Objects can also have properties that are, in their own right, objects. For example, you could define an object named person like this:

function Person(name, age, sex) {

  this.name = name;

  this.age = age;

  this.sex = sex;

}

Then you could instantiate two new objects of Person, like this:

var rand = new Person('Simon Templar', 45, 'M');

var ken = new Person('Billy Bunter', 29, 'M');

The definition of Car could then be rewritten to include a new property called owner which would, in turn, take a person object:

function Car(make, model, year, owner) {

  this.make = make;

  this.model = model;

  this.year = year;

  this.owner = owner;

}

You would do this to instantiate the objects:

var car1 = new Car('Mercedes', 'Compressor', 2000, rand);

var car2 = new Car('BMW', 'X5', 2005, ken);

Note that when we create a new object instead of passing an integer value or a literal string, the statements we used to pass the objects, simon and billy, as the owner arguments. If you then wanted to find out who owned car2, you would access this property:

car2.owner.name

A property can be added to an object you defined previously, like this:

car1.color = 'blue';

This statement adds a color property to car1 and then assigns a value of 'blue' to it. This will NOT have an effect on any other object. If you wanted to add a property to all of the objects sharing the same type, you would need to add that property into the object type definition.

Using Object.create

Lastly, the Object.create() method can be used to create your object. This is a useful method because you get to pick what prototype you want without needing to define the constructor function:

// Animal properties and method encapsulation

var Animal = {

  type: 'Invertebrates', // Default value of properties

  displayType: function() { // Method which will display type of Animal

    console.log(this.type);

  }

};

// Create new animal type called animal1

var animal1 = Object.create(Animal);

animal1.displayType(); // Output:Invertebrates

// Create new animal type called Fish

var fish = Object.create(Animal);

fish.type = 'Fish';

fish.displayType(); // Output:Fish

Inheritance

Every JavaScript object will inherit from one or more objects. The object that inherits is called the prototype and the properties that are inherited are stored in the constructor's prototype object – to be discussed later.

Indexing an Object Property

Object properties can be referred to in two ways – by the name of the property or by the ordinal index. If a property is defined by name it must be referred to at all times by that name; in the same way, if it is defined by its index, that index must be used to refer to it.

This restriction is applicable when an object's properties are created using a constructor function and when individual properties are explicitly defined, for example, myCar.color = "black". If you use an index to define the object, for example, myCar[3] = "55mpg", you would refer to it only as myCar[3].

There is one exception to this – array-like objects that are reflected from HTML, like forms, which is an array-like object. Objects in an array-like object can be referred to by the position they are in the document (ordinal number) or by name if it has been defined. For example, if you have a document with two <FORM> tags and the second has a NAME attribute called "myform", you can refer to it in three ways:

document.forms[1]

document.forms["myform"]

document.forms.myform

Defining Object Type Properties

The prototype property can be used to add properties to objects you previously defined. This will define a property shared by all the objects with the type specified instead of just by single object instances.

The next example adds a property called "color" to all objects that have a type of Car, then, a value is assigned to the new property of the object called car1:

Car.prototype.color = null;

car1.color = 'black';

Method Definition

Methods are functions associated with an object. In other words, methods are properties or objects are functions. You define a method in the same way a standard function is defined, but they must be assigned as an object property.

Here's an example:

objectName.methodname = functionName;

var myObj = {

  myMethod: function(params) {

    // ...do something

  }

  // THIS WILL WORK AS WELL

  myOtherMethod(params) {

    // ...do something else

  }

};

In this example, objectName is an object that already exists, methodname is the name you are giving the method, and functionName is the name given to the function.

The method is then called in the object context, like this:

object.methodname(params);

You can also add a method definition into the constructor function for an object as another way of defining an object type's methods. For example, a function could be defined to format the properties of the Car objects you defined earlier, and then display them, like this:

function displayCar() {

```
var result = 'A Wonderful ' + this.year + ' ' + this.make

   + ' ' + this.model;

pretty_print(result);

}
```

In this, pretty_print is the name of a function that displays a string and a horizontal ruling. Note that we used the *this* keyword to reference the object the method belongs to.

This function can be made into a method of the Car object with the addition of this statement to the object definition:

this.displayCar = displayCar;

The definition of Car should now look like:

```
function Car(make, model, year, owner) {

   this.make = make;

   this.model = model;

   this.year = year;

   this.owner = owner;

   this.displayCar = displayCar;

}
```

The displayCar method may then be called for each object, like this:

car1.displayCar();

car2.displayCar();

Referencing Objects with the *this* Keyword

The *this* keyword in JavaScript can be used inside a method as a way of referencing the current object. For example, if you had a function named validate that was used to authenticate the value properties of an object, with the object and its low and high values specified, like this:

```
function validate(obj, lowval, hival) {

   if ((obj.value < lowval) || (obj.value > hival)) {
```

alert('Invalid Value!');

}

}

You could then call the validate function in the onChange event handler for each form element, using the *this* keyword to pass the function to the relevant function, like this:

<input type="text" name="age" size="5"

onChange="validate(this, 21, 99)">

Generally this would refer to a method's calling object.

When you combine the *this* keyword with the form property, it would refer to the parent form of the current object. In the next example, the form called myForm has a button and a Text object. When the button is clicked by a user, the Text object value will be set to the name of the form. The onClick event handler will use this.form to reference myForm, which is the parent form:

<form name="myForm">

<p><label>Form name:<input type="text" name="text1" value="Beluga"></label>

<p><input name="button1" type="button" value="Show Form Name"

onclick="this.form.text1.value = this.form.name">

</p>

</form>

Defining the Getters and Setters

Getters are methods used for getting the value of a specified property while setters are methods used for setting the value of a specified property. Getters and setters can be defined on any core object already predefined or on any user-defined object so long as support is there to add new properties.

The syntax to define both uses the syntax for object literals.

In the following example, you can see getters and setters at work on a user-defined object called 'o':

var o = {

a: 7,

```
  get b() {

    return this.a + 1;

  },

  set c(x) {

    this.a = x / 2;

  }

};
```

```
console.log(o.a); // 7

console.log(o.b); // 8

o.c = 50;

console.log(o.a); // 25
```

The properties for the o object are:

- o.a – this is a number

- o.b – this is a getter that will return o.a + 1

- o.c – this is a setter that will set o.a's value as half of the value that o.c is set as

Note, that where a getter or setter is defined inside an object literal, using [gs]et property(), rather than ___define[GS]etter___, the function names are not the getter or setter names themselves. You may be led to believe this by the syntax [gs]et propertyName(){} but, in fact, if you used that syntax to define a getter you would need to use Object.defineProperty to programmatically define a named function explicitly.

In the following example, you can see how getters and setters are used to extend the Data prototype so a property called year is added to every instance of the Date class (predefined). The Date class has existing methods called getFullYear and setFullYear and these are used to support the getter and setter in the year property. The statements in the example are defining the year property getter and setter:

```
var d = Date.prototype;
```

```
Object.defineProperty(d, 'year', {

  get: function() { return this.getFullYear(); },

  set: function(y) { this.setFullYear(y); }

});
```

While these statements are using the getter and setter in an object called Date:

```
var now = new Date();

console.log(now.year); // 2019

now.year = 2019; // 987617605170

console.log(now);

// Sun Feb 24 11:13:25 GMT-0700 (Pacific Daylight Time) 2019
```

Principally, a getter or setter can be:

- defined by object initializers, OR

- added to an object later using either a getter or a setter adding method.

When you use an object initializer to define a getter or a setter, all that is needed is the getter method prefixed with get and the setter method prefixed with set. The getter method will not take any parameters while the setter method will only take one, which is the new value being set. For example:

```
var o = {

  a: 7,

  get b() { return this.a + 1; },

  set c(x) { this.a = x / 2; }

};
```

You can also add a getter or setter to an object whenever you want after the object is created by using the method Object.defineProperties. The first parameter for this method is an object with properties named as the getter or setter names and property values which are the objects used to define the functions for the getter/setter.

This example shows the same getter/setter that we used in the last example being defined:

```
var o = { a: 0 };
```

```
Object.defineProperties(o, {
    'b': { get: function() { return this.a + 1; } },
    'c': { set: function(x) { this.a = x / 2; } }
});
```

```
o.c = 10; // Runs the setter, which will assign 10 / 2 (5) to the 'a' property
console.log(o.b); // Runs the getter, which will yield  a + 1 or 6
```

Which form you use will depend on what you are doing and what your programming style is. If you choose to use the object initializer when you define the prototype, the first form is probably the best one for most occasions. It is more natural and more compact. If you need your getters and setters added later, perhaps because you are adding to a prototype or object written by another programmer, you would use the second form. This is more representative of how dynamic JavaScript is but it can also make your code harder to understand.

Deleting a Property

So long as a property is non-inherited, you can use the delete operator to remove it, as in the following example:

```
// Create a new object called myobj, with two properties named a and b.
var myobj = new Object;
myobj.a = 5;
myobj.b = 12;
```

```
// Remove the a property, leaving myobj with only the b property.
delete myobj.a;
console.log ('a' in myobj); // yields "false"
```

Global variables can also be deleted using the delete operator so long as the variable was not declared using the var keyword:

g = 17;

delete g;

Comparing Objects

Objects are reference types in JavaScript and two distinct objects will never be equal, even if their properties are the same. The only way to yield true is to compare an object reference with itself:

// Two variables, two distinct objects but with the same properties

var fruit = {name: 'peach'};

var fruitbear = {name: 'peach'};

fruit == fruitbear; // return false

fruit === fruitbear; // return false

// Two variables, one single object

var fruit = {name: 'peach'};

var fruitbear = fruit; // assign fruit object reference to fruitbear

// here fruit and fruitbear both point to same object

fruit == fruitbear; // return true

fruit === fruitbear; // return true

fruit.name = 'blueberry';

console.log(fruitbear); // yields { name: "blueberry" } instead of { name: "peach" }

The Object Model

JavaScript is not a class-based language; it is object and prototype-based and, because of this, it might be harder to create object hierarchies and set up the inheritance of properties and values. In this section, we are going to look at how this is done.

The Difference between Class-Based and Prototype-Based Languages

The class-based programming languages, like C++ and Java, are based on a concept involving two entities – the class and the instance.

- Classes define all properties used to characterize a specific object or set of objects. Classes are abstract; they not a specific member of an object set they are describing. For example, the Employee class represents all employees in a set, not just one.

- Instances are instantiations of classes, i.e. members of the class. For example, Simon may be an Employee class instance, representative of one individual as one employee. Instances share the exact same properties as the parent class – they have no more and no fewer properties.

With JavaScript and other prototype-based languages, this distinction is not made. Instead, it only has objects. These languages have the notion of prototypical objects, i.e. an object that can be used as a template to retrieve properties for new objects. Any object may specify its own set of properties, either at the time of creation or at runtime. As well, any object may be associated as another object's prototype, which lets the second object share the properties of the first object.

Defining Classes

In a class-based language, classes are defined in separate definitions. Constructors may be specified in the definition so class instances may be created. Constructor methods will specify what the initial values are for the instance properties and will also carry out any appropriate processing at creation time. The new operator is used with the constructor method to create instances of a class.

JavaScript does something similar but the class definition and constructor are not separate from one another. Instead, a constructor function is defined to create an object with a specific set of initial properties and their values. You can use any function in JavaScript as a constructor and the new operator is always used with the constructor function to create new objects.

The Subclass and Inheritance

In class-based languages, class definitions are used to create class hierarchies. Inside a class definition, it can be specified that a newly created class is a subclass of a class that already exists. The subclass will then inherit all properties from its superclass and can also modify properties it inherited or add new ones. For example, let's say the Employee class contains just two properties – name and dept. Employee has a subclass called Manager and this adds another property called reports. Any instance of the Manager class would automatically contain all of the properties – name, dept, and reports.

The way that inheritance is implemented in JavaScript is to let you associate prototypical objects with constructor functions. For example, you could construct the Employee/Manager example exactly as it is above with slightly different terminology. First, the Employee constructor function is defined with the name and dept properties specified. Next, the Manager constructor function is defined with a call to the Employee constructor and with the reports property specified. Lastly, a new object is derived from the Employee.prototype to become a Manager constructor function prototype. When a new Manager is then created, it will inherit the properties of name and dept from the Employee object.

Add and Remove Properties

With a class-based language, classes tend to be created at compile time, followed by instantiation of class instances at compile or runtime. The number of properties and the type of properties cannot be changed once the class has been defined. By contrast, in JavaScript, it is possible to add object properties or remove them at runtime. If a property is added to a prototype object (for a set of objects), those objects will also receive the added property.

For the rest of this section, we will look at creating an object hierarchy using constructors and prototypes in JavaScript with a comparison of how it would be done in Java. We will also be using the employee hierarchy from here on in.

The employee Hierarchy

The employee hierarchy is a very simple one with these objects:

            Employee

Manager   Worker

      Salesperson   Engineer

- Employee contains two properties – name, with a value defaulting to the empty string, and dept with a value defaulting to "general".

- Manager is based on the employee class, adding a new property of reports, with a value defaulting to an array (empty) – the value is intended to be EmployeeObjects array.

- Also based on Employee is Worker which brings a property called reports, with value also defaulting to an empty array – the value is intended to be a string array.

- And Salesperson is also based on Worker, adding a property called quota, with a value defaulting to 100. This will override dept with a value of "sales", which indicates all the Salespersons work for the same department.

- Lastly, Engineer is also based on Worker. It brings the property called machine, with a value that defaults to an empty string and will also override dept with a value of "engineering".

Create the Hierarchy

There are various ways to define the right constructor function for the implementation of your Employee hierarchy. The method you choose will depend almost entirely on what you are trying to do with your application.

This shows how simple and relatively inflexible definitions are used to get inheritance working. When the object is created, no property values can be specified; the new object will just have the default values, but you can change these later.

These are just dummy applications, but when you write your own, your constructors would likely be defined in a way that lets you provide the values for the properties at the time you create the object; for now, we will just look at a simple way to ensure that inheritance occurs.

Both the definitions below are similar – the first is for JavaScript and the second for Java. The difference is that for Java, the property type must be specified; you don't need to do this in JavaScript.

JavaScript

function Employee() {

this.name = '';

this.dept = 'general';

```
}
```

Java

```
public class Employee {

  public String name = "";

  public String dept = "general";

}
```

In the Worker and Manager definitions, you can see the difference in how the next object higher up the inheritance chain is specified. With JavaScript, a prototypical instance is added as the constructor function prototype property value. This can be done any time after the constructor is defined. The prototype.constructor for the construction function is then overridden. With Java, the superclass is specified in the class definition and that superclass cannot be changed outside of the class definition.

JavaScript

```
function Manager() {

  Employee.call(this);

  this.reports = [];

}

Manager.prototype = Object.create(Employee.prototype);

Manager.prototype.constructor = Manager;


function Worker() {

  Employee.call(this);

  this.projects = [];

}

Worker.prototype = Object.create(Employee.prototype);

Worker.prototype.constructor = Worker;
```

Java

```java
public class Manager extends Employee {

  public Employee[] reports =

    new Employee[0];

}
```

```java
public class Worker extends Employee {

  public String[] projects = new String[0];

}
```

Objects are created in the Salesperson and Engineer definitions; these objects are descendants of Works and, as a result, from Employee. An object of any of these types will have the properties of all the objects coming before it in the hierarchy chain. The definitions also override the dept property inherited values using new values that are specific to the objects.

JavaScript

```javascript
function Salesperson() {

  Worker.call(this);

  this.dept = 'sales';

  this.quota = 100;

}

Salesperson.prototype = Object.create(Worker.prototype);

Salesperson.prototype.constructor = Salesperson;


function Engineer() {

  Worker.call(this);
```

```
    this.dept = 'engineering';

    this.machine = '';

}

Engineer.prototype = Object.create(Worker.prototype)

Engineer.prototype.constructor = Engineer;
```

Java

```
public class Salesperson extends Worker {

    public String dept = "sales";

    public double quota = 100.0;

}
```

```
public class Engineer extends Worker {

    public String dept = "engineering";

    public String machine = "";

}
```

With these definitions, object instances can be created to receive the default property values.

The Object Hierarchy

This hierarchy is created using the code example below:

Employee

Manager   Worker

        Salesperson   Engineer

The individual objects are John, Shelley, Michael, George, Julie, etc., and the instances are created from the constructor:

```
var John = new Employee;
// You can leave the parentheses out if the
// constructor Doesn't take any arguments.
// John.name is ''
// John.dept is 'general'


var Shelley = new Manager;
// Shelley.name is ''
// Shelley.dept is 'general'
// Shelley.reports is []


var Michael = new Worker;
// Michael.name is ''
// Michael.dept is 'general'
// Michael.projects is []


var George = new Salesperson;
// George.name is ''
// George.dept is 'sales'
// George.projects is []
// George.quota is 100


var Julie = new Engineer;
// Julie.name is ''
```

// Julie.dept is 'engineering'

// Julie.projects is []

// Julie.machine is "

Object Properties

Now we are going to look at the way an object will inherit the properties from one or more other objects within the prototype chain and then look at the result if you are adding properties at runtime.

Inheriting Properties

Let's say that you create a Worker object called Michael using this statement:

var Michael = new Worker;

On seeing the new operator, JavaScript will create a generic object and set the internal property [[Prototype]] value implicitly to Worker.prototype; this object is then passed to the Worker construction function as the *this* keyword value. The internal [[prototype]] property will determine which type of prototype chain will return the values for the properties; one these properties have been set, the new object is returned and the variable called Michael is set to the object using the assignment statement.

This doesn't place values explicitly into the Michael object for those properties inherited from the prototype chain. When you request a property value, JavaScript will first check if the value is in the object. If it is, it will be returned. If there is no property of the requested name, JavaScript will state there is no property in the object. By doing this, the object called Michael will have these properties and corresponding values:

Michael.name = ";

Michael.dept = 'general';

Michael.projects = [];

The Employee constructor assigns the local values for the properties called name and dept to the Michael object and the Worker constructor assigns the property of the project's local value to the object as well. This provides for the inheritance of the properties and corresponding values.

Because you cannot supply values that are instance-specific, the information is always going to be generic. Property values will continuously be default values shared by any new object created from the Worker constructor; these values can be changed later. You can now provide more specific information for the Michael object:

Michael.name = 'Donalds, Michael';

Michael.dept = 'admin';

Michael.projects = ['navigator'];

Adding Properties

In JavaScript, properties can be added to an object at runtime and you are not limited to only using those properties the constructor function provides. Adding a property that is specific to one object is done by assigning the object with a value, like this:

Michael.bonus = 2500;

We have now provided a property called bonus to the Michael object; none of the other Workers will have this property.

When adding a property to an object used as a constructor function prototype, that property is added to every object that can inherit the prototype properties. For example, you can use the statement below to add a property called specialty to every employee:

Employee.prototype.specialty = 'none';

Once this statement has been executed, the Michael object will have this new property.

Flexible Constructors

So far, our constructor functions have not allowed us to specify any values for the properties when an instance is created. JavaScript allows you to provide constructors with arguments for the purpose of initializing the instance property values. This can be done in this way:

JavaScript

function Employee(name, dept) {

  this.name = name || '';

  this.dept = dept || 'general';

}

Java

public class Employee {

  public String name;

```java
    public String dept;
    public Employee () {
        this("", "general");
    }
    public Employee (String name) {
        this(name, "general");
    }
    public Employee (String name, String dept) {
        this.name = name;
        this.dept = dept;
    }
}
```

JavaScript

```javascript
function Worker(projs) {

    this.projects = projs || [];
}
Worker.prototype = new Employee;
```

Java

```java
public class Worker extends Employee {
    public String[] projects;
    public Worker () {
        this(new String[0]);
    }
    public Worker (String[] projs) {
```

```
      projects = projs;

   }

}
```

JavaScript

```javascript
function Engineer(mach) {

   this.dept = 'engineering';

   this.machine = mach || '';

}

Engineer.prototype = new Worker;
```

Java

```java
public class Engineer extends Worker {

   public String machine;

   public Engineer () {

     dept = "engineering";

     machine = "";

   }

   public Engineer (String mach) {

     dept = "engineering";

     machine = mach;

   }

}
```

A special jargon is sourced by JavaScript for the definitions used in setting the default values:

```javascript
this.name = name || '';
```

The logical OR (||) operator will evaluate the first argument; if it evaluates to true, it is returned. If false, the second argument value is returned. As such, that single code line is checking whether a name has a useful value in its name property. If it does, this.name is set to the value; if not, it is set to empty string.

Note

You might find this doesn't work as you expect if you call the constructor with arguments that evaluate false, such as 0 or an empty string. In cases like this, the default value is given.

Using these definitions, you can specify a value for your local defined properties when creating object instances. The following statement, for example, can be used to create a new Engineer:

var Julie = new Engineer('belau');

Julie now has properties of:

Julie.name == '';

Julie.dept == 'engineering';

Julie.projects == [];

Julie.machine == 'belau';

By using these definitions, initial values cannot be specified for inherited properties. To do that, more code should be added in the constructor function.

So, we have a generic object created by the constructor function which then specifies local properties and corresponding values for the newly created object. More properties can be added by the constructor by calling the constructor function directly for objects higher up the chain.

Let's now take a more detailed look at one of the definitions; this is a new definition for the constructor called Engineer:

function Engineer(name, projs, mach) {

  this.base = Worker;

  this.base(name, 'engineering', projs);

  this.machine = mach || '';

}

Suppose an Engineer object was created like this:

var Julie = new Engineer('Donalds, Julie', ['navigator', 'javascript'], 'belau');

These are the steps that JavaScript takes:

1. A generic object is created by the new operator and the __proto__ property is set as Engineer.prototype.

2. The new object is passed to the Engineer constructor as the *this* keyword value by the new operator.

3. A new property named base is created for the object by the constructor and the Worker constructor value is assigned to the new property. This, in turn, makes the worker constructor into an Engineer object method.

4. The base method is called by the constructor, which passes two of the constructor arguments as the method arguments – "Donalds, Julie" and –["navigator", "javascript"], along with the string named "engineering". By using "engineering" explicitly in the constructor, it indicates that all the Engineer objects share the same value for the dept property that is inherited. The value that was inherited from Employee is overridden by the dept property value.

5. The method called base is an Engineer method and because of this, when the base is called, the *this* keyword is bound to the new object created in the first step. As such, the Worker function will then pass the two arguments to the Employee constructor function. On return from this function, the Worker function will set the property called projects using the remaining argument.

6. On return from the method called base, the Engineer constructor will initialize the machine property for the object to "belau".

7. Lastly, on return from the constructor, the new object is assigned by JavaScript to the variable called Julie.

You could be mistaken that once the Worker constructor has been called from the Engineer constructor, inheritance has been correctly set up for all Engineer objects. However, you aren't. When you call the Worker constructor, make sure an Engineer object has the properties specified in every constructor function that is called right from the start. However, if you were to add new properties at a later date to the Worker or Employee prototypes, the Engineer object will not inherit the new properties. Let's assume we have these statements, for example:

function Engineer(name, projs, mach) {

* this.base = Worker;*

```
    this.base(name, 'engineering', projs);

    this.machine = mach || '';

}
```

var Julie = new Engineer('Donalds, Julie', ['navigator', 'javascript'], 'belau');

Employee.prototype.specialty = 'none';

The object called Julie doesn't inherit the property called specialty. You must still set the prototype up explicitly to be sure of dynamic inheritance. Instead of the previous statements, assume you have these:

```
function Engineer(name, projs, mach) {

    this.base = Worker;

    this.base(name, 'engineering', projs);

    this.machine = mach || '';

}
```

Engineer.prototype = new Worker;

var Julie = new Engineer('Donalds, Julie', ['navigator', 'javascript'], 'belau');

Employee.prototype.specialty = 'none';

Now the specialty property value of the Julie object is set to "none".

Another inheritance method is to use the call() and apply() methods. The code below is equivalent:

```
function Engineer(name, projs, mach) {

    this.base = Worker;

    this.base(name, 'engineering', projs);

    this.machine = mach || '';

}

function Engineer(name, projs, mach) {

    Worker.call(this, name, 'engineering', projs);
```

```
  this.machine = mach || '';

}
```

When you use the call() method in JavaScript, your implementation is a lot cleaner because you no longer need the base.

Local vs. Inherited Values

As a quick overview, when you access a property of an object, these steps are carried out by JavaScript:

1. First, a check is made whether there is a local value; if there is, that value is returned.

2. If there is no local value, the prototype chain is checked using the property called __proto__.

3. If there is an object in the chain that provides a value for the property specified, that value will be returned.

4. If there is no property found in the chain, the object doesn't have a property of that name.

How this turns out will depend on the way you define things in the code. These definitions were used in the first example:

```
function Employee() {

  this.name = '';

  this.dept = 'general';

}


function Worker() {

  this.projects = [];

}

Worker.prototype = new Employee;
```

Using these definitions, let's now create an instance of Worker, called annie, using this statement:

var annie = new Worker;

The object called annie has got a local property called projects. Right now, the name and dept property values are not local to the new object and, as a result, they are derived from the ___proto___ property for annie. This means annie has the following property values:

annie.name == '';

annie.dept == 'general';

annie.projects == [];

Now let's say you want to make a change to the name property value in the prototype linked to Employee:

Employee.prototype.name = 'Unknown';

You might suppose the new value will propagate to every Employee instance but it doesn't.

When an Employee object instance is created, regardless of what it is, the instance's name property is given a local value. This means when you create a new object for Employee, thus setting the Worker prototype, Worker.prototype is given a local value for the name property. As such, when JavaScript looks for the name property of annie, which is a Worker instance, it finds a local value in Worker-prototype; it will not look in Employee.prototype which is further up the chain.

If, at runtime, you wanted to make a change to an object property value and ensure all object descendants inherit that new value, do not define the property in the constructor function; instead, it should be added to the prototype for the constructor. For example, let's say we want to change our last piece of code to this:

function Employee() {

  this.dept = 'general';   // this.name (a local variable) won't not appear here

}

Employee.prototype.name = '';   // A single copy

function Worker() {

  this.projects = [];

}

Worker.prototype = new Employee;

var annie = new Worker;

Employee.prototype.name = 'Unknown';

Now, the name property of the annie object becomes "Unknown".

As you can see from these examples, if you want the object properties to have default values, and you want the option to change the values when it comes to runtime, those properties must be set in the prototype and not in the constructor function.

Determine Instance Relationships

In JavaScript, property lookup involves looking inside the object's own properties; if a specified property name can't be found, JavaScript will move to the __proto__ property, the special property of that object. This will carry on recursively and is known as "lookup in the prototype chain".

The __proto__ property is set at the time an object is constructed and is set as the value of the prototype property for the constructor. As such, an expression of new Foo() will create an object that has a __proto__ called ==Foo.prototype. As a result, any changes made to the Foo.prototype will change the lookup for any object that new Foo() created.

All objects have their own __proto__ property, with the exception of Object; this means that all functions have the prototype object property. Because of this, an object may be related to one or more other objects through prototype inheritance. Inheritance can be tested for through a comparison of the __proto__ for an object and the prototype object for a function. In JavaScript, there is a shortcut for this – you can use the instanceof operator to test objects against functions and, if the object is inheriting from the function, true will be returned. For example:

var f = new Foo();

var isTrue = (f instanceof Foo);

To go a bit deeper on this, let's say we have the same set of definitions we used earlier in the section on Inheriting Properties. Now we want to create an Engineer object, like this:

var charlie = new Engineer('Bucket, Charlie', ['jsd'], 'fiji');

All the following statements will evaluate true:

charlie.__proto__ == Engineer.prototype;

charlie.__proto__.__proto__ == Worker.prototype;

charlie.__proto__.__proto__.__proto__ == Employee.prototype;

charlie.__proto__.__proto__.__proto__.__proto__ == Object.prototype;

charlie.__proto__.__proto__.__proto__.__proto__.__proto__ == null;

We could now write our instanceOf function like this:

```
function instanceOf(object, constructor) {

  object = object.__proto__;

  while (object != null) {

    if (object == constructor.prototype)

      return true;

    if (typeof object == 'xml') {

      return constructor.prototype == XML.prototype;

    }

    object = object.__proto__;

  }

  return false;

}
```

With this function, all the following expressions will evaluate true:

instanceOf(charlie, Engineer)

instanceOf(charlie, Worker)

instanceOf(charlie, Employee)

instanceOf(charlie, Object)

But this one will be false:

instanceOf(charlie, Salesperson)

Using Global Information in a Constructor

When creating a constructor, take care if you are setting global information in it. For example, let's say you want each new employee to be assigned automatically with a unique ID number; this definition could be used for Employee:

var idCounter = 1;

function Employee(name, dept) {

   this.name = name || '';

   this.dept = dept || 'general';

   this.id = idCounter++;

}

Using this definition, when a new Employee is created, the constructor automatically assigns the next ID in a sequence, incrementing the ID counter (global). If the next statement were you next, shania.id will be 1 and ben.id will be 2:

var shania = new Employee('Comfrey, Shania', 'pubs');

var ben = new Employee('Stilman, Ben', 'sales');

That all looks fine, doesn't it? Not really. Each time a new Employee object is created, we also increment idCounter. If you were to create the whole Employee hierarchy we are covering in this section, you would be calling the Employee constructor whenever a prototype is set up. Let's say we have this code:

var idCounter = 1;

function Employee(name, dept) {

   this.name = name || '';

   this.dept = dept || 'general';

   this.id = idCounter++;

}

function Manager(name, dept, reports) {...}

Manager.prototype = new Employee;

function Worker(name, dept, projs) {...}

Worker.prototype = new Employee;

function Engineer(name, projs, Timh) {...}

Engineer.prototype = new Worker;

function Salesperson(name, projs, quota) {...}

Salesperson.prototype = new Worker;

var Tim = new Engineer('Compton, Tim');

Now let's take that further and assume the definitions we left out have the property called base and will call the constructor that is above them in the chain. If this were the case, by the time we get to create the tim object, it will be tim.id5

Much will depend on what the application is and whether the fact the counter has been incremented additional times is important or not. If it is essential the counter value is exact, you could get around it with this constructor:

function Employee(name, dept) {

  this.name = name || '';

  this.dept = dept || 'general';

  if (name)

    this.id = idCounter++;

}

When creating Employee instances for use as prototypes, the constructor is not given any arguments. If you use this constructor definition and you don't assign arguments, no value is assigned to id by the constructor and, as a result, the counter is not updated.

Because of this, if you want an Employee to be assigned an id, a name must be specified. In the current example, tim.id would be 1.

Another way to do it would be to create a copy of the prototype object for Employee and assign it to Worker:

Worker.prototype = Object.create(Employee.prototype);

// instead of Worker.prototype = new Employee

Multiple Inheritance

While some of the OOP (object-oriented) languages support multiple inheritances, JavaScript does not. Multiple inheritances are where objects inherit properties and corresponding values from parent objects that are not related.

In JavaScript, property value inheritance happens at runtime when the program looks in an object's prototype chain for a value. Because objects only have one prototype associated, it is not possible for JavaScript to dynamically inherit from any more than a single chain.

You can write a constructor function that will call one or more other constructor functions, which provides you with the illusion of multiple inheritances. Look at these statements as an example:

function Hobbyist(hobby) {

  this.hobby = hobby || 'diving';

}

function Engineer(name, projs, Timh, hobby) {

  this.base1 = Worker;

  this.base1(name, 'engineering', projs);

  this.base2 = Hobbyist;

  this.base2(hobby);

  this.Timhine = Timh || '';

}

Engineer.prototype = new Worker;

var dennis = new Engineer('Donalds, Dennis', ['collabra'], 'hugo');

Now let's assume the Worker definition is the same as we used earlier, but this time the object called dennis has these properties:

dennis.name == 'Donalds, Dennis';

dennis.dept == 'engineering';

dennis.projects == ['collabra'];

dennis.Timhine == 'hugo';

dennis.hobby == 'diving';

Dennis inherits the property of hobby from the constructor called Hobbyist. However, let's say we add a new property to the prototype for the Hobbyist constructor:

Hobbyist.prototype.equipment = ['mask', 'fins', 'regulator', 'bcd'];

The Donalds property of the dennis object will not inherit the newly added property.

Promises

Promises are objects representing the final outlook, be it failure or completion, of asynchronous operations. In this section, we will look at returned promises and consumption before we go ahead and create them.

In essence, a promise is an object that is returned, to which callbacks are attached rather than the callback being passed to a function.

Imagine you have a function called createAudioFileAsync(); this will generate sound files asynchronously with the provision of two callback functions and .a configuration record. One callback function will be called upon successful creation of the audio file and the other will be called if it fails and an error occurs.

The code below uses the createAudioFileAsync() function:

```
function successCallback(result) {

  console.log("Audio file ready at URL: " + result);

}



function failureCallback(error) {

  console.log("Error generating audio file: " + error);

}



createAudioFileAsync(audioSettings, successCallback, failureCallback);
```

A modern function would return promises to which callbacks can be attached. For example, if we rewrote the function to return the promise, we could use it as simply as this:

```
createAudioFileAsync(audioSettings).then(successCallback, failureCallback);
```

This is a shortened version of:

```
const promise = createAudioFileAsync(audioSettings);

promise.then(successCallback, failureCallback);
```

This is known as an asynchronous function call. Using this convention has a few advantages that we will explore now:

Guarantees

Promises have certain guarantees the old method of passed-in callbacks didn't have:

- A callback will not be called before the current run of the JS event loop has completed.

- A callback added using the *them* method will be called as it is above, even if the asynchronous operation has failed.

- To add several callbacks, just use the then() method for each one (4 callbacks = 4 then() methods, for example). Each of the callbacks is executed in order of insertion, one after the other.

One of the best things about promises is chaining,

Chaining

Executing at least two asynchronous operations back-to-back is a common requirement. Each operation will start only when the previous one has succeeded, using the returned result from the successful operation. This is done with a promise chain.

Here's how it works. A new promise is returned by the then() function and it is a different promise to the original one:

const promise = doSomething();

const promise2 = promise.then(successCallback, failureCallback);

or

const promise2 = doSomething().then(successCallback, failureCallback);

The second promise, called promise2, is representative of doSomething() completing and of either successCallback() or failureCallback(), both passed in and both may be another asynchronous function returning a promise. In that case, if you add any callbacks to promise2, they are queued behind the promise the success or failure function returns.

In short, a promise is a representative of when an asynchronous step in the promise chain is completed.

Previously, if you tried to do multiple asynchronous operations together, you would get the well-known "pyramid of doom":

```
doSomething(function(result) {
  doSomethingElse(result, function(newResult) {
    doThirdThing(newResult, function(finalResult) {
      console.log('Got the final result: ' + finalResult);
    }, failureCallback);
  }, failureCallback);
}, failureCallback);
```

These days, callbacks get attached to returned promises, thus forming the chain:

```
doSomething()
.then(function(result) {
  return doSomethingElse(result);
})
.then(function(newResult) {
  return doThirdThing(newResult);
})
.then(function(finalResult) {
  console.log('Got the final result: ' + finalResult);
})
.catch(failureCallback);
```

catch(failureCallback is a shortened version of then(null, failureCallback, while the then() arguments are optional. If this were expressed using arrow functions, it would look like this:

```
doSomething()
.then(result => doSomethingElse(result))
.then(newResult => doThirdThing(newResult))
.then(finalResult => {
```

```
console.log(`Got the final result: ${finalResult}`);
})
.catch(failureCallback);
```

It is important to remember that results must always be returned; if not, the callbacks cannot catch the result from the last promise. Using arrow functions, () => x is a shortened version of () => {return x;}).

Chaining After Catches

Chaining is still possible even after a catch or failure, and this can be very useful when you want new actions done even when one action on the chain has failed. Look at this example:

```
new Promise((resolve, reject) => {

  console.log('Initial');


  resolve();
})
.then(() => {

  throw new Error('Something failed');


  console.log('Do this');
})
.catch(() => {

  console.log('Do that');
})
.then(() => {

  console.log('Do this, whatever happened earlier');
});
```

The output will be:

Initial

Do that

Do this, whatever happened earlier

You do not see the Do this text displayed because rejection was caused by the Something failed error.

Error Propagation

Thus, look back to the "pyramid of doom" shown earlier; do you recall that failureCallback appeared three times, as opposed to a single time at the end of our promise chain?

doSomething()

.then(result => doSomethingElse(result))

.then(newResult => doThirdThing(newResult))

.then(finalResult => console.log(`Got the final result: ${finalResult}`))

.catch(failureCallback);

A promise chain will halt if an exception occurs and will look down the promise chain to see if there are any catch handlers; this is how synchronous code works:

try {

* const result = syncDoSomething();*

* const newResult = syncDoSomethingElse(result);*

* const finalResult = syncDoThirdThing(newResult);*

* console.log(`Got the final result: ${finalResult}`);*

} catch(error) {

* failureCallback(error);*

}

The symmetry between asynchronous and synchronous code results in the ECMAScript 2017 syntactic sugar of async/_await:

async function foo() {

```
try {

  const result = await doSomething();

  const newResult = await doSomethingElse(result);

  const finalResult = await doThirdThing(newResult);

  console.log(`Got the final result: ${finalResult}`);

} catch(error) {

  failureCallback(error);

}

}
```

Promises evolved to fix a basic flaw in the "pyramid of doom" and will catch every error, even programming, and thrown exceptions. This is imperative to ensure asynchronous operations are functionally composed.

Creating Promises around Old Callback APIs

Using a constructor, it is possible to create a promise scratch, but you should only do this if you have old APIs that need to be wrapped.

Ideally, every asynchronous function would return a Promise, but there are some APIs that expect the success and/or failure callbacks passed in an old-fashioned way. The best example is the setTimeout() function:

```
setTimeout(() => saySomething("10 seconds passed"), 10000);
```

It causes problems if you mix promises with the old-style callbacks. Let's say that saySomething() has failed or it has an error in the programming; nothing would catch it and the only thing to blame is the setTimeout() function.

However, there is a way to wrap a promise around setTimeout. Best practice says that functions causing problems should be wrapped at the lowest level, and then never be directly called:

```
const wait = ms => new Promise(resolve => setTimeout(resolve, ms));
```

```
wait(10000).then(() => saySomething("10 seconds")).catch(failureCallback);
```

In short, a promise constructor can take an executor function allowing us to manually accept or reject promises. Because setTimeout() hasn't really failed, in our case, we didn't include reject.

Composition

Both Promise.reject() and Promise.resolve() are shorter ways to create promises that are already rejected or resolved. There are times when this could be quite useful.

As well, Promise.race() and Promise.all() are both composition tools that allow parallel running of asynchronous operations.

Operations can be started in parallel and then we can wait while they all finish, as in this example:

Promise.all([func1(), func2(), func3()])

.then(([result1, result2, result3]) => { /* use result1, result2 and result3 */ });

You can use a bit of clever JavaScript to create sequential composition:

[func1, func2, func3].reduce((p, f) => p.then(f), Promise.resolve())

.then(result3 => { /* use result3 */ });

All we have done is reduced an array containing asynchronous functions to a promise chain equivalent of Promise.resolve().then(func1).then(func2).then(func3).

We can turn this into a reusable function commonly used in programming, especially functional programming:

const applyAsync = (acc,val) => acc.then(val);

const composeAsync = (...funcs) => x => funcs.reduce(applyAsync, Promise.resolve(x));

The function called composeAsync() can take one or more arguments in the form of functions and return another function taking an initial value passed down the composition pipeline:

const transformData = composeAsync(func1, func2, func3);

const result3 = transformData(data);

With ECMAScript 2017, we can do sequential composition quite simply using async/wait:

let result;

```
for (const f of [func1, func2, func3]) {

  result = await f(result);

}

/* use last result (i.e. result3) */
```

Timing

As a way of avoiding the unexpected, any function that is passed to then() will not be asynchronously called, even when you have a promise it has already been resolved:

```
Promise.resolve().then(() => console.log(2));

console.log(1); // 1, 2
```

Rather than running immediately, the function that is passed in is placed into a microtask queue; that is, it will run later on, once the queue has emptied when the current event loop run finishes.

```
const wait = ms => new Promise(resolve => setTimeout(resolve, ms));


wait().then(() => console.log(4));

Promise.resolve().then(() => console.log(2)).then(() => console.log(3));

console.log(1); // 1, 2, 3, 4
```

Nesting

It is much better not to nest simple chains because nesting is often the result of careless of lazy composition.

Nesting is one of the control structures used to limit catch statement scope. More specifically, nested catches will not catch errors that fall outside of the nested scope or higher in the chain. When you use it the right way, it can provide much better error recovery:

```
doSomethingImportant()

.then(result => doSomethingOptional()

  .then(optionalResult => doSomethingReallyNice(optionalResult))

  .catch(e => {})) // Ignore this if optional things fail; proceed.
```

.then(() => moreImportantStuff())

.catch(e => console.log("Critical failure: " + e.message));

Note the nesting of the optional steps; this isn't a result of indentation, rather the result of risky placement of the parentheses surrounding them.

The inner catch statement, which is neutralizing, can only catch a failure from doSomethingReallyNice() and doSomethingOptional(); after these, the code will continue with moreImportantStuff(). Perhaps more significantly, if a failure occurs with doSomethingImportant(), the outer catch is the only one that will catch it – this is the last catch.

Common Mistakes

There are a few common blunders you need to watch for when you compose a promise chain. You can see some of those mistakes in this example:

doSomething().then(function(result) {

  doSomethingElse(result) // Didn't return the promise from the inner chain and unnecessary nesting

  .then(newResult => doThirdThing(newResult));

}).then(() => doFourthThing());

// The chain wasn't terminated with a catch!

The first error is in neglecting to chain everything as it should be. This tends to happen when new promises are created but don't return. As a result of this, the chain is broken; what we actually have is a pair of racing independent chains. This means doFourthThing() will not wait until doThirdThing() or doSomethingElse() has finished, instead of running parallel to them and very likely totally unintended. And, if you have separate chains, it leads to separate error handling and that can lead to errors going uncaught.

The second error is unnecessary nesting, which is what allows the first error to happen. Nesting also puts limits on the scope of the inner error handlers and this, if not tended to, can also result in errors going uncaught. The promise constructor anti-pattern is another variation of this, a combination of the somewhat redundant use of a promise constructor wrapping code that has promises already and nesting.

The final mistake in the example is neglecting to terminate a chain using catch. If a promise chain goes unterminated, most browsers will kick up an uncaught promise rejection.

As a rule, a promise chain should be returned or terminated and new promises must be immediately returned to keep things flat:

doSomething()

.then(function(result) {

  return doSomethingElse(result);

})

.then(newResult => doThirdThing(newResult))

.then(() => doFourthThing())

.catch(error => console.log(error));

In this, () => x is a shorter version of () => {return x;}

What we have now is one chain that is deterministic and has the correct error handling. When you use async/_wait, most problems, of not all of them, can be addressed and the tradeoff is commonest mistake – forgetting to use the *await* keyword in that syntax.

Iterators and Generators

One of the most common operations is processing each item within a collection. In JavaScript, there are several methods of iteration, from a simple *for* loop to the filter() and map() functions. We talked about these earlier in the section but now we go a bit more in-depth to discuss how iterators and generators drag iteration straight to the heart of the language, providing a way for the *for...of* loop to be customized.

Iterators

A JavaScript iterator is simply an object that can define sequences and, on termination, possibly a return value too. More specifically, iterators are any object that can implement the iterator protocol using the next() method; this method will return objects with two properties – value, which is the next sequence value, and done, which evaluates true if the final sequence value is consumed. If value and done are present together, it will result in the return value of the iterator.

Once an iterator object has been created, it can be explicitly iterated and this is done through the repeated calling of next(). When you iterate over an iterator, it is known as "consuming the iterator," because generally this can be done only once. Once the terminating value yields, any further calls to next() should move on to return {done: true}.

The Array iterator is the most commonly used one in JavaScript and all it does is return individual values in sequence from the array. It is easy enough to think that we could express all iterators as arrays but that simply isn't true. An Array has to be allocated as a whole whereas an iterator is consumed only when needed and, as such, it can express unlimited sizes of arrays, like the integer range between 0 and Infinity.

Below is an example that does exactly that, letting us create a range iterator to define an integer sequence from start to finish inclusive and spaced a step apart. The return value is the sequence size and a variable called iterationCount tracks that size:

```
function makeRangeIterator(start = 0, end = Infinity, step = 1) {

    let nextIndex = start;

    let iterationCount = 0;


    const rangeIterator = {
```

```
  next: function() {

    let result;

    if (nextIndex <= end) {

      result = { value: nextIndex, done: false }

      nextIndex += step;

      iterationCount++;

      return result;

    }

    return { value: iterationCount, done: true }

  }

};

return rangeIterator;

}
```

When you use the iterator, it will look like this:

```
let it = makeRangeIterator(1, 10, 2);


let result = it.next();

while (!result.done) {

console.log(result.value); // 1 3 5 7 9

result = it.next();

}


console.log("Iterated over sequence of size: ", result.value); // 5
```

Generator Functions

While the custom iterators are great tools, creating them requires cautious programming because it is important the internal state is explicitly maintained. A generator function is an incredibly powerful alternative because it allows you to write one function with non-continuous execution that defines an iterative algorithm. We use the function* syntax to write generator functions, and, when they are first called, none of the code is executed; instead, an iterator type known as a generator is returned. When the next() method for the generator is called, the value is consumed and the function will execute until it comes against the *yield* keyword.

You can call this function as many times as you need and each time a new generator will be returned. However, you can only iterate over a generator once.

Now we can adapt our earlier example with code that behaves in exactly the same way, but with a much nicer implementation:

function* makeRangeIterator(start = 0, end = Infinity, step = 1) {

   let iterationCount = 0;

   for (let i = start; i < end; i += step) {

     iterationCount++;

     yield i;

   }

   return iterationCount;

}

Iterables

Objects are classed as iterable only if they define their own iteration behavior, i.e. the values a *for...of* construct will loop over. Some the types built-in to JavaScript, such as Map or Array, already contain default behavior for iteration while others, like the Object type, do not.

To be considered as iterable, the @@ iterator method must be implemented by the object; this means the object, or an object up the prototype chain, has a property containing the Symbol.iterator key.

User-Defined Iterables

Defining your own iterable is prepared like this:

var myIterable = {

   *[Symbol.iterator]() {

```
    yield 1;

    yield 2;

    yield 3;

  }

}


for (let value of myIterable) {

  console.log(value);

}
// 1

// 2

// 3


or


[...myIterable]; // [1, 2, 3]
```

Built-in Iterables

The iterables built-in to JavaScript are Map, Set, Array, String, and TypedArray because the prototype object for each one has the Symbol.iterator method.

A syntax that Expects an Iterable

There are expressions and statements that will expect an iterable, like the *for...of* loop, and *yield** for example:

```
for (let value of ['a', 'b', 'c']) {

  console.log(value);

}
// "a"
```

```
// "b"

// "c"


[...'abc']; // ["a", "b", "c"]


function* gen() {

  yield* ['a', 'b', 'c'];

}


console.log(gen().next()); // { value: "a", done: false }


[a, b, c] = new Set(['a', 'b', 'c']);

console.log(a); // "a"
```

Advanced Generators

A generator will compute its yielded value when needed and this is why they are so efficient at representing sequences that take too much to compute, and even an infinite sequence like the example above.

The next() method will also take a value that can be used for the modification of the generator's internal state. When you pass a value to next() it is treated as the result from the yield expression that stopped the generator.

In this example, the Fibonacci generator uses next(x) to get the sequence going again:

```
function* fibonacci() {

  var fn1 = 0;

  var fn2 = 1;

  while (true) {

    var current = fn1;

    fn1 = fn2;
```

```
    fn2 = current + fn1;

    var reset = yield current;

    if (reset) {

      fn1 = 0;

      fn2 = 1;

    }

  }

}


var sequence = fibonacci();

console.log(sequence.next().value);    // 0

console.log(sequence.next().value);    // 1

console.log(sequence.next().value);    // 1

console.log(sequence.next().value);    // 2

console.log(sequence.next().value);    // 3

console.log(sequence.next().value);    // 5

console.log(sequence.next().value);    // 8

console.log(sequence.next(true).value); // 0

console.log(sequence.next().value);    // 1

console.log(sequence.next().value);    // 1

console.log(sequence.next().value);    // 2
```

You can also call the throw() method of a generator to force it into throwing an exception, but you must specify the exception value to be thrown. This will be thrown from the generator's current suspended context, just as if yield were a throw() value statement instead.

If the exception is not caught in the generator, it continues up through the throw() call and all succeeding next() calls result in the property called done evaluating as true.

A generator also has a method called return(value) to return the specified value and stop the generator.

Meta-Programming

With ECMA 2015, support was provided in JavaScript for two new objects – Proxy and Reflect. These objects intercept basic operations, such as assignment, lookup, invoking functions, enumeration, etc., and define customized behavior. These objects allow for meta-level programming in JavaScript.

Proxies

Proxies were first introduced with ECMAScript. A Proxy object lets you intercept some operations, define custom behavior, and implement it. In the example below, Proxy is used to get a property onto an object:

```
var handler = {

  get: function(target, name) {

    return name in target ? target[name] : 49;

  }

};



var p = new Proxy({}, handler);

p.a = 1;

console.log(p.a, p.b); // 1, 49
```

A target, which is an empty object, has been defined by the Proxy object along with a handler object. In the handler object, a get trap has been implemented. An object that has been proxied won't return a value of undefined when it receives undefined properties; instead, it will return the number 49.

Terminology

When we talk about Proxy functionality, you can expect to come across these terms:

- **handler** – a placeholder object with traps in it

- **traps** – methods used for providing access to properties. This is much the same as the traps used in operating systems.

- **target** – this is the object being virtualized by the Proxy. Targets tend to be storage backends for proxies. Invariants, which are semantics that does not change, regarding properties that cannot be configured or objects that cannot be extended are verified against targets.

- **Invariants** – these are semantics that does not change when a custom operation is implemented. If a handler's invariants are violated, a TypeError is thrown.

Handlers and Traps

Below are the traps available to a Proxy object:

- **handler.getPrototypeOf()** – has interceptions of Object.getPrototypeOf(). Reflect.getPrototypeOf(), __proto__, Object.prototype.isPrototypeOf(), and instanceOf(). The invariant is get.PrototypeOf() and the a null or object must be returned by the method.

- **handler.setPrototypeOf()** – has interceptions of Object.setPrototypeOf() and Reflect.setPrototypeOf(). If the target is non-extensible then the prototype parameter has to have the same value Object.getPrototypeOf(target) has.

- **Handler,isExtensible()** – has interceptions of Object.isExtensible() and Reflect.isExtensible(). The invariant is Object.isExtensible(proxy) and it must return the value Object.isExtensible(target) returns.

- **handler.preventExtensions()** – has interceptions of Object.preventExtensions() and Reflect.preventExtensions(). The invariant is Object.preventExtensions(proxy) which will return true only if Object.isExtensible(proxy) returns false.

- **Handler.getOwnPropertyDescriptor()** – has interceptions of Object.getOwnPropertyDescriptor() and Reflect.getOwnPropertyDescriptor(). It has an invariant of getOwnPropertyDescriptor() which must return either undefined or an object. If a property exists as a target object own property that cannot be configured, it can't be reported as a non-existent property. It also can't be reported as non-existent if it exists as a target object own property where the target is non-extensible. It cannot be reported as existent if it doesn't exist as a target object own property where the target is non-extensible and property may not be reported as not being configurable if it doesn't exist as a target object own property, or if it a target object own property that can be configured. The Object.getOwnPropertyDescriptor(target) result may be applied, using Object.defineProperty, to the target object and no exception will be thrown.

- **handler.defineProperty()** – has interceptions of Object.defineProperty() and Reflect.defineProperty(). If the target object is non-extensible, a property may not be added. Nor may it be added as non-configurable or modified to non-configurable if the property is not a target object non-configurable property. It also can't be non-configurable if a target object configurable property corresponding to it exists. If the corresponding property exists no exception will be thrown by Object.defineProperty(target, prop, descriptor). If the defineProperty handler returns a false value in strict mode, a TypeError exception is thrown.

- **handler.has()** – has interceptions of Object.create(proxy) and Reflect.has() with a property called query: foo in the proxy and an inherited property of query: foo in both interceptions. Properties may not be reported as non-existent if they exist as a target object's non-configurable own property or if it exists as a target object own property and the object itself is non-extensible.

- **handler.get()** – has property access of proxy.bar and proxy[foo] with inherited access in Object.create(proxy[foo] and an interception of Reflect.get(). A property's reported value has to be the same as the target object that corresponds to it, where the target property is a data property that cannot be written to or configured. The property value has to be undefined where the target object that corresponds to it is an accessor property that cannot be configured and that has a [[Get]] attribute of undefined.

- **handler.set()** – has a property assignment of proxy[foo] = bar and one of proxy.foo = bar. It has inherited property assignment in Object.create(proxy[foo] = bar and an interception of Reflect.set(). The property value cannot be changed to a value different to the target object value that corresponds to it where the corresponding object is a data property that cannot be written to or configured. A property value cannot be set if the target object that corresponds to it is an accessor property that cannot be configured and has a [[Set]] attribute if undefined. If a set handler returns a false value in strict mode, a TypeError exception is thrown.

- **handler.deleteProperty()** – has interceptions of Property proxy[foo] and delete of Reflect.deleteProperty(). Deletion is via deletion: proxy.foo. Properties cannot be deleted if they exist as target object non-configurable own properties.

- **handler.enumerate()** – has property enumeration of /for...in (var name in proxy) {...} and interception of Reflect.enumerate(). An object must be returned by the enumerate method.

- **handler.ownKeys()** – has interceptions of Object.getOwnPropertyNames(), Object.keys(), Object.getOwnPropertySymbols() and Reflect.ownKeys. ownKeys will result in a list and the Type of each of the elements in the list will be a symbol or a string. The List result must have the keys of target object non-configurable own properties. If the target object isn't extensible, List must have the keys for the target object own properties – there must not be any other values.

- **handler.apply()** – has interceptions of proxy(...args). Reflect.apply(), Function.prototype.call() and Function.prototype,apply(). The handler.apply() method does not have any invariants.

- **handler.construct()** - has interceptions of proxy(...args) and Reflect.construct(). The result of handler.construct() must always be an object.

Revocable Proxy

The method called Proxy.revocable() is used when creating a Proxy object that is revocable. This means using the revoke function to revoke the proxy and switch it off. After this, any proxy operation will result in a TypeError being thrown.

```
var revocable = Proxy.revocable({}, {

  get: function(target, name) {

    return '[[' + name + ']]';

  }
});

var proxy = revocable.proxy;

console.log(proxy.foo); // "[[foo]]"


revocable.revoke();


console.log(proxy.foo);  // TypeError gets thrown

proxy.foo = 1;        // Another TypeError

delete proxy.foo;     // still a TypeError

typeof proxy;         // "object", typeof won't trigger any trap
```

Reflection

One of the built-in objects is Reflect; an object that provides us with methods for JavaScript operations that can be intercepted. Those methods are the same as the ones from the proxy handlers and you should remember that Reflect isn't a function object.

Reflect helps us to forward a default operation to the target from the handler.

For example, Reflect.has() provides us with a function in the shape of the in operator:

Reflect.has(Object, 'assign'); // true

A Much Better Apply Function

With ECMAScript 5, we tend to use the method called Function.prototype.apply() to call function given a value for this and arguments provided in the form of an array-like object or an array:

Function.prototype.apply.call(Math.floor, undefined, [1.75]);

Using the method, Reflect.apply, this gets easier to understand:

console.log(Reflect.apply(Math.floor, undefined, [1.75]));

// 1;

console.log(Reflect.apply(String.fromCharCode, undefined, [104, 101, 108, 108, 111]));

// "hello"

console.log(Reflect.apply(RegExp.prototype.exec, /ab/, ['confabulation']).index);

// 4

console.log(Reflect.apply(".charAt, 'ponies', [3]));

// "i"

Checking Property Definitions for Success

Object.defineProperty will return object if it is successful, otherwise a TypeError exception is thrown. You could use a try...catch block for catching errors that occur while you are defining properties. Reflect.defineProperty returns a success status of a Boolean value so an *if...else* block is sufficient:

```
if (Reflect.defineProperty(target, property, attributes)) {

  // success

} else {

  // failure

}
```

For the rest of this section, we will look at what JSON is and how to work with it. After that, we'll build a Bouncing Ball game to give you some practice using what you already learned and then have a brief look at APIs.

Working with JSON

JSON stands for JavaScript Object Notation and it is a text-based format used to represent structured data founded on the object syntax in JavaScript. JSON tends to be used for the transmission of data in a web application, for example, when data is sent from server to client, enabling it to be displayed on the page and vice versa. You will come across this quite a lot on your JavaScript and web building journey, so I will give you the information you need to work with it in JavaScript.

Consequently, what is JSON?

The object syntax was made popular by Douglas Crockford and JSON is a text-based way of following it. It is similar to the syntax for the JS object literal but it can be used independent of JavaScript with many environments providing the ability to parse JSON and generate it.

JSON exists in string format, which is useful for the purpose of transmitting data across networks. When you want or need to access the data held in it, it must first be converted into a native object, and there is a global JSON object in JavaScript providing the required methods to convert between them.

Note

Converting strings to native objects is known as parsing and converting native objects to strings for transmission across a network is known as stringification.

JSON objects can be stored within their own files, which are nothing more than test files with a file extension of .json.

The Structure of JSON

JSON is a string format that appears like the object literal format in JavaScript. The same data types included in a standard object can also be contained within JSON – numbers, strings, Booleans, arrays, and other object literals. Using these, you can construct a JSON data hierarchy like this:

```
{

  "squadName": "Super hero Avengers",

  "homeTown": "New York City",

  "formed": 2012,
```

```json
"secretBase": "Avengers tower",
"active": true,
"members": [
  {
    "name": "Iron Man",
    "age": 49,
    "secretIdentity": "Tony Stark",
    "powers": [
      "Industrial genius",
      "Enhanced mental processes",
      "Expert engineer"
    ]
  },
  {
    "name": "Black Widow",
    "age": 39,
    "secretIdentity": "Natasha Romanoff",
    "powers": [
      "World class athlete",
      "Martial artist",
      "Weapons specialist"
    ]
  },
  {
    "name": "Captain America",
```

```
  "age": 1000000,

  "secretIdentity": "Steve Rogers",

  "powers": [

    "Superhuman strength",

    "Superhuman mobility",

    "Superhuman resilience",

    "Advanced healing",

    "Advanced mental capacity"

    ]

   }

  ]

 }
```

If we were to load this into a JS program, and parse a variable in with the name of superHeroes, we would be able to access the data in it with the same bot and bracket notation we use with JavaScript objects. For example:

superHeroes.homeTown

superHeroes['active']

If we want to have access to data down in the hierarchy, we would need to chain together the names of the properties and the array indexes. For example, if we wanted to access the third of the superpowers attributed to the second hero on the members' list, we would do this:

superHeroes['members'][1]['powers'][2]

Breaking this down:

- First comes the name of the variable – superheroes.

- Next, we want access to the members' property in the variable so ["members"] is used.

- Inside "members" is an array that has been populated with objects. We want the second of those objects in the array so [1] is used.

- Within that object, we want access to the property called powers so ["powers"] is used.

- In the powers property, there is an array that has the superpowers for the chosen hero. We want the third superpower so [2] is used.

Arrays as JSON

While it is mostly correct that JSON text is like the syntax for JavaScript objects, arrays are also valid JSON, like this:

```
[

 {

   "name": "Iron Man",

   "age": 29,

   "secretIdentity": "Tony Stark",

   "powers": [

     "Industrial genius",

     "Enhanced mental processes",

     "Expert engineer"

   ]

 },

 {

   "name": "Black Widow",

   "age": 39,

   "secretIdentity": "Natasha Romanoff",

   "powers": [

     "World class athlete",

     "Martial artist",

     "Weapons specialist"
```

```
    ]
  }
]
```

This is all valid JSON; start with an array index to access the array items in the parsed version, i.e. [0]["powers"][0]

Other Things to Know

The following are important points to know about using JSON:

- JSON is a data format only, containing no methods, only properties.

- A requisite of JSON is the use of double quotation marks around the names of properties and around strings. You cannot use single quotation marks as they are invalid.

- If you misplace even one colon or comma in a JSON file, things can go wrong and the file won't work. Whenever you attempt to use data, validate it using an application such as JSONLint. As a side note, there is little chance of errors appearing in JSON generated by the computer, so long as the generator program is working as it should be.

- JSON is able to take on any data type form while that data type can be validly included in JSON. It doesn't just take objects and arrays. For example, one string or one number would be valid as a JSON object.

- In JavaScript, object properties can be left unquoted but in JSON, you can only use strings that are quoted as properties.

A JSON Example

Let's do a bit of practical work now and go through an example that shows how JSON data could be used on a website.

Getting Started

First of all, head to GitHub and make copies of these files – style.css and heroes.html. These are the official MDN files and the Style file has some CSS we can use on the webpage, while the heroes file contains a bit of body HTML:

<header>

</header>

<section>

</section>

Also included is a <script> element containing all of the code you write in this practical example. Right now, it only has two lines used for grabbing references to <> elements and the <header> and then stores the references in variables:

var header = document.querySelector('header');

var = document.querySelector(");

For the purposes of this exercise, we'll use the MDN superheroes.json file you can get from <u>here</u>.

Getting the JSON

We will use the XMLHttpRequest API, often shortened to XHR, to get the JSON. This is one of the most useful of all objects in JavaScript because it allows us to make requests to the network to get resources from a server using JavaScript, i.e. text, image, JSON, HTML snippets, etc. This means we can easily update small bits of our content without reloading the whole page every time. The result of this is web pages that are far more responsive, but that is something we'll be delving into later in the book.

Let's get started.

1. The first thing we need to do is store the URL for JSON we will be retrieving and this is stored in a variable. Add this to the bottom of the JavaScript code:

var requestURL = 'https://mdn.github.io/learning-area/javascript/oojs/json/superheroes.json';

2. Next, we create a request object instance to create a new request. This is done from the XMLHttpRequest constructor and we use the new keyword to do it. Add this line to the bottom of your code

var request = new XMLHttpRequest();

3. Now we use open() to open a new request, so add this line:

request.open('GET', requestURL);

This takes a minimum of two parameters; there are quite a few optional ones to choose from but, for this example, the mandatory ones are sufficient. They are:

- The HTTP method – used for the request to the network. In our case, using GET is okay because all we want is a little simple data.

- The URL the request is being made to. For our example, that URL is for the JSON file that was stored earlier.

Once you have done this

4. Add these two lines to set our responseType as JSON. That way, XHR will know that JSON will be returned from the server and is to be converted in the background into an object. Then we use send() to send our request:

request.responseType = 'json';

request.send();

5. Lastly, we wait for the server to return the response and then we can deal with it. Add these lines to the bottom of your code:

request.onload = function() {

var superHeroes = request.response;

populateHeader(superHeroes);

showHeroes(superHeroes);

}

What we have done here is store the response to the request, which is available inside the response property, inside a variable named superHeroes. The variable will now have the JSON-based JavaScript object. Next, we pass the object to a pair of function calls; the first is going to fill <header> with the right data and the second creates an info card for each of the heroes and inserts each between the <>.

The code has been wrapped in an event handler that will run whenever the load event fires on our request object. This happens because the load event will only fire when the response is returned successfully. Doing it this way is a form of guaranteeing that request.response will categorically be available when we want to do something with it.

Populating the Header

We have our JSON data and we have converted it to a JavaScript object. Now we can use it by writing our functions that were referenced earlier. First, the following lines need to be added to the bottom of your code – this is a function definition:

function populateHeader(jsonObj) {

```
var myH1 = document.createElement('h1');

myH1.textContent = jsonObj['squadName'];

header.appendChild(myH1);


var myPara = document.createElement('p');

myPara.textContent = 'Hometown: ' + jsonObj['homeTown'] + ' // Formed: ' +
jsonObj['formed'];

header.appendChild(myPara);

}
```

The parameter has been named as jsonObj as a reminder that the object originally came from JSON. First we used createElement() to create the <h1> element; next, its textContent is set to equal the object property called squadName, and then it was appended, using appendChild(), to the header. A similar operation is then done with a paragraph; it is created, its text content set, and appended to the header. The difference is that the text for the paragraph is set to a concatenated string that has both the homeTown and the formed property objects.

Creating Information Cards

To create and display the information cards, we add this function to the bottom of our code:

```
function showHeroes(jsonObj) {

 var heroes = jsonObj['members'];


 for (var i = 0; i < heroes.length; i++) {

  var myArticle = document.createElement('article');

  var myH2 = document.createElement('h2');

  var myPara1 = document.createElement('p');

  var myPara2 = document.createElement('p');

  var myPara3 = document.createElement('p');
```

```
var myList = document.createElement('ul');


myH2.textContent = heroes[i].name;

myPara1.textContent = 'Secret identity: ' + heroes[i].secretIdentity;

myPara2.textContent = 'Age: ' + heroes[i].age;

myPara3.textContent = 'Superpowers:';


var superPowers = heroes[i].powers;

for (var j = 0; j < superPowers.length; j++) {

  var listItem = document.createElement('li');

  listItem.textContent = superPowers[j];

  myList.appendChild(listItem);

}


myArticle.appendChild(myH2);

myArticle.appendChild(myPara1);

myArticle.appendChild(myPara2);

myArticle.appendChild(myPara3);

myArticle.appendChild(myList);


section.appendChild(myArticle);

 }

}
```

To begin with, the object members property is now stored inside a new variable. The array has several objects and each contains information for the superheroes. A *for* loop is then used for looping through each individual array object. For each of these, we did the following:

- Several new elements are created – one <article>, one <h2>, one <ul> and three <p>s

- The <h2> is set so it has the name of the current hero.

- The three paragraphs (<p>) are filled with the secretIdentity, the age and a line that says "superpowers". This introduces some of the list information.

- The property called powers is stored in a new variable named superPowers, which has an array listing the superpowers of the current hero.

- Another for loop is used to loop through the superpowers for the current hero; we create one <li> element for each one, place the superpower into the element and then use appendChild() to place the listItem into the <ul> element, (myList).

- Lastly, we append the three <p>s, the <h2> and the <ul> in the <article>, (myArticle). The <article> is then appended in the <>. Be vigilant of the order you append things as this will be the order they get displayed in the HTML.

Note

If you are struggling to follow our dot/bracket notation in use here, it might help if you open the superheroes.json file in a separate tab or inside your text editor and refer to it as you work through this. You can also go back over the section on Objects to get more information on this kind of notation.

Conversion between Text and Objects

This was quite a simple example showing how the JavaScript object is accessed, and it was made so because the XHR request was set to directly convert our JSON response into the JavaScript object like this:

request.responseType = 'json';

Sometimes things aren't so easy; on occasion, you will get a Raw JSON string that needs to be manually converted to the object. And when an object is to be sent across the network it needs to be converted to a JSON string first. These are common problems in the world of web development and, to help out, a JSON object has been made available in web browsers containing these two methods:

- **parse()** - this will take a parameter of a JSON string and return the JavaScript object that corresponds to it.

- **stringify()** – this will take a parameter of an object and will return the JSON string form that corresponds to it.

Taking the example we drew up earlier - if we set the XHR to return raw text (JSON) and then parse() converts it into the JS object. The key piece of code is:

request.open('GET', requestURL);

request.responseType = 'json'; // now we get a string!

request.send();

request.onload = function() {

  var superHeroesText = request.response; // get the string from the response

  var superHeroes = JSON.parse(superHeroesText); // convert it to an object

  populateHeader(superHeroes);

  showHeroes(superHeroes);

}

As you probably guessed, the stringify() method works the opposite way. Input these lines into the JavaScript console in your browser, one at a time, and see what happens:

var myJSON = { "name": "Chris", "age": "38" };

myJSON

var myString = JSON.stringify(myJSON);

myString

A JavaScript object has been created; we check to see what is in it and then use stringify to convert it into a JSON string. The return value is saved in a new variable and then we check again.

That completes our basic guide to JSON and how to use it in a program, how to create JSON and parse it, and how to gain access to the data that is locked in it. Next, we look at building a simple bouncing ball game.

The Bouncing Ball Game

It's time to put your newfound JavaScript knowledge to the test. You learned about objects and the syntax to use, so now we're going to build a game, a simple bouncing balls game to give you some practice in building custom objects in JavaScript.

Let's Get Bouncing

We're going to write a demo for a classic bouncing balls game that will demonstrate the usefulness of JavaScript objects. We will have balls bouncing all over the screen and, whenever one ball touches another, both will change color.

We are going to use an API called Canvas to draw the balls and an API called requestAnimationFrame to animate the entire display. You won't need prior knowledge of either API and, by the time you have built this game, hopefully, you will want to look into them some more. As we continue, we'll also introduce a couple of neat techniques, such as bouncing a ball off a wall and looking to see whether one hit another – that's collision detection – and we'll be using some cool objects too.

Getting Started

To start with, you will need to make a local copy of each of these files - index.html, style.css, and main.js files. These files contain:

- **Index.html** – a simple document in HTML that has one <h1> element, one <canvas> element for drawing the balls, and some elements to help apply the JavaScript and CSS to the HTML.
- **Style.css** – a few simple styles which we will use for styling and positioning the <h1> and remove any margins or scrollbars from the edges of the page, leaving it looking neat and tidy.
- **Main.js** – some JavaScript that will help us to set up our <canvas> element and give us a general function we can use.

So far, our script looks like this:

var canvas = document.querySelector('canvas');

var ctx = canvas.getContext('2d');

var width = canvas.width = window.innerWidth;

var height = canvas.height = window.innerHeight;

In this script, we have referenced the <canvas> element, and then we called the getContext() method so we have some kind of context on which to draw the balls. The variable that results from this is ctx and this is the object that provides direct representation of the canvas drawing area and gives us the ability to draw some 2D shapes.

Next, the width and height variables were set along with the height and width of the canvas element, which is represented by the properties called canvas.height and canvas.width so they equal the browser viewport height and width. This is the area the webpage will display on and we used the properties called Window.innerHight() and Window.innerWidth() for this.

You may have spotted that we have chained several assignments together; this is fine because it helps us get all the variables set much quicker.

The final part of the script so far now looks like this:

function random(min, max) {

  *var num = Math.floor(Math.random() * (max - min + 1)) + min;*

  return num;

}

The function accepts two arguments in the form of numbers and will return one random number from somewhere in between the two argument numbers.

Modeling the Ball

Our program is going to have quite a few balls bouncing on the screen. Because they all behave in pretty much the same way, the easiest way of representing them is to use an object. We'll start by including this constructor at the end of our code:

function Ball(x, y, velX, velY, color, size) {

  this.x = x;

  this.y = y;

  this.velX = velX;

  this.velY = velY;

  this.color = color;

  this.size = size;

}

We have a few parameters here used to define the properties that every ball must have in the program:

- **x and y coordinates** – these are the coordinates in horizontal and vertical terms that the balls will first be on the screen. The range of this is between 0, which is the top-left corner, to the height and width of the viewport on the browser, which is the bottom-right corner.

- **velX and velY** – this is the horizontal velocity and the vertical velocity of each ball. In real-world terms, the values will be added regularly to the x and y coordinate values when the balls are animated, stating how much each ball is to move on each frame.

- **Color** – each ball is given a specific color.

- **Size** – each ball is given a specific size, the radius of the ball in pixels.

That's the properties for the balls sorted out, now we need to look at the methods. Obviously, we want the balls to do something in this program.

Drawing the Balls

The first step is to include the draw() method below to prototype for Ball():

Ball.prototype.draw = function() {

  ctx.beginPath();

  ctx.fillStyle = this.color;

  ctx.arc(this.x, this.y, this.size, 0, 2 * Math.PI);

  ctx.fill();

}

With this function, the ball is being told to draw itself on the screen. To do this, several members of the 2D canvas context (ctx) that we defined a while ago are called. The context can be seen as a piece of paper and we tell the pen to start drawing:

- The first step is to use the beginPath() method; this states we want a shape drawn on our paper.

- Second, we define the color we want our shape by using fillStyle(). This gets set to the property of the color of the ball.

- Then the arc() method is used to draw an arc on the paper. This has four parameters:

    - X and y position for the center of the arc – these are the x and y properties for the ball.

    - The arc radius – this is the property for the size of the ball.

    - The final two are used to specify the beginning and end number of degrees that the arc is drawn around the circle. We have specified 0 degrees and also 2 * PI. This is equal to 360 degrees and you must use radians to specify this, providing one whole circle. If you had put 1 * PI you would only get half a circle of 180 degrees.

- Finally, the fill() method is used to tell the program we want the path stared with beginPath() to be finished and that the color we specified is used to fill in the area.

Now you can begin to test your object.

1. Save your code and then open the HTML file in your browser.

2. Go the JavaScript console in your browser and refresh the page; the canvas size should change to a small viewport when the console is opened.

3. Type this in so a new ball instance is created:

var testBall = new Ball(50, 100, 4, 4, 'blue', 10);

4. Call the members:

testBall.x

testBall.size

testBall.color

testBall.draw()

5. When the last line of that code is input, the ball should be drawn on the canvas.

Update the Ball Data

The ball can be drawn in the start position but we want it to move. We do that by using an update function. The following code goes at the end of the JS file to give the prototype for Ball() an update method:

Ball.prototype.update = function() {

```
if ((this.x + this.size) >= width) {

  this.velX = -(this.velX);

}


if ((this.x - this.size) <= 0) {

  this.velX = -(this.velX);

}


if ((this.y + this.size) >= height) {

  this.velY = -(this.velY);

}


if ((this.y - this.size) <= 0) {

  this.velY = -(this.velY);

}


  this.x += this.velX;

  this.y += this.velY;

}
```

The four parts at the start of the function will check to see if the ball got to the canvas edge. If yes, the polarity is reversed on the relevant velocity so the ball will go in the opposite direction. For example, if the ball is moving up, which is positive velY, the vertical or down velocity is altered so the ball moves down which is negative velY.

In each of the four parts, we:

- Check if the x coordinate is more than the canvas width, i.e. the ball is going off the page at the right edge.

- Check if the x coordinate is less than 0, i.e. the ball is going off the page at the left edge.

- Check if the y coordinate is more than the canvas height, i.e. the ball is going off the page at the bottom edge.

- Check if the y coordinate is less than 0, i.e. the ball is going off the page at the top edge.

In each of the four cases, the ball size is included in the calculation. This is because the x and y coordinates are at the ball's center but we need the edge of the ball to bounce from the perimeter of the canvas area. The last thing we want is it going off the screen before it begins bouncing back again.

The final two lines of the code are giving the x coordinate the velX value and the y coordinate the velY value, in effect, moving the ball every time the method is called.

That's enough for now; let's move on to a bit of animation.

Animating the Ball

Now we're going to have a bit of fun. We'll add some balls onto the canvas and provide some animation to them.

1. The first step is to create a place to store the balls and we do that with the array below, so add it to the end of your code:

var balls = [];

2. Any program that has animated objects typically has some kind of animation loop. This loop keeps the program information updated, rendering the view resulting from the update onto each animation frame. This is basic for almost any game or animated program. Add the code below to the end of your program:

function loop() {

ctx.fillStyle = 'rgba(0, 0, 0, 0.25)';

ctx.fillRect(0, 0, width, height);

while (balls.length < 25) {

var size = random(10,20);

var ball = new Ball(

```
  // ball position always drawn at least one ball width

  // away from the edge of the canvas, to avoid drawing errors

  random(0 + size,width - size),

  random(0 + size,height - size),

  random(-7,7),

  random(-7,7),

  'rgb(' + random(0,255) + ',' + random(0,255) + ',' + random(0,255) +')',

  size

  );

  balls.push(ball);

 }


for (var i = 0; i < balls.length; i++) {

  balls[i].draw();

  balls[i].update();

 }


  requestAnimationFrame(loop);

}
```

This loop function does this:

- The canvas fill color is set to semi-transparent black. A rectangle in that color is
  then drawn to cover the entire height and width of the canvas. This is done using
  fillRect() which has four parameters providing a starting coordinate, a height and
  a width for the rectangle. What this does is covers the drawing on the previous
  frame before the next can be drawn. If this is missed out, you won't see any balls
  on your screen, only long worms squiggling about! The fill color is set as
  rgba(0,0,0,0.25), which is semi-transparent, and lets the last few frames show
  through a little; this is what provides the trails as the balls move. If you were to

put a 1 instead of 0.25, you would no longer see them. Play around with this number and see what effect it has.

- A new instance of Ball() is created with random values that the random() function generates. The new instance is added to the end of the balls array using the push() function, but that only happens when there are fewer than 25 balls in the array. So, when 25 balls are on the screen, more won't be added. Again, play around with the number in balls.length<25 to see what happens – either more or fewer balls on your screen. One thing to be aware of is the amount of processing power your computer and/or browser has; if you specify a few thousand balls then you might find the animation slows down significantly!

- Next, all the balls contained in the array are looped through and the draw() function and update() function are run for each ball resulting in the ball being drawn on the screen. Then the position and velocity are updated ready for the next frame to appear.

- The requestAnimationFrame() method is used to run the function one more time. When you run this method constantly and the same function name is continuously passed, the function runs a specified number of times every second so a smooth animation is created. This is usually done recursively, meaning, every time the function runs it calls itself it results in it running repeatedly.

3. Finally, type this code at the end of your JS program so that can call the function; this will start the animation:

loop();

That's the basics taken care of. Save and refresh to get those balls bouncing!

Adding the Collision Detection

Now for some more fun. We're going to add a bit of collision detection into our program; each ball needs to know when it has collided with another.

1. Add this method definition to the place where you defined the Ball.prototype.update() method block:

Ball.prototype.collisionDetect = function() {

for (var j = 0; j < balls.length; j++) {

if (!(this === balls[j])) {

var dx = this.x - balls[j].x;

```
    var dy = this.y - balls[j].y;

    var distance = Math.sqrt(dx * dx + dy * dy);


    if (distance < this.size + balls[j].size) {

      balls[j].color = this.color = 'rgb(' + random(0, 255) + ',' + random(0, 255) + ',' +
random(0, 255) +')';

    }

   }

  }

 }
```

This is a somewhat more complex method so don't be alarmed if it doesn't make much sense to you at first glance. This is how it works:

- For every ball, we need to look at all of the other balls on the screen to see if one collided with another. We do this by opening a *for* loop that will loop through every ball in the balls[] array.

- Inside the *for* loop, an *if* statement is used to see if the ball that is being looped through currently is the ball that we are checking. What we don't want to do is check if a ball collided with itself! We do this by checking to see if the current ball, that's the one whose collisionDetect() method is currently being checked, is the same as the ball being looped through (the ball the current for loop iteration refers to in the collisionDetect() method). Then ! is used as a way of negating the check; that way, the *if* statement code will run only if they aren't the same.

- Next, a common algorithm is used to check the collision between two circles. What we are checking for here is whether any of the circles overlap.

- If we do detect a collision, the inner *if* statement code is run. All we are doing here is setting the color property to a random color for each of the circles. We could have made this more complex and perhaps made the balls bounce more realistically off each other but that would be a great deal more complex to implement. For now, we'll keep things simple.

2. This method also needs to be called for every frame in the animation; so add the code below to the line where it says balls[i].update();

balls[i].collisionDetect();

Save and refresh once more, and when your balls collide they should change color.

Hopefully, you had some fun writing a demo of random bouncing balls. We used a number of objects and object-oriented techniques and this should have provided you with some good practice at both the use of objects and of real-world context.

In the next section, we'll go a little further and add some more features to the demo.

Adding More Features

We're going to continue by adding some more features to the bouncing balls game as a way of testing your understanding of objects in JavaScript and of object-oriented constructs.

Before we start, make local copies (new ones) of these files:

- index-finished.html

- style.css

- main-finished.js

Project Outline

While our current demo is fun in itself, we want to make it even more so. We're going to add some interactivity with an evil circle controlled by the user. This evil ball will eat any ball it catches.

As well, we are going to put your object-building skills to the test; we'll create a generic object called Shape() from which both the evil circle and the balls can inherit. Lastly, we'll be adding a score counter to keep track of how many balls are left to be captured.

Create the New Object

The first step is to modify the Ball() constructor you already have and turn it into a Shape() constructor, and then we add another Ball() constructor:

1. Make sure your Shape() constructor defines the x, the y, the velX, and the velY properties in the exact same way that Ball() did but not the properties for size and color.

2. Make sure it also defines a brand new property named *exists*. This will track the existence of the balls in the demo- those that haven't been consumed by our evil circle. This must be a Boolean that returns True or False.

3. Make sure your Ball() constructor can inherit the properties of x, y, velX, and velY, as well as the *exists* property from Shape().

4. Color and size properties must be defined in the same way that the first Ball() constructor did.

5. Make sure the prototype for the Ball() constructor and the constructor are set correctly.

The method definitions in ball for draw(), collisionDetect(), and update() can stay as they were.

A new parameter will need to be added to the new constructor call, Ball() (...), ensuring that *exists* is the 5th parameter and it has a value of True.

Once you have done all this, reload your code. It should work like before but with the objects redesigned.

Define the Evil Circle

Now we get to meet the bad boy – our EvilCircle(). We are only going to have one of these but we will define it with a constructor that will inherit from Shape(). This is to give you a little bit of practice.

Later, you could add another circle that another player can control, or you can add several circles controlled by the computer. Obviously, one evil circle isn't going to rule the world but, for our purposes, it will do nicely.

Our EvilCircle() constructor needs to inherit several things from Shape() – x, y, exist, velY and velX. Keep in mind that both velY and velX must always equal 20 and that can be done with something like – Shape.call(this, x, y, 20, 20, exists).

The constructor also has to define the following *own* properties:

- Size – 10

- Color – 'white'

Don't forget that the inherited properties must be defined as parameters within the constructor, and the constructor and the prototype properties are set correctly.

EvilCircle() Methods

There should be four methods in EvilCircle()

draw()

This has the exact same purpose as the draw() method in Ball() – the object instance is drawn on the canvas. It also works in much the same way so the easiest way to start is to copy the definition from Ball.prototype.draw and then make these changes to it:

- We don't want our evil circle filled in; it just needs an outer line or stroke. Do this by updating fill() to stroke() and fillStyle() to strokeStyle().

- We also need that stroke to be thicker so it's easier to see the evil circle on the screen. Do this by giving lineWidth() a value of 3 somewhere after the call to beginPath().

checkBounds()

This one will do the same thing as the first bit of the update() function in Ball() – it checks whether our evil circle is going to disappear off the screen edge and, if it is, change it. Again, same as the definition for Ball.prototype.update with the following changes:

Remove the two lines at the end so the position of the evil circle will not be updated every single frame. We don't need to do this as it will be moved in a different way, as you will soon see.

In the *if* statements, if our tests return a value of true, we don't want velX/velY updated. Instead, the value of x/y needs to be changed resulting in the evil circle bouncing back on-screen a little. It would make sense here to add or subtract the size property of the evil circle as needed.

setControls()

The setControls() method adds an event listener called onkeydown to our window object. This way, when specific keys on the keyboard are pressed, the evil circle can be moved around the screen. Add the code below to the method definition:

```
var _this = this;

window.onkeydown = function(e) {

  if (e.keyCode === 65) {

    _this.x -= _this.velX;

  } else if (e.keyCode === 68) {

    _this.x += _this.velX;

  } else if (e.keyCode === 87) {

    _this.y -= _this.velY;

  } else if (e.keyCode === 83) {

    _this.y += _this.velY;

  }
```

}

With this, the keycode property for the event object is consulted when a key is pressed; it will check which key it is and if it is one of the four keys that specified keycodes represent, the circle will move up, down, left, or right.

A couple of things to think about – which keys do the specified codes map to? And why did we set var_this=this; in the position that we did? A clue – it is to do with the function scope.

collisionDetect()

This method works much the same as the collisionDetect() method in Ball() so copy that method definition and then make these changes:

- There is no longer a need to check that the ball being iterated over is the one that is checking because we no longer have a ball – we have an evil circle. So, in the outer if statement, we need to include some kind of test that looks to see if the ball being checked actually exists – think about the property you would use to do this. If it doesn't, the evil circle has already consumed it so you don't need to run the check again.

- We no longer need to make the objects change their color when they collide. Instead, in the inner if statement, you can set any ball that collides with your evil circle to no longer exist – again, think hard about how that would be done.

Bringing it All Together

Now that the evil circle has been defined, we want it to appear in the game. To do this, a few things need to be changed in the loop() function:

- First, we need a new object instance of the evil circle with the required parameters specified. Next we call the setControls() method. These need to be done just once; there's no need to repeat them on every loop iteration.

- Where the loop goes through every ball and the functions draw(), update() and collisionDetect() are called for each of them, we need to change it so the functions are only called if the current ball is in existence.

- Lastly, the draw(), checkBounds(), and collisionDetect() method for the evil circle instance should be called on each loop iteration.

The Score Counter

The last thing to do is implement our score counter so follow these steps carefully:

1. Opening your HTML file, go to the <h1> element that has the "Ball count" text and add a <p> element just below it

2. Open your CSS file and add this rule at the end of the code:

```
p {
  position: absolute;
  margin: 0;
  top: 35px;
  right: 5px;
  color: #aaa;
}
```

3. Now go to your JavaScript file and make these changes:

   o Create a new variable that will store a paragraph reference.

   o In some way, keep a count of how many balls are on the screen.

   o The count must be incremented and the updated number of balls should display each time a new ball is added.

   o The count should be decremented and the updated number of balls displayed whenever the evil circle consumes a ball so it no longer exists.

Be sure to work through this slowly and one step at a time. Make a copy of the demo each time you get a stage working. Should you run into trouble later, you can refer back to it.

To finish our look at JavaScript, we'll take a brief look at Client-side APIs.

Client-side Web APIs

When you start to write client-side JavaScript for applications or websites, one of the first things you will come across are APIs or Application Programming Interfaces. These are features allowing you to manipulate different parts of the operating system and the browser that the website or application will run on or manipulate the data from other services and websites. We're going to have a brief look at what an API is and how you can make use of some frequent ones that will come across on your development journey.

We've spent some considerable time looking at JavaScript objects as they are modules tending to involve API usage on a fairly simple level because its client-side examples of JavaScript are tough to write without them.

Introduction to the Web API

We'll start by taking a high-look at the API, discovering what they are, how they work, how they are used in your code and their structure. We'll have a look at the main API classes and what their uses are.

What is an API?

An Application Programming Interface is a construct available in computer programming languages that allows the program/application developer to better create functionality with more complexity. An API will abstract a lot of intricate code away and provide you with much easier syntax to use instead.

To put this in real-world terms, focus your thoughts on the electricity that supplies wherever you live or work. When you want to use something, like a kettle, an iron, a computer, etc., you plug the appliance into a socket. You don't need to write the appliance straight into the mains power supply – that would be an incredibly inefficient way of doing things and, if you are not a registered electrician, it would also be difficult, not to mention hazardous.

In much the same way, let's say you want to program a few graphics in 3D. Using an API written in one of the higher-level languages, such as Python or JavaScript will make this much easier to do than attempting to write low-level code, such as C++ directly to control the GPU and other graphical functions in your computer.

The official glossary entry describes the API as a set of rules and features that exist in an application (software program). These rules and features make it possible for the software to be interacted with using software and not a human user interface. An API could be viewed as being a contract between the application that offers it and third-party software, hardware, or other items.

In terms of web development, APIs are sets of code features, such as properties, methods, URLs, and events used by a developer so tier application interacts with specified parts of the user web browser or the other hardware or software on the system, or even third-party services and websites.

An example of some of the APIs:

- **getUserMedia** – This API is used for grabbing video and audio from a webcam on the user system. This can then be used however the developer wants to use it, i.e. recording audio and video, broadcasting it via a conference call, capturing image stills from the webcam, and so on.
- **Geolocation** – This API is used for the retrieval of location information from the services available on the user's device, for example, GPS. This information could then be used with the Google Maps APIs to plot locations on maps, show routes and show tourist attractions, for example.
- **Twitter** – These APIs are used to get data from a Twitter account, for example, the latest tweets by a user which then is displayed on a page.
- **Web Animations** – These are used to animate sections of web pages, for example, to make images move or rotate.

Using APIs in Client-Side JavaScript

Client-side APIs are everywhere and JavaScript has a large number built-in. These APIs are not actually a part of the language; instead, they build on the core of the language and provide you with much more powerful features to use when you write your applications. Generally, these APIs come under two categories:

Browser APIs

These are built-in to the web browser and can be used for the exposure of browser data and data from the environment surrounding the computer providing the ability to do complex and useful things. For example, the Web Audio API contains constructs that allow audio to be manipulated in a browser, for example, taking audio tracks, changing their volume, applying new and different effects to them, etc. What the browser is doing in the background is using lower-level code, quite complex, such as Rust or C++, to process the audio. You don't see that because the API has abstracted the complexity away.

Third-Party APIs

These are not in the web browser as default APIs; generally, you need to get the code and the related information from somewhere else on the internet. For example, take the Twitter API. You can do lots of things with this, such as displaying your tweets on your blog or social media page. This third-party API gives a special group of constructs that are used for querying Twitter and returning specified information.

The Relationship between JavaScript, JavaScript Tools, and APIs

We explained what a JavaScript client-side API is and how it relates to the programming language. To make it clearer, we'll do a quick recap so you can also see where other tools in JavaScript might fit in:

- **JavaScript** – This is high-level language (scripting) that is built into a web browser. JavaScript allows you to add different feature and functionality to a web application or web page. JavaScript is also made available in other environments, like Node.

- **Browser APIs** – These are constructs that are already built-in to the browser on top of the language allowing for much easier implementation of functionality.

- **Third-Party APIs** – These are constructs that are built-in to third-party service and platforms, like Twitter, Facebook, and others. These give you the tools to use functionality from those platforms in your own web page or application, for example, showing your Tweets or Facebook posts on your own website.

- **JavaScript Libraries** – These are JavaScript files that have custom functions in them. These functions can be attached to your application or web page to help you write common functionality or speed up existing functionality. Examples of libraries include jQuery, React, and Mootools.

- **JavaScript Frameworks** – These are next up the ladder from the libraries. Examples include Ember and Angular and they are packages containing CSS, HTML, JavaScript, and some other technologies you need to install and use for writing a web application from the ground up. The biggest difference between the framework and the library is something called "Inversion of Control". When a method is called from a library, the developer controls the process by things inverted with a framework – the developer's code is called by the framework.

What Can An API Do?

Modern browsers contain vast numbers of APIs, allowing you to do so much with your code. The commonest browser categories are:

- **Document Manipulation APIs** – These will manipulate any document loaded into the browser. The obvious one is the DOM API (Document Object Model) allowing manipulation of CSS and HTML, for example, creating HTML, removing it and changing it, applying new styles dynamically to a web page, and so on. Whenever a popup window shows up on a web page or you see new content, for example, that is the DOM API at work.

- **APIS for Fetching Data from Servers** – These update small bits of a webpage by themselves and are very common APIs. One tiny detail can make all the difference to the way a website performs; for example, if you wanted a stock listing updated, or a list of books, it is much better to have it done instantly without reloading the whole page or website from the server – it makes your website look snappier and more responsive to the user. Some of the APIs in this category include Fetch and XMLHttpRequest. You might also see Ajax as a term describing this kind of technique and we'll be looking at that later in the guide.

- **APIs used to Manipulate Graphics and Draw Graphics** – These have now been given a lot of support in browsers with the most common APIs being WebGL and Canvas, both of which let you update pixel data inside a <canvas> element (HTML) to create both 2d and 3D scenes. As an example, you might draw circles, rectangles, or other shapes, import images to the canvas, apply filters to them, such as greyscale or sepia with the Canvas API and, with the WebGL API, you could create a highly complex scene in 3D including textures, lighting, and so on. These type of APIS tend to be used in combination with others that help create animation loops, like window.requestAnimationFrame() and those that help to make continuous updates to scenes like games and cartoons.

- **Video and Audio APIs** – These include the Web Audio API, HTMLMediaElement, and WebRTC and allow you to do some cool things with multimedia. You can create customized user-interface controls to play audio and video, you can display text with your videos showing the name of the tracks, subtitles, captions and so on. You can grab video from a web camera and use another API to manipulate it using a canvas to display it in a conference call on another computer. You can even give audio tracks certain effects, like distortion, panning, gain, etc.

- **Device APIs** – These are APIs used for the manipulation or and retrieval of data from hardware in a way so it can be used in a web app in a handy way. An example of this would be informing users by way of a system notification that there is an update available using the Notification APIs or, as in the case of mobile devices, using a Vibration API.

- **APIs for Client-Side Storage** – These are becoming more common in browsers. Being able to store data client-side is incredibly useful when you want an app that saves its own state between each page-load and even works when the device is not online. There are a few options to choose from, such as using the Web Storage API to save name and value data, and the IndexedDB API for data storage that is more complex, like tabular data.

Third-Party APIs

There is a large range of third-party APIs, some more popular than others and these are the ones you are likely to use at some point:

- **Twitter API** - allows you to display Tweets on your webpage.

- **Map APIs** – such as Google Maps API and MapQuest that let you do all manner of things on your website with maps.

- **Facebook API Suite** – These let you use part of Facebook in a way that benefits your applications, such as allowing people to log into your app using Facebook, taking payments in-app, targeted ad campaigns, and so on.

- **YouTube API** – This lets you embed videos from YouTube into your website, build up YouTube playlists, search YouTube, and so on.

- **Twilio API** – This gives you a framework to build the functionality for video and voice calls into your application, send MMS and SMS from the app, and much more.

All the different APIs in JavaScript work in different ways but, in general, they share common themes and features in how they work.

- **Object-Based**

Any code you write using APIs will use at least one JavaScript object to interact with those APIs. The objects can be seen as containers that hold the data the API is using (object properties) and hold the functionality made available by the API (object methods).

To better describe this, we'll look at the Web Audio API again. This is quite complex as APIs go, and it has quite a few objects in it. The obvious objects are:

- **AudioContext** – This represents an audio graph for the manipulation of audio playing in the browser. There are several methods and properties to use for audio manipulation.

- **MediaElementAudioSourceNode** – This represents an <audio> element with the sounds that want to be played and you want to manipulate into the audio context.

- **AudioDestinationNode** – This represents the audio destination, for example, the device that is going to output the audio, usually headphones or speakers connected to the computer.

What is the interaction between all these objects? Look at the following HTML code:

<audio src="outfoxing.mp3"></audio>

<button class="paused">Play</button>

*
*

<input type="range" min="0" max="1" step="0.01" value="1" class="volume">

First of all, an <audio> element has been included. Using this, an MP3 is embedded to the webpage; we have not added in any default controls for the browser. Next, we added a <button> to use to start and stop the audio, along with an >=<input> element. This is a type range and we use this to adjust the track volume while it plays.

The following is the JavaScript code example:

The first thing we do is create an AudioContext instance and it is from inside this our track will be manipulated:

const AudioContext = window.AudioContext || window.webkitAudioContext;

const audioCtx = new AudioContext();

Next, constants used to store references to the <button>, <audio>, and <input> element are created and the AudioContext.createMediaElementSource() method is used to create the MediaElementAudioSourceNode; this represents the audio source – the <audio> element from which the track is played:

const audioElement = document.querySelector('audio');

const playBtn = document.querySelector('button');

const volumeSlider = document.querySelector('.volume');

```
const audioSource = audioCtx.createMediaElementSource(audioElement);
```

Next, two event handlers are included that will toggle from play to pause and back whenever the relevant button is pressed, and to reset the display all the way back to the start when the audio track finishes:

```
// play/pause audio

playBtn.addEventListener('click', function() {

    // check if context is in suspended state (autoplay policy)

    if (audioCtx.state === 'suspended') {

        audioCtx.resume();

    }


    // if the track is stopped, play it

    if (this.getAttribute('class') === 'paused') {

        audioElement.play();

        this.setAttribute('class', 'playing');

        this.textContent = 'Pause'

    // if track is playing, stop it

    } else if (this.getAttribute('class') === 'playing') {

        audioElement.pause();

        this.setAttribute('class', 'paused');

        this.textContent = 'Play';

    }

});


// if track ends

audioElement.addEventListener('ended', function() {
```

playBtn.setAttribute('class', 'paused');

this.textContent = 'Play'

});

Note

You might have spotted the play() method and the pause() method that we use to play and pause the track are nothing to do with the Web Audio API; instead they are part of HTMLMediaElement, which, although related, is dissimilar.

Next, the GainNode object is created using the method called AudioContext.createGain(). This is to adjust the volume of any audio going through it. We also create a further event handler to change the audio graph gain, or volume value when the slider value is changed:

const gainNode = audioCtx.createGain();

volumeSlider.addEventListener('input', function() {

gainNode.gain.value = this.value;

});

The last thing that needs to be done to get this working is to get all the different nodes from the audio graph connected. To do this, we use the AudioNode.connect() method available on all node types:

audioSource.connect(gainNode).connect(audioCtx.destination);

The audio will begin in the source. Then it is connected to the gain node allowing for the volume to be adjusted as needed. That gain node at that point is connected to the destination node allowing the sound to be played on the device (your computer) – the property called AudioContext.destination is representative of whatever default AudioDestinationNode is available on your hardware, i.e. your computer speakers.

- **Recognizable Entry Points**

When you use an API, be certain that you know exactly where the entry point is. For example, the Web Audio API for this entry point is quite simple – the AudioContext object – and it has to be used whenever you do any kind of audio manipulation.

Another one is the DOM API, or the Document Object Model. This also is a simple entry point; you can usually find the features with the Document object or with an HTML element instance you want to change in some way. FO=or example:

var em = document.createElement('em'); // create a new em element

var para = document.querySelector('p'); // reference an existing p element

em.textContent = 'Hello there!'; // give em some text content

para.appendChild(em); // embed em inside para

The Canvas API can only manipulate things using a context object although, this time, it is not an audio context but a graphical context. To create the context object, a reference needs to obtained so the <canvas> element to be drawn on and then the HTMLCanvasElement.getContext() method should be called:

var canvas = document.querySelector('canvas');

var ctx = canvas.getContext('2d');

At that juncture, whatever you plan on doing to that canvas must be done by calling the content object properties and related methods. The content object is a CanvasRenderingContext2D instance.

For example:

Ball.prototype.draw = function() {

ctx.beginPath();

ctx.fillStyle = this.color;

*ctx.arc(this.x, this.y, this.size, 0, 2 * Math.PI);*

ctx.fill();

};

You may recognize this piece of code – we used it in the bouncing ball game we created earlier.

- **Events are Used for Handling Changes in State**

An event is an occurrence or an action that occurs in the system you are programming. The system will tell you about the event or occurrence to respond in the correct way if necessary. For example, if a user clicks on a button on your webpage, you may want to respond by, for example, showing a box with some information in it.

Not all Web APIs have events in them but most have at least one. Event handlers and their properties are what allow the functions to run when the events fire.

We used event handlers when we drew up our Web Audio API example earlier and, to give you a further example, some XMLHttpRequest object instances (each of which represents one HTTP request sent to a server to get a resource of some type) also have several available events. For example, a load event is fired when a successful response is returned with the resource that was requested, making it available.

This simple example shows how to use this:

```
var requestURL = 'https://mdn.github.io/learning-area/javascript/oojs/json/superheroes.json';

var request = new XMLHttpRequest();

request.open('GET', requestURL);

request.responseType = 'json';

request.send();


request.onload = function() {

  var superHeroes = request.response;

  populateHeader(superHeroes);

  showHeroes(superHeroes);

}
```

The first five lines of this code specify where the resource we want to be retrieved is, using the XMLHttpRequest() constructor to create a brand-new instance of the request object, opening an HTTP Get request so the indicated resource can be retrieved, specifying that JSON format should be used for the response and then sending the request.

Next, the onload handler function states exactly what will happen with the response. We know it will be returned successfully and available once the load event has finished unless some error happens, so the response is saved. That response should contain the

JSON from the variable called superHeroes. We then pass it for more processing to two separate functions.

- **Extra Security Mechanisms Where Needed**

The features in Web APIs are subject to all the same security as JavaScript and other technologies related to the web, for example, Same-Origin policy. However, they may also have extra security methods where they are needed. For example, some modern Web APIS won't work on a page that is not served over HTTPS because they may contain sensitive data.

As well as that, there are Web APIs that need to ask for permission from the user to be enabled when calls are made in your code. For example, the Notifications API will show a popup dialog box asking for user permission.

Both the HTMLMediaElement and Web Audio APIs are subject to the autoplay policy security mechanism. This means audio can't be played automatically when a web page loads; your users must initiate it using a control of some kind, like a button. This is because having audio autoplay can be quite irritating and users should never be subjected to it.

Note

Some of these security mechanisms can even stop an example from locally running, although that depends on the level of strictness of your browser, for example, if a local example file is loaded in the browser rather than having it run from a web server.

That concludes our brief look at client-side web APIs. You should now have a good idea of what they are, how they work, and how to make use of them in your code.

In the next part of this guide, we will be taking an in-depth look at jQuery.

Part 2: Getting to Grips with jQuery

What is jQuery?

jQuery is a JavaScript library, fast, full of features and lightweight. It is based on the "write less, do more" principle" and contains APIs that are uncomplicated to use and make some things much easier to do, such as traversal and manipulation of HTML documents, adding animation effects, and event handling. In addition, it works seamlessly over all the major web browsers.

jQuery also lets you create applications based on Ajax quickly and effortlessly. Some of the biggest companies in the world, like Microsoft, Google, and IBM, use jQuery to build their applications so you can understand how popular it is.

jQuery was created early in 2006 by John Resig and is currently run as an open-source project by a distributed and dedicated developer group.

What can jQuery be used for?

jQuery can be used for many things including:

- Selecting elements for manipulation purposes
- Creating effects, such as showing or hiding elements, transition sliding, and more
- Using less code to create complex animations using CSS
- Easy manipulation of DOM elements, along with their attributes
- Easy implementation of Ajax for the asynchronous exchange of data between client and server
- Easy traversal of a DOM tree to find specified elements
- Multiple actions can be performed on any element using just one line of code
- Set or get HTML element dimensions

This is just the tip of the iceberg; we'll be going over what jQuery can do throughout this section and how you can use it to your benefit.

Talking of advantages...

Advantages of using jQuery

If you are not au fait with jQuery, you might wonder why it is so special. Well, that's all down to the pluses you get when you use jQuery:

- **It saves time** – a lot of it, not to mention energy when you use the efforts and selectors built into jQuery, leaving you free to concentrate on the rest of your work.

- **It simplifies common tasks in JavaScript** – uses fewer lines of code to create web pages that are full of features and interactive. One easy example is using jQuery to implement Ajax so your web pages can be updated without refreshing the entire page.
- **It's simple to use** – If you have a working knowledge of the basics of CSS, HTML, and JavaScript, you won't grapple using jQuery.
- **It is compatible with all major browsers** – jQuery was created and kept updated with all major browsers in mind. It can easily be used with Chrome, Safari, Edge, Internet Explorer, and Mozilla, among others.
- **It's free** – there is and never will be any charge to download and use jQuery.

Note

When you use JavaScript to select elements in HTML documents, it often requires several lines of code; with jQuery, you simply make use of the selector mechanism to traverse DOM trees and get your elements for manipulation straightforward and swiftly.

What This Section Covers

We'll be covering all the main jQuery features, such as event handling, the selector mechanism, effect methods used to add interactivity to a webpage, showing/hiding elements, element animation, and much more.

We'll also look later at how multiple methods can be chained together, how DOM manipulation tasks are done, such as getting or setting HTML element content and values, adding and removing elements and/or attributes, getting and setting element CSS properties, getting or setting element height and width, and much more.

Lastly, we will look at an incredibly powerful jQuery feature – traversal of a DOM tree. This will allow you to get the sibling, parent and child elements, along with a selection of the filters for elements, implementation of Ajax for information retrieval form servers, how to update the content of a page without having to refresh, and how to stop conflict arising between jQuery ad other libraries in JavaScript.

We will be introducing many real-word examples for you to try. These are designed to help you understand jQuery better, along with some good workarounds, notes, and tips to make life easier for you.

Getting Started

We'll kick right off with a web page powered by jQuery but, before we can do that, we need to download jQuery.

Go to https://jquery.com/download/ and download jQuery onto your computer. You will see a choice of two versions – compressed or uncompressed. Choose the uncompressed version for development and debugging; the compressed version is best for production because it uses less bandwidth and provides better performance.

The file has a .js extension; this is because jQuery is a JavaScript library. This means it can easily be included in an HTML document the same way as any other JavaScript file would be included – with the <script> element.

If you want to play along, input the following code into an online editor:

```
<!DOCTYPE html>

<html>

<head>

    <meta charset="utf-8">

    <title>Simple HTML Document</title>

    <link rel="stylesheet" type="text/css" href="css/style.css">

    <script src="js/jquery-1.11.3.min.js"></script>

</head>

<body>

    <h1>Hello, World!</h1>

</body>

</html>
```

Always ensure that the jQuery file is added BEFORE you add your custom scripts. If you don't, your code cannot access the jQuery APIs.

Tip

You probably spotted that we skipped the type= "text/javascript" attribute in the <script> tag and this is because HTML 5 does not require it. The default language of HTML5 and most browsers is JavaScript but you can still use the attribute to make your code easier to read and understand.

jQuery from CDN

jQuery can also be included via Content Delivery Network links if you would rather not download jQuery yourself. These offer certain benefits in terms of performance because hosting is spread over several global servers and it comes from the nearest one to the requester.

Let's create a jQuery Web Page

So far, we have looked at what purpose jQuery has and how to add it into a document. Now we can put it to some real use.

What we are going to do here is perform a simple operation in jQuery – change the color of the header text from black, which is the default color, to red:

```
<!DOCTYPE html>

<html>

<head>

  <meta charset="utf-8">

  <title>My First jQuery Web Page</title>

  <link rel="stylesheet" type="text/css" href="css/style.css">

  <script src="js/jquery-1.11.3.min.js"></script>

  <script type="text/javascript">

    $(document).ready(function(){

      $("h1").css("color", "#0088ff");

    });

  </script>

</head>
```

```
<body>

  <h1>Hello, World!</h1>

</body>

</html>
```

All we did was changed the heading color, which is the <h1> element, by using the css() method and the element selector in jQuery and we do this when the document is ready using an event known as the document-ready event. We'll cover more detail about events, selectors, and methods later.

jQuery Syntax

It's time to learn how to use jQuery to write code.

Standard Syntax:

jQuery statements usually begin with a $ (dollar sign), and they end with ; (a semicolon).

The following code is a demo of basic jQuery use:

```
<script type="text/javascript">

  $(document).ready(function(){

    // the code to be executed...

    alert("Hello World!");

  });

</script>
```

All this does is displays a message to a user saying, "Hello World!"

Explanation

Let's break this code down and see exactly what it did:

- **<script> element** – Because jQuery is nothing more than a JavaScript library, we can place the jQuery code inside our <script> element. You can add it into an external JS file if you want, which is the most preferred method, and in this case, you would simply remove this section.

- **$(document).ready(handler)** – This is the ready event statement. The handler is nothing more than a function passed to the method called ready(), where it will be safely executed once the document is ready for manipulation, for example, once full construction of the DOM hierarchy has been completed.

The ready() method in jQuery is generally used with anonymous functions so, you could also write the code above like this:

```
<script type="text/javascript">

  $(function(){

    // the code to be executed...

    alert("Hello World!");

  });

</script>
```

It doesn't matter which one of these you use as both are relevant. However, the ready event code is easier to read.

You can also add jQuery statements into an event handler function to carry out basic actions, for example, $(selector).action();

In this, $(selector) chooses the HTML elements in the DOM tree for manipulation and action() is applying a specified action on those elements. That could be something like changing the values for CSS properties, setting the contents of the element, and so on.

Here's another example; this one is setting paragraph text once the DOM is ready:

```
<!DOCTYPE html>

<html>

<head>

  <meta charset="utf-8">

  <title>jQuery Document Ready Demo</title>

  <link rel="stylesheet" type="text/css" href="css/style.css">

  <script src="js/jquery-1.11.3.min.js"></script>

  <script type="text/javascript">

    $(document).ready(function(){

      $("p").text("Hello World!");
```

```
        });

    </script>

</head>

<body>

    <p>Not loaded yet.</p>

</body>

</html>
```

In this example, in the jQuery statement of $("p").text("Hello World!");, the p is the selector. This selects all the <p> elements, which are the paragraphs, in the document. The text() method is used to set the text content of the paragraph to "Hello World!"

When the document is ready, the paragraph text is automatically replaced; but what would happen if we wanted a user to do a specific action before the jQuery code was executed to replace the text?

Look at this example:

```
<!DOCTYPE html>

<html>

<head>

    <meta charset="utf-8">

    <title>jQuery Click Handler Demo</title>

    <link rel="stylesheet" type="text/css" href="css/style.css">

    <script src="js/jquery-1.11.3.min.js"></script>

    <script type="text/javascript">

        $(document).ready(function(){

            $("button").click(function(){

                $("p").text("Hello World!");

            });

        });
```

```
    </script>

</head>

<body>

  <p>Not loaded yet.</p>

  <button type="button">Replace Text</button>

</body>

</html>
```

What we have in this instance is the paragraph text being replaced ONLY when a click event happens on the button for "Replace Text", i.e. when the user clicks the button.

That concludes a look at the basics of jQuery; now we'll go a bit more in-depth.

Note

Make sure your jQuery code is inside the document ready event otherwise the code will not execute when the document is ready to be worked on.

jQuery Selectors

In this section, we will look at using jQuery to select HTML elements.

The most common use of JavaScript is to get or modify content or values of HTML elements on a page, followed by applying effects, such as show/hide, animation, etc. Before you can do any of this, you need to find your target HTML element and select it.

You could use a typical JavaScript approach, but it will be incredibly agonizing! This is where jQuery makes things wonderfully simple. One of the most powerful of all jQuery features is that it makes it easy to select DOM elements quickly.

Tip

jQuery offers support for almost every selector the CSS3 specifications define and it also includes its own selectors. The custom selectors provide the ability to enhance the selection of the HTML elements.

In the next couple of sections, we will look at the more common methods to select elements and what you can do with them using jQuery.

Selection using ID

The ID selector can be used to make single element selections using the unique ID. Case in point, the next command will select an element and highlight it, provided it has the id="mark" attribute, once the document is ready for manipulation:

```
<script type="text/javascript">

$(document).ready(function(){

    // Highlight element with id mark

    $("#mark").css("background", "yellow");

});

</script>
```

In this example, the $(document).ready() event is used for the safe manipulation of pages using jQuery. Any code inside this event will run ONLY when the page DOM is properly ready – more about events later.

Selection by Class Name

If we want to select an element with a specified class, we would use the class selector. For example, the next piece of code will select and highlight the elements that have the class="mark" attribute once the document is ready:

```
<script type="text/javascript">

$(document).ready(function(){

    // Highlight elements with class mark

    $(".mark").css("background", "yellow");

});

</script>
```

Selection by Name

If you want to select an element based on its name, we would use the element selector. The next code will select and then highlight any paragraph or <p> element when the document is ready:

```
<script type="text/javascript">

$(document).ready(function(){

    // Highlight paragraph elements

    $("p").css("background", "yellow");

});

</script>
```

Selection by Attribute

The attribute selector is used to select elements based on their HTML attributes, for example, the target attribute of a link or the type attribute of an input. In the next code, we select and then highlight all text input or <input> elements that have the type="test" attribute, when the document is ready:

```
<script type="text/javascript">

$(document).ready(function(){

    // Highlight paragraph elements
```

```javascript
    $('input[type="text"]').css("background", "yellow");
});
```

```
</script>
```

Selection by Compound CSS Selector

The CSS selectors can also be combined to make things even more precise. For example, the class selector can be united with one of the element selectors to find all document elements that have specified types and classes.

```html
<script type="text/javascript">
```

```javascript
$(document).ready(function(){

    // Highlight paragraph elements with class mark

    $("p.mark").css("background", "yellow");


    // Highlight span elements inside the element with ID mark

    $("#mark span").css("background", "yellow");


    // Highlight li elements inside the ul elements

    $("ul li").css("background", "red");


    // Highlight li elements inside the ul element with id mark

    $("ul#mark li").css("background", "yellow");


    // Highlight li elements inside all the ul elements with class mark

    $("ul.mark li").css("background", "green");


    // Highlight all anchor elements with target blank

    $('a[target="_blank"]').css("background", "yellow");
```

```
});

</script>
```

Custom Selector

As well as the selectors defined by CSS, there are also custom selectors in jQuery to make element selection even better.

For example:

```
<script type="text/javascript">

$(document).ready(function(){

    // Highlight table rows appearing in odd places

    $("tr:odd").css("background", "yellow");


    // Highlight table rows appearing in even places

    $("tr:even").css("background", "orange");


    // Highlight first paragraph element

    $("p:first").css("background", "red");

});

</script>
```

jQuery Events

In this section, we will take a look at jQuery events. An event tends to be triggered when a user interacts with a web page; perhaps they click on a link or click a mouse button, type text into a box, make a selection in a box, press a key on their keyboard, or move their mouse pointer, for example. Sometimes, the browser will trigger the events, like refreshing or reloading the page.

Basic event-handling is enhanced when you use jQuery because you get to use events methods such as:

- ready()

- click()

- keypress()

- focus()

- change()

- blur()

For example, if you wanted to execute JS code when the DOM is ready, you could use the ready() method from jQuery, like the example below:

<script type="text/javascript">

$(document).ready(function(){

// Code to be executed

alert("Hello World!");

});

</script>

Note

$(document).ready() event is used for safe manipulation of a page using jQuery. Any code that is included in the event will run ONLY when the page DOM is ready, for example, ready for manipulation.

Generally, we can place events into four groups:

1. mouse events

2. keyboard evets

3. form events

4. document or window events

In the next section, we'll look at each group in a bit more detail, as well as providing some of the related jQuery methods.

Mouse Events

Mouse events are fired when users click on a page element or move their mouse pointer, for example. Some of the jQuery methods commonly used to handle these events include:

Click()

This method attaches event handler functions to the chosen elements for any click event. The function is only executed when a user clicks on the specified element. For example, in this code, the <p> elements on the page are hidden when clicked on:

```
<script type="text/javascript">

$(document).ready(function(){

    $("p").click(function(){

        $(this).slideUp();

    });

});

</script>
```

Note

The *this* keyword has been used in the jQuery function (event handler) and is used to reference the element for the event.

dblclick()

This method attached event handler functions to given elements for any dblclick event. The function will only be executed when a user has double-clicked the given element. In the next example, when the <p> elements are double clicked, they are hidden:

```
<script type="text/javascript">

$(document).ready(function(){

    $("p").dblclick(function(){

        $(this).slideUp();

    });

});

</script>
```

hover()

This method attaches at least one, usually two event handler functions to the given elements. The functions will be executed only when the mouse pointer has entered and left the specified elements. The first function will be executed when the user's mouse pointer is placed over an element while the second one is executed when the mouse pointer is moved away from the element.

In the next example, the <p> elements are highlighted when the mouse pointer is placed on them and the highlighting disappears when the mouse cursor is moved.

```
<script type="text/javascript">

$(document).ready(function(){

    $("p").hover(function(){

        $(this).addClass("highlight");

    },function(){

        $(this).removeClass("highlight");

    });

});

</script>
```

Tip

The hover() method could be considered a combination of two other jQuery methods – mouseenter() and mouseleave()

mouseenter()

This method attached an event handler to a given element. This function is executed only when the mouse enters the element, for example, the mouse cursor is placed over it. This example shows the <p> element highlighted when the cursor is placed on it:

```
<script type="text/javascript">

$(document).ready(function(){

   $("p").mouseenter(function(){

      $(this).addClass("highlight");

   });

});

</script>
```

mouseleave()

This method attaches an event handler to a given element; the element will be executed when the mouse cursor is moved away from the element. In this example, the <p> element will no longer be highlighted when the mouse cursor is moved away:

```
<script type="text/javascript">

$(document).ready(function(){

   $("p").mouseleave(function(){

      $(this).removeClass("highlight");

   });

});

</script>
```

Keyboard Events

Keyboard events are powered when users press a key on the keyboard or when they release the key. Some of the jQuery methods commonly used for handling keyboard events are:

keypress()

The keypress() method will attach event handler functions to specified elements, which tend to form controls. These functions are executed only when keyboard input is received by the browser from a user. In the next example, when a keypress event is fired, a message is displayed, telling you how many times the event fired when a specified key is pressed on the keyboard:

```
<script type="text/javascript">

$(document).ready(function(){

    var i = 0;

    $('input[type="text"]').keypress(function(){

        $("span").text(i += 1);

        $("p").show().fadeOut();

    });

});

</script>
```

Note

The keypress() event is much like the keydown() event with one exception – the modified keys and non-printing keys – Esc, SHIFT, Del, Backspace, the arrow keys, etc. – will not trigger a keypress) event, only a keydown() event.

keydown()

The keydown() method will attach event handler functions to specified elements, which are usually form controls. These are executed only after the first press of a key on the keyboard. In the next example, a message is displayed when the event is fired telling you how many times it was fired when a key is pressed on the keyboard.

```
<script type="text/javascript">

$(document).ready(function(){

    var i = 0;

    $('input[type="text"]').keydown(function(){

        $("span").text(i += 1);
```

```
$("p").show().fadeOut();

    });

});

</script>
```

keyup()

This method will attach event handler functions to specified elements, usually a form control. It will only be executed when a user releases the key they are pressing on the keyboard. In the next example, when the key is released on the keyboard, the event is fired and a message is displayed to confirm it, and how many times it was fired.

```
<script type="text/javascript">

$(document).ready(function(){

    var i = 0;

    $('input[type="text"]').keyup(function(){

        $("span").text(i += 1);

        $("p").show().fadeOut();

    });

});

</script>
```

Tip

You can attach keyboard events to any element but they will only be set to an element that has the focus. This is why keyboard events are usually attached to form controls, like textarea or text input box.

Form Events

Form events are fired when form controls receive focus or lose it, or when a form control value is modified by a user, perhaps when they type some text into a text input, choose one of the options in a select box, and so on. Some of the more commonly used jQuery methods with form events are:

change()

The change() method will attach event handler functions to one of three elements - <textarea>, <input>, and <select>. These will be executed only when the value of the element changes. As you can see in the next example, an alert message is displayed when any of the options in the dropdown select menu are chosen:

```
<script type="text/javascript">

$(document).ready(function(){

   $("select").change(function(){

      var selectedOption = $(this).find(":selected").val();

      alert("You have selected - " + selectedOption);

   });

});

</script>
```

Notes

For check boxes, select boxes and rainbow buttons, events are fired the second the user has made their selection using the mouse. For textarea and text input, the event is only fired once the element has lost focus.

focus()

The focus() method attaches event handler functions to specified elements, which are usually a link or a form control. The function executes only when focus is gained. In the next example, a message is displayed as soon as focus us received by the text input:

```
<script type="text/javascript">

$(document).ready(function(){

   $("input").focus(function(){

      $(this).next("span").show().fadeOut("slow");

   });

});

</script>
```

blur()

The blur() method is used to attach event handler functions to form elements, like <select>, <textarea>, and <input>. Execution only happens when focus is lost. In the next example, a message is displayed when focus is lost from the <text input:

```
<script type="text/javascript">
$(document).ready(function(){
  $("input").blur(function(){
    $(this).next("span").show().fadeOut("slow");
  });
});
</script>
```

submit()

The submit() method is used to attach event handler functions to form elements. These are executed only when a user tries to submit a form. In the next example, a message is displayed dependent on the value entered when the form is submitted:

```
<script type="text/javascript">
$(document).ready(function(){
  $("form").submit(function(event){
    var regex = /^[a-zA-Z]+$/;
    var currentValue = $("#firstName").val();
    if(regex.test(currentValue) == false){
      $("#result").html('<p class="error">Not valid!</p>').show().fadeOut(1000);
      // Preventing form submission
      event.preventDefault();
    }
  });
});
```

```
</script>
```

Tip

Forms may be submitted in two ways – either a submit button is clicked or the Enter key is pressed when focus is on certain form elements.

Document and Window Events

Events may also be triggered in situations where the Page document object model, or DOM is ready, or when the browser is scrolled or resized by a user, for example. Some of the more commonly used methods with these events are:

ready()

The ready() method is used to specify the function that should execute on full loading of the DOM. In this example, the text will be replaced when the DOM hierarchy has been constructed and is ready for manipulation:

```
<script type="text/javascript">

$(document).ready(function(){

    $("p").text("The DOM is now loaded and can be manipulated.");

});

</script>
```

resize()

The resize() method is used to attach event handler functions to window elements. These will only be executed when a change is made to the size of the browser window. In the next example, the width and height of a browser window is displayed when an attempt is made to drag the corners to resize it:

```
<script type="text/javascript">

$(document).ready(function(){

  $(window).resize(function() {

    $(window).bind("resize", function(){

      $("p").text("Window width: " + $(window).width() + ", " + "Window height: " +
$(window).height());

    });
```

```
    });

});

</script>
```

scroll()

The scroll() method is used to attach event handler functions to a window, or to an element or iframe that can be scrolled. This will be executed when the scroll position of the element changes. In the next example, a message is displayed when the browser window is scrolled:

```
<script type="text/javascript">

$(document).ready(function(){

    $(window).scroll(function() {

        $("p").show().fadeOut("slow");

    });

});

</script>
```

jQuery Show and Hide

We'll now take a brief look at how to use jQuery to show and hide HTML elements. We use two methods for this – show() and hide(). With the hide() method, all you do is set the inline style display: none for the specified elements. By contrast, show() will restore those display properties for matched element sets to what they were to start with, usually inline, block, or inline-block, before display: none was applied. Look at this example:

```
<script type="text/javascript">

$(document).ready(function(){

    // Hide displayed paragraphs

    $(".hide-btn").click(function(){

        $("p").hide();

    });
```

```
    // Show hidden paragraphs

    $(".show-btn").click(function(){

        $("p").show();

    });

});

</script>
```

Optionally, you may specify the duration or speed parameter so the show hide effect is animated over a given time period. You can specify the durations using predefined strings of 'slow' or fast'; you can also choose to use milliseconds for much better precision. The higher the value, the slower the animation will be:

```
<script type="text/javascript">

$(document).ready(function(){

    // Hide displayed paragraphs with different speeds

    $(".hide-btn").click(function(){

        $("p.normal").hide();

        $("p.fast").hide("fast");

        $("p.slow").hide("slow");

        $("p.very-fast").hide(50);

        $("p.very-slow").hide(2000);

    });


    // Show hidden paragraphs with different speeds

    $(".show-btn").click(function(){

        $("p.normal").show();

        $("p.fast").show("fast");
```

```javascript
        $("p.slow").show("slow");

        $("p.very-fast").show(50);

        $("p.very-slow").show(2000);

    });

});

</script>
```

Note

Using the 'fast' string for speed or duration indicates that 200 milliseconds is the duration, while 'slow' indicates that 600 milliseconds is the duration.

Callback functions may also be specified for execution after show() or hide() has finished – more about that later.

```javascript
<script type="text/javascript">

$(document).ready(function(){

    // Display alert message after hiding paragraphs

    $(".hide-btn").click(function(){

        $("p").hide("slow", function(){

            // Code to be executed

            alert("The hide effect is completed.");

        });

    });


    // Display alert message after showing paragraphs

    $(".show-btn").click(function(){

        $("p").show("slow", function(){

            // Code to be executed

            alert("The show effect is completed.");
```

```
        });

    });

});

</script>
```

toggle()

We use the toggle() method for showing or hiding elements in a way that, if displayed initially, the element is hidden whereas, if it is hidden, it will be displayed. In other words, it will toggle between the visibilities.

```
<script type="text/javascript">

$(document).ready(function(){

    // Toggles paragraphs display

    $(".toggle-btn").click(function(){

        $("p").toggle();

    });

});

</script>
```

In much the same way, the duration parameter for toggle() may be specified so it is animated, like show() and hide():

```
<script type="text/javascript">

$(document).ready(function(){

    // Toggles paragraphs with different speeds

    $(".toggle-btn").click(function(){

        $("p.normal").toggle();

        $("p.fast").toggle("fast");

        $("p.slow").toggle("slow");

        $("p.very-fast").toggle(50);
```

```
    $("p.very-slow").toggle(2000);
  });
});
</script>
```

And callback functions can also be specified for toggle():

```
<script type="text/javascript">
$(document).ready(function(){
    // Display alert message after toggling paragraphs
    $(".toggle-btn").click(function(){
        $("p").toggle(1000, function(){
            // Code to be executed
            alert("The toggle effect is completed.");
        });
    });
});
</script>
```

jQuery Fading Effects

Now it is time to learn how to fade elements in and out in jQuery.

jQuery fadeIn() and fadeout() Methods

These two methods can be used to display HTML elements by increasing opacity gradually or hiding them by gradually decreasing opacity.

Here's an example:

```
<script type="text/javascript">

$(document).ready(function(){

    // Fading out displayed paragraphs

    $(".out-btn").click(function(){

        $("p").fadeOut();

    });


    // Fading in hidden paragraphs

    $(".in-btn").click(function(){

        $("p").fadeIn();

    });

});

</script>
```

Like any of the other effects methods in jQuery, you have the option of specifying a duration parameter for both methods. This gives you some control over the length of time the fade animation lasts for. You can use a predefined "slow" or "fast" string or you can use milliseconds – the higher the value, the slower the animation.

Here's an example

```
<script type="text/javascript">

$(document).ready(function(){
```

```
// Fading out displayed paragraphs with different speeds

$(".out-btn").click(function(){

    $("p.normal").fadeOut();

    $("p.fast").fadeOut("fast");

    $("p.slow").fadeOut("slow");

    $("p.very-fast").fadeOut(50);

    $("p.very-slow").fadeOut(2000);

});


// Fading in hidden paragraphs with different speeds

$(".in-btn").click(function(){

    $("p.normal").fadeIn();

    $("p.fast").fadeIn("fast");

    $("p.slow").fadeIn("slow");

    $("p.very-fast").fadeIn(50);

    $("p.very-slow").fadeIn(2000);

  });

});

</script>
```

Note

You might spot that the effects of both fadeIn() and fadeOut() methods are similar in looks to the show() and hide() methods; the difference is, the fadeIn() and fadeOut() methods will animate only the opacity of the specified elements and not their dimensions like the show() and hide() methods do.

Callback functions can also be specified for execution after the effect method has finished – more about these later.

For now, look at this example:

```
<script type="text/javascript">
$(document).ready(function(){
    // Display alert message after fading out paragraphs
    $(".out-btn").click(function(){
        $("p").fadeOut("slow", function(){
            // Code to be executed
            alert("The fade-out effect is completed.");
        });
    });


    // Display alert message after fading in paragraphs
    $(".in-btn").click(function(){
        $("p").fadeIn("slow", function(){
            // Code to be executed
            alert("The fade-in effect is completed.");
        });
    });
});
</script>
```

jQuery fadeToggle() Method

The fadeToggle() method is used to display or hide elements through animation of opacity in a way a displayed element will fade out and a hidden element will fade in:

```
<script type="text/javascript">
$(document).ready(function(){
    // Toggles paragraphs display with fading
    $(".toggle-btn").click(function(){
```

```
      $("p").fadeToggle();

  });

});
```

</script>

Again, the duration parameter can be specified to control how long the fade toggle animation lasts.

<script type="text/javascript">

```
$(document).ready(function(){

  // Fade Toggles paragraphs with different speeds

  $(".toggle-btn").click(function(){

    $("p.normal").fadeToggle();

    $("p.fast").fadeToggle("fast");

    $("p.slow").fadeToggle("slow");

    $("p.very-fast").fadeToggle(50);

    $("p.very-slow").fadeToggle(2000);

  });

});
```

</script>

Once again, the callback function may be specified to execute once the method has completed.

<script type="text/javascript">

```
$(document).ready(function(){

  // Display alert message after fade toggling paragraphs

  $(".toggle-btn").click(function(){

    $("p").fadeToggle(1000, function(){

      // Code to be executed
```

```
        alert("The fade-toggle effect is completed.");
      });
    });
  });
</script>
```

jQuery fadeTo() Method

The fadeTo() method is much like the fadeIn() method but with a difference – this one allows you to fade elements to a specified level of opacity.

$(selector).fadeTo(speed, opacity, callback);

The opacity parameter is required and it will specify the opacity of the target elements – it can be set to any number between 0 and 1. The duration parameter is also a requirement to specify how long the animation will last.

```
<script type="text/javascript">
$(document).ready(function(){
  // Fade to paragraphs with different opacity
  $(".to-btn").click(function(){
    $("p.none").fadeTo("fast", 0);
    $("p.partial").fadeTo("slow", 0.5);
    $("p.complete").fadeTo(2000, 1);
  });
});
</script>
```

jQuery Sliding Effects

There are two methods to use.

jQuery slideUp() and slideDown()

The slideUp() method is used for showing HTML elements while slideDown() is used to hide HTML elements by increasing or decreasing their height.

Here's an example:

```
<script type="text/javascript">

$(document).ready(function(){

    // Slide up displayed paragraphs

    $(".up-btn").click(function(){

        $("p").slideUp();

    });


    // Slide down hidden paragraphs

    $(".down-btn").click(function(){

        $("p").slideDown();

    });

});

</script>
```

Again, the duration parameter is optional, controlling the length of time the animations will last. The predefined "fast" or "slow" string can be used or you can use milliseconds to specify the duration- higher equals slower animations.

Here's an example:

```
<script type="text/javascript">

$(document).ready(function(){
```

```javascript
// Sliding up displayed paragraphs with different speeds
$(".up-btn").click(function(){
    $("p.normal").slideUp();
    $("p.fast").slideUp("fast");
    $("p.slow").slideUp("slow");
    $("p.very-fast").slideUp(50);
    $("p.very-slow").slideUp(2000);
});


// Sliding down hidden paragraphs with different speeds
$(".down-btn").click(function(){
    $("p.normal").slideDown();
    $("p.fast").slideDown("fast");
    $("p.slow").slideDown("slow");
    $("p.very-fast").slideDown(50);
    $("p.very-slow").slideDown(2000);
  });
});
</script>
```

As usual, the callback function can be specified for execution after the method completes.

```javascript
<script type="text/javascript">
$(document).ready(function(){
    // Display alert message after sliding up paragraphs
    $(".up-btn").click(function(){
        $("p").slideUp("slow", function(){
```

```
        // Code to be executed
        alert("The slide-up effect is completed.");
    });
  });


  // Display alert message after sliding down paragraphs
  $(".down-btn").click(function(){
    $("p").slideDown("slow", function(){
      // Code to be executed
      alert("The slide-down effect is completed.");
    });
  });
});

</script>
```

jQuery slideToggle() Method

The slideToggle() method will show or hide an element by way of animation of the height; if an element is displayed, it will be hidden and, if already hidden, it will be displayed. In other words the slideToggle() method toggles between the slideDown() and slideUp() methods.

For example:

```
<script type="text/javascript">
$(document).ready(function(){
  // Toggles paragraphs display with sliding
  $(".toggle-btn").click(function(){
    $("p").slideToggle();
  });
```

});

</script>

In the same way, the duration parameter can be specified to control how long the animation runs, i.e. its speed.

```
<script type="text/javascript">
$(document).ready(function(){
    // Slide Toggles paragraphs with different speeds
    $(".toggle-btn").click(function(){
        $("p.normal").slideToggle();
        $("p.fast").slideToggle("fast");
        $("p.slow").slideToggle("slow");
        $("p.very-fast").slideToggle(50);
        $("p.very-slow").slideToggle(2000);
    });
});
</script>
```

And, yes, the callback function can be specified for this method too.

For example:

```
<script type="text/javascript">
$(document).ready(function(){
    // Display alert message after slide toggling paragraphs
    $(".toggle-btn").click(function(){
        $("p").slideToggle(1000, function(){
            // Code to be executed
            alert("The slide-toggle effect is completed.");
        });
```

```
    });
});
</script>
```

jQuery Animation Effects

Now we'll take a quick look at how to use jQuery to animate CSS properties.

jQuery animate() Method

We use the animate() method to create customized animations. Typically, it is used for the animation of numeric CSS properties, such as height, width, padding, margin, top, left, opacity, etc. You cannot use basic jQuery functionality to animate background-color, color, or any other non-numeric property.

Note

You cannot animate all CSS properties. Generally, if a CSS property accepts a value of a length, a number, a percentage, or a color, it can be animated. However, there is no support for color animation in the core jQuery library. You need to use the jQuery color plugin to do this.

Syntax

The basic animate() method syntax is:

$(selector).animate({ properties }, duration, callback);

Each parameter for the method has these meanings:

- The parameter for the required properties will define which CSS properties are to be animated.

- The duration parameter is optional; if used, it specifies the length of time an animation runs. You can use two ways to specify the duration – milliseconds, in which a higher value equals a slower animation, or using a predefined string of "slow" or "fast".

- The callback parameter is also optional and is a function that is called when the animation method has completed.

Below is a simple example of the animate() method being used to animate an image so it moves from its position 300 pixels to the right just by a button click:

<script type="text/javascript">

$(document).ready(function(){

  $("button").click(function(){

```
    $("img").animate({

        left: 300

    });

  });

});
```

</script>

Note

HTML elements all have static positions by default. Because the nature of a static position dictates it can't be moved, the element's CSS position property is to be set as fixed, relative, or absolute so the position can be manipulated or animated.

Simultaneous Animation of Multiple Properties

It is also possible to animate several properties of one element simultaneously with the animate() method. All properties selected will be animated at the same time with no delays:

```
<script type="text/javascript">

$(document).ready(function(){

  $("button").click(function(){

    $(".box").animate({

      width: "300px",

      height: "300px",

      marginLeft: "150px",

      borderWidth: "10px",

      opacity: 0.5

    });

  });

});

</script>
```

Note

When you use the CSS properties with the animate() method, the names must be written in camel case. For example, if you wanted the font size animated, you would use 'fontSize' and not font-size and by the same token, marginRight instead of margin-right borderHeight instead of border-height.

Tip

The border-style property must be set for the element BEFORE you animate the property for border-width. Elements need to have borders before the border-width can be animated simply because the border-style property has a default value of none.

Queued Animation

Several properties of a single element may also be animated one at a time by queueing them using the chaining feature in jQuery. We will be looking at this in more depth shortly but, first, here's an example of a chained animation in jQuery. Each animation begins when the previous animation has completed:

```
<script type="text/javascript">

$(document).ready(function(){

  $("button").click(function(){

    $(".box")

      .animate({width: "300px"})

      .animate({height: "300px"})

      .animate({marginLeft: "150px"})

      .animate({borderWidth: "10px"})

      .animate({opacity: 0.5});

  });

});

</script>
```

Using Relative Values

Relative values may also be defined for animated properties. If you use a leading += or -= prefix to specify the value, the target value will be calculated through addition or subtraction of the number to or from the current property value.

For example

```
<script type="text/javascript">

$(document).ready(function(){

  $("button").click(function(){

    $(".box").animate({

      top: "+=50px",
```

```
        left: "+=50px",

        width: "+=50px",

        height: "+=50px"

    });

  });

});

</script>
```

Using Pre-Defined Values

As well as numeric values, properties may also take three strings – "hide", "show" and "toggle". This is helpful when you have a situation where all you want to do is animate a property from the value it has now to the initial value or the other way around.

For example:

```
<script type="text/javascript">

$(document).ready(function(){

  $("button").click(function(){

    $(".box").animate({

      width: 'toggle'

    });

  });

});

</script>
```

jQuery Stop Animations

Now we will look at how we use jQuery to stop the animations from running.

jQuery stop() Method

We use the stop() method to stop effects or animations already running on elements before they can complete.

The syntax used is:

$(selector).stop(stopAll, goToEnd);

The parameters used in the syntax mean:

- The stopAll Boolean parameter is optional and is used to specify whether queued animations should be removed or not. It has a default value of false and this means the only animation stopped is the current one; the remaining animations will continue running until completed.
- The goToEnd Boolean parameter is also optional and is used to specify whether the current animation should be immediately completed. It has a default value of false.

Below is an example showing the stop() method in use – animation is started and stopped with a button click:

<script type="text/javascript">

$(document).ready(function(){

  // Start animation

  $(".start-btn").click(function(){

   $("img").animate({left: "+=150px"}, 2000);

  });

  // Stop running animation

  $(".stop-btn").click(function(){

   $("img").stop();

```javascript
});

// Start animation in the opposite direction
$(".back-btn").click(function(){
   $("img").animate({left: "-=150px"}, 2000);
});

// Reset to default
$(".reset-btn").click(function(){
   $("img").animate({left: "0"}, "fast");
 });
});
</script>
```

Note

The stop() method works for all the jQuery effects, like sliding, fading, show and hide, and on custom animations.

Here's another example of the stop() method; in this one, if the 'Slide Toggle' button is clicked after the animation starts but before it completes; the animations turn in the opposite direction from the starting point that was saved:

```javascript
<script type="text/javascript">
$(document).ready(function(){
   // Kill and toggle the current sliding animation
   $(".toggle-btn").on("click", function(){
      $(".box").stop().slideToggle(1000);
   });
});
```

```
</script>
```

Creating the Smooth Hover Effect

When you create an animated hover effect, there is one problem you are likely to face – multiple animations queued up when the mouse cursor is placed and removed rapidly. The reason this happens is the mouseleave and mouseenter events are triggered very quickly before completion of the animation. To stop this from transpiring and to create a smooth hover, add another method to the chain – the stop(true, true) method.

For example:

```
<script type="text/javascript">

$(document).ready(function(){

  $(".box").hover(function(){

    $(this).find("img").stop(true, true).fadeOut();

  }, function(){

    $(this).find("img").stop(true, true).fadeIn();

  });

});

</script>
```

Note

The stop(true, true) method will clear all of the animations queued up and will jump the animation directly to the final value.

jQuery Chaining

Another great feature in jQuery is method chaining. This method lets us perform several actions on one set of elements using just one line of code. We can do this because most methods in jQuery return jQuery objects and these can then be used to call other methods.

For example:

```
<script type="text/javascript">

$(document).ready(function(){

    $("button").click(function(){

        $("p").animate({width: "100%"}).animate({fontSize:
"46px"}).animate({borderWidth: 30});

    });

});

</script>
```

What we have here is a demonstration of three animate() methods being chained together. When the trigger button is clicked by the user, the <p> is expanded to 100% width. Once this has been done, font-size will begin animating and, once that has finished the border animation starts.

Tip

Method chaining serves two purposes; first, it makes your jQuery code a good deal cleaner and easier to read and, second, your script will perform much better because the browser won't have to look for the same element time and time again to perform an action on them.

Single lines of code can also be broken down into several lines to make reading it much easier. Take a look at the next example that shows a different way of writing the method sequence than the last example:

```
<script type="text/javascript">

$(document).ready(function(){

    $("button").click(function(){
```

```
$("p")

    .animate({width: "100%"})

    .animate({fontSize: "46px"})

    .animate({borderWidth: 30});

  });

});

</script>
```

Some of the methods in jQuery will not return a jQuery object. Generally, a setter, which is a method that assigns a value when selected, will return a jQuery object and you can carry on calling methods on the selection. A getter, on the other hand, will return the value requested, so methods can no longer be called on that value.

An example of this is the html() method. If the method doesn't have any parameters passed to it, the contents of the specified element are returned, not a jQuery object.

For example:

```
<script type="text/javascript">

$(document).ready(function(){

  $("button").click(function(){

    // This will work

    $("h1").html("Hello World!").addClass("test");


    // This will NOT work

    $("p").html().addClass("test");

  });

});

</script>
```

jQuery Callback

We've mentioned callbacks a few times so far; now it's time to learn how to define the callback function for an effect.

jQuery Callback Function

All statements in Javascript are executed one line at a time. However, jQuery effects can take a while to finish, so the next code line may start executing while the first one is running. You can stop this by using a callback function for each of your effect methods.

Callback functions are executed as soon as the effect has completed. We pass the callback function to the effect method as an argument; typically, they will be the last method argument. Let's take the jQuery slideToggle() method; adding a callback function to the basic syntax would look like this:

$(selector).slideToggle(duration, callback);

Look at this example. We have inserted two statements next to one another – slideToggle() and alert(). Running this code would result in the alert being displayed immediately when the trigger button is clicked; it will not wait until the slide toggle effect has finished:

<script type="text/javascript">

$(document).ready(function(){

  $("button").click(function(){

    $("p").slideToggle("slow");

    alert("The slide toggle effect has completed.");

  });

});

</script>

Now we have a modified version of this example; the alert() statement is inside a callback function for slideToggle(). Here the slideToggle() will finish before the alert message is displayed:

<script type="text/javascript">

```
$(document).ready(function(){

    $("button").click(function(){

        $("p").slideToggle("slow", function(){

            // Code to be executed once effect is complete

            alert("The slide toggle effect has completed.");

        });

    });

});

</script>
```

In much the same way, callback functions can be displayed for many of the other jQuery effect methods, such as fadeIn(), fadeOut(), show(), hide(), animate(), etc.

Note

If you apply the effect method to several elements, the callback function will be called one time for each of the specified elements, as opposed to just once for all of them.

For example:

```
<script type="text/javascript">

$(document).ready(function(){

    $("button").click(function(){

        $("h1, p").slideToggle("slow", function(){

            // Code to be executed once effect is complete

            alert("The slide toggle effect has completed.");

        });

    });

});

</script>
```

Try this code and the same alert is displayed twice – one time for the <h1> element and once for the <p> element – when the trigger button is clicked.

jQuery Getters and Setters

Now we will look at how to use jQuery to get or set the content and attribute values for an element along with the value for the form control.

jQuery Get or Set Contents and Values

Some methods in jQuery can be used to assign or read selection values. That includes the html(), text(), val() and attr() methods.

When we call these methods without using arguments, we call them getters because they will get or read an element's value. When we call them with a value, they are called setters because they will set or assign the value.

jQuery text() Method

We use the text() method to either get the text contents from all the specified elements including all descendants or to set the text of the specified elements.

The next example shows how to get the text from paragraphs:

```
<script type="text/javascript">

$(document).ready(function(){

   // Get combined text contents of all paragraphs

   $(".btn-one").click(function(){

     var str = $("p").text();

     alert(str);

   });


   // Get text contents of the first paragraph

   $(".btn-two").click(function(){

     var str = $("p:first").text();

     alert(str);

   });
```

311

```
});
```

```
</script>
```

Note

The text() method is also used to retrieve values of all specified elements whereas some of the other getters, for attr(), val(), and html(), for example, will only return the value of the first specified element.

The next example shows how to set text for paragraphs:

```
<script type="text/javascript">
$(document).ready(function(){
    // Set text contents of all paragraphs
    $(".btn-one").click(function(){
        $("p").text("This is demo text.");
    });


    // Set text contents of the first paragraph
    $(".btn-two").click(function(){
        $("p:first").text("This is another demo text.");
    });
});
</script>
```

Note

When the text(), attr(), html(), and val() methods are called using values as the arguments, the value is set to all the elements that match.

jQuery html() Method

We use the html() method to get or set html content for specified elements.

The next example shows you how to get the paragraph element HTML contents and the <div> element container:

```
<script type="text/javascript">

$(document).ready(function(){

    // Get HTML contents of first selected paragraph

    $(".btn-one").click(function(){

        var str = $("p").html();

        alert(str);

    });


    // Get HTML contents of an element with ID container

    $(".btn-two").click(function(){

        var str = $("#container").html();

        alert(str);

    });

});

</script>
```

Note

If you select multiple elements, the html() method will return only the HTML content from the first element in the set of specified elements.

The next example shows how to set the <body> element HTML contents:

```
<script type="text/javascript">

$(document).ready(function(){

    // Set HTML contents for document's body

    $("button").click(function(){

        $("body").html("<p>Hello World!</p>");

    });

});
```

</script>

jQuery attr() Method

The attr() method is used to get an element attribute value or set at least one attribute for a specified element.

The following example shows how to get a hyperlink's href attribute, i.e. the <a> element, along with the specified <img> element's alt attribute:

<script type="text/javascript">

$(document).ready(function(){

  // Get href attribute value of first selected hyperlink

  $(".btn-one").click(function(){

    var str = $("a").attr("href");

    alert(str);

  });

  // Get alt attribute value of an image with ID sky

  $(".btn-two").click(function(){

    var str = $("img#sky").attr("alt");

    alert(str);

  });

});

</script>

Note

If you select several parameters, only the first element from the set will be returned by the attr() method.

How the checked attribute is set for the checkbox is shown here:

<script type="text/javascript">

```
$(document).ready(function(){

    // Check all the checkboxes

    $("button").click(function(){

        $('input[type="checkbox"]').attr("checked", "checked");

    });

});

</script>
```

You can also use the attr() method to set several attributes at the same time. This example shows how title and class attributes are set for the <img> elements:

```
<script type="text/javascript">

$(document).ready(function(){

    // Add a class and title attribute to all the images

    $("button").click(function(){

        $("img").attr({

            "class" : "frame",

            "title" : "Hot Air Balloons"

        });

    });

});

</script>
```

jQuery val() Method

The val() method is used mostly to get or set current element values, such as for <textarea>, <select>, and <input>.

This example shows how to get the form control values:

```javascript
<script type="text/javascript">
$(document).ready(function(){
    // Get value of a text input with ID name
    $("button.get-name").click(function(){
        var name = $('input[type="text"]#name').val();
        alert(name);
    });


    // Get value of a textarea with ID comment
    $("button.get-comment").click(function(){
        var comment = $("textarea#comment").val();
        alert(comment);
    });


    // Get value of a select box with ID city
    $("button.get-city").click(function(){
        var city = $("select#city").val();
        alert(city);
    });
});
</script>
```

Note

If you select several elements, only the value of the first element from the set will be returned by the val() method.

The next example shows how form control values are set:

```
<script type="text/javascript">

$(document).ready(function(){

   // Set value of all the text inputs

   $("button").click(function(){

      var text = $(this).text();

      $('input[type="text"]').val(text);

   });

});

</script>
```

jQuery Insert Content

Now we turn our attention to using jQuery to insert new content or elements in a document.

jQuery Insert New Content

jQuery gives a number of techniques to add new content into an already-existing element including:

- append()
- prepend()
- html()
- text()
- before()
- after()
- wrap()
- and others

The text() and html() methods have already been covered previously so we'll talk about the others instead.

jQuery append() Method

The append() method is used to insert new content at the end of a specified element. This example shows how to append HTML to all of the paragraphs on document ready and some text to the container element when a button is clicked:

```
<script type="text/javascript">

$(document).ready(function(){

  // Append all paragraphs

  $("p").append(' <a href="#">read more...</a>');


  // Append an element with ID container

  $("button").click(function(){

    $("#container").append("This is demo text.");

  });
```

});

</script>

Note

When the append() or prepend() methods are used to insert content or elements, they are added inside the specified elements.

jQuery prepend() Method

We use the prepend() method to insert content at the start of the specified elements. In the next example, we prepend HTML to every paragraph on document ready and text to a container element when the button is clicked.

<script type="text/javascript">

$(document).ready(function(){

   // Prepend all paragraphs

   $("p").prepend("Note: ");

   // Prepend an element with ID container

   $("button").click(function(){

     $("#container").prepend("This is demo text.");

   });

});

</script>

Using append() and prepend() to Insert Multiple Elements

Both methods can be used to pass several arguments in at once as the input. In the next example, the jQuery coded needed to insert three elements into a body element – the <h1>, <p>, and <img> elements, are all added as child nodes.

<script type="text/javascript">

$(document).ready(function(){

   var newHeading = "<h1>Important Note:</h1>";

```
    var newParagraph = document.createElement("p");

    newParagraph.innerHTML = "<em>Lorem Ipsum is dummy text...</em>";

    var newImage = $('<img src="images/smiley.png" alt="Symbol">');

    $("body").append(newHeading, newParagraph, newImage);

});

</script>
```

jQuery before() Method

The before() method is used to insert content in front of specified elements. This example shows how to insert a paragraph in front of the container element and insert an image in front of the <h1> element when a button is clicked:

```
<script type="text/javascript">

$(document).ready(function(){

    // Add content before an element with ID container

    $("#container").before("<p>&mdash; The Beginning &mdash;</p>");


    // Add content before headings

    $("button").click(function(){

        $("h1").before('<img src="images/marker-left.gif" alt="Symbol">');

    });

});

</script>
```

Note

When the before() and after() methods are used to insert the content, it is inserted outside the specified elements.

jQuery after() Method

The after() method is used to insert the content after the specified elements. In this example, a paragraph is inserted following the container element and an image is inserted after the <h1> element when a button is clicked:

```
<script type="text/javascript">

$(document).ready(function(){

    // Add content after an element with ID container

    $("#container").after("<p>&mdash; The End &mdash;</p>");


    // Add content after headings

    $("button").click(function(){

        $("h1").after('<img src="images/marker-right.gif" alt="Symbol">');

    });

});

</script>
```

Using before() and after() To Insert Multiple Elements

The before() and after() methods can be used to pass several arguments as the input. In this example, three elements are inserted in front of the <p> elements – an <h1>, a <p>, and an <img>:

```
<script type="text/javascript">

$(document).ready(function(){

    var newHeading = "<h2>Important Note:</h2>";

    var newParagraph = document.createElement("p");

    newParagraph.innerHTML = "<em>Lorem Ipsum is dummy text...</em>";

    var newImage = $('<img src="images/smiley.png" alt="Symbol">');

    $("p").before(newHeading, newParagraph, newImage);

});
```

</script>

jQuery wrap() Method

Lastly, the wrap() method is used to wrap HTML structures around specified elements.

In the next example, the code is wrapping a <div> element around the container elements and using a <b> element to wrap the inner contents of all the paragraph elements before wrapping them again in an <em> element:

<script type="text/javascript">

$(document).ready(function(){

// Wrap elements with class container with HTML

$(".container").wrap('<div class="wrapper"></div>');

// Wrap paragraph's content with HTML

$("button").click(function(){

$("p").contents().wrap("<em><b></b></em>");

});

});

</script>

jQuery Remove Elements And Attribute

In this part, we'll look at how jQuery can be used to remove HTML elements, their contents, and the attribute from the document.

There are several methods in jQuery, like remove(), empty() and unwrap() to remove the HTML elements or contents out of the document.

jQuery empty() Method

This method is used to eliminate all the child elements, descendent elements, and text content from the specified DOM elements. In the following instance, we will empty the elements with the class called .container of their contents on the click of a button:

```
<script type="text/javascript">

$(document).ready(function(){

    // Empty container element

    $("button").click(function(){

        $(".container").empty();

    });

});

</script>
```

Note

The World Wide Web Consortium DOM spec states that any text string inside an element is considered to be a child node of the containing element.

jQuery remove() Method

The jQuery remove() method is used to remove the specified element plus all its contents from the DOM. Also removed are any bound events and jQuery data that are associated with the elements.

Look at this example where, with one button click, we remove every <p> element that has the class called .hint from the DOM, as well as removing all nested elements from within the <p> elements:

```
<script type="text/javascript">
```

```
$(document).ready(function(){

    // Removes paragraphs with class "hint" from DOM

    $("button").click(function(){

        $("p.hint").remove();

    });

});

</script>
```

This method may also have an optional parameter of a selector that will let you filter the elements being removed. For example, we could rewrite our previous example like this:

```
<script type="text/javascript">

$(document).ready(function(){

    // Removes paragraphs with class "hint" from DOM

    $("button").click(function(){

        $("p").remove(".hint");

    });

});

</script>
```

Note

The selector expression may also be included as a parameter in the remove() method as a way of filtering several elements, for example remove(',hint", .demo").

jQuery unwrap() Method

The unwrap() method lets us remove parent elements from specified DOM elements. It is usually the opposite of the wrap() method. In the example below, we are removing the <p> element parent elements with a single button click:

```
<script type="text/javascript">

$(document).ready(function(){

    // Removes the paragraph's parent element
```

```
$("button").click(function(){

    $("p").unwrap();

  });

});

</script>
```

jQuery removeAttr() Method

The removeAttr() is used to remove attributes from specified elements. In the next example, the attribute called href is removed from the <a> elements when a button is clicked:

```
<script type="text/javascript">

$(document).ready(function(){

  // Removes the hyperlink's href attribute

  $("button").click(function(){

    $("a").removeAttr("href");

  });

});

</script>
```

jQuery Add and Remove CSS Classes

Now it is time to look at how jQuery can be used to add and remove CSS classes.

There are a few methods in jQuery to manipulate CSS classes that have been assigned to HTML elements, like addClass(), toggleClass(), removeClass(), etc.

jQuery addClass() Method

The addClass() method is used to add at least one class to the specified elements and the following example shows just that. The class called .page-header is added to the <h1> element and the class called .highlight is added to the <p> elements that have the class called .hint, with one click of the button.

```
<!DOCTYPE html>

<html lang="en">

<head>

<meta charset="utf-8">

<title>jQuery addClass() Demo</title>

<style type="text/css">

  .page-header{

    color: red;

    text-transform: uppercase;

  }

  .highlight{

    background: yellow;

  }

</style>

<script src="https://code.jquery.com/jquery-1.12.4.min.js"></script>

<script type="text/javascript">

$(document).ready(function(){
```

```
    $("button").click(function(){

        $("h1").addClass("page-header");

        $("p.hint").addClass("highlight");

    });

});

</script>

</head>

<body>

    <h1>Demo Text</h1>

    <p>Lorem ipsum dolor sit amet, consectetur adipiscing elit...</p>

    <p class="hint"><strong>Tip:</strong> Lorem Ipsum is dummy text.</p>

    <button type="button">Add Class</button>

</body>

</html>
```

It is also possible to add several classes to an element simultaneously. Remember to specify the list of classes, separated by spaces, inside the addClass() method, like this:

```
<!DOCTYPE html>

<html lang="en">

<head>

<meta charset="utf-8">

<title>jQuery addClass() Demo</title>

<style type="text/css">

    .page-header{

        color: red;

        text-transform: uppercase;

    }
```

```
    .highlight{
        background: yellow;
    }
</style>
<script src="https://code.jquery.com/jquery-1.12.4.min.js"></script>
<script type="text/javascript">
$(document).ready(function(){
    $("button").click(function(){
        $("h1").addClass("page-header highlight");
    });
});
</script>
</head>
<body>
    <h1>Hello World</h1>
    <p>The quick brown fox jumps over the lazy dog.</p>
    <button type="button">Add Class</button>
</body>
</html>
```

jQuery removeClass() Method

In much the same way, the removeClass() method is used to remove the classes. This method can be used for the removal on one class, several classes, or all classes from an element at the same time. The example below shows the class called .page-header being removed from the <h1> element and the classes called .hint and .highlight from all <p> elements with one click of the button:

```
<!DOCTYPE html>

<html lang="en">
```

```
<head>

<meta charset="utf-8">

<title>jQuery removeClass() Demo</title>

<style type="text/css">

  .page-header{

    color: red;

    text-transform: uppercase;

  }

  .highlight{

    background: yellow;

  }

</style>

<script src="https://code.jquery.com/jquery-1.12.4.min.js"></script>

<script type="text/javascript">

$(document).ready(function(){

  $("button").click(function(){

    $("h1").removeClass("page-header");

    $("p").removeClass("hint highlight");

  });

});

</script>

</head>

<body>

  <h1 class="page-header">Demo Text</h1>

  <p>Lorem ipsum dolor sit amet, consectetur adipiscing elit...</p>
```

```
<p class="hint highlight"><strong>Tip:</strong> Lorem Ipsum is dummy text.</p>

<button type="button">Remove Class</button>

</body>

</html>
```

When the removeClass() method is called without any arguments, all classes will be removed from the specified elements, as in this example:

```
<!DOCTYPE html>

<html lang="en">

<head>

<meta charset="utf-8">

<title>jQuery removeClass() Demo</title>

<style type="text/css">

  .page-header{

    color: red;

    text-transform: uppercase;

  }

  .highlight{

    background: yellow;

  }

</style>

<script src="https://code.jquery.com/jquery-1.12.4.min.js"></script>

<script type="text/javascript">

$(document).ready(function(){

  $("button").click(function(){

    $("h1").removeClass();

    $("p").removeClass();
```

```
    });
});
</script>
</head>
<body>
    <h1 class="page-header">Demo Text</h1>
    <p>Lorem ipsum dolor sit amet, consectetur adipiscing elit...</p>
    <p class="hint highlight"><strong>Tip:</strong> Lorem Ipsum is dummy text.</p>
    <button type="button">Remove Class</button>
</body>
</html>
```

jQuery toggleClass() Method

The toggleClass() method adds or removes at least one class from specified elements in a way that, if the class is already in the chosen element, it will be removed. If the class is not in the element, it is added.

Look at this example:

```
<!DOCTYPE html>
<html lang="en">
<head>
<meta charset="utf-8">
<title>jQuery toggleClass() Demo</title>
<style type="text/css">
  p{
    padding: 10px;
    cursor: pointer;
    font: bold 16px sans-serif;
```

```
        }
    .highlight{
        background: yellow;
    }
</style>
<script src="https://code.jquery.com/jquery-1.12.4.min.js"></script>
<script type="text/javascript">
$(document).ready(function(){
    $("p").click(function(){
        $(this).toggleClass("highlight");
    });
});
</script>
</head>
<body>
    <p>Click on me to toggle highlighting.</p>
    <p class="highlight">Click on me to toggle highlighting.</p>
    <p>Click on me to toggle highlighting.</p>
</body>
</html>
```

jQuery Get and Set CSS Properties

Now we will look at using jQuery for getting and setting style properties.

jQuery css() Method

The css() method is used to obtain the computed value of a specified CSS property or to set a minimum of one CSS property for the specified elements. This method provides a quick and easy way to directly apply styles to the HTML elements that either haven't been or defined in a stylesheet or can't be defined in a straightforward way.

Get a CSS Property Value

Getting a computed value of a CSS property for a specified element is as simple as passing the css()method a parameter of the property name. The syntax to use is:

$(selector).css("propertyName");

The next example shows how to retrieve the computed value for a specified <div> element CSS color property and display it with the click of a button:

<!DOCTYPE html>

<html lang="en">

<head>

<meta charset="utf-8">

<title>jQuery css() Demo</title>

<style type="text/css">

* div{*

*   width: 100px;*

*   height: 100px;*

*   margin: 10px;*

*   cursor: pointer;*

*   display: inline-block;*

* }*

```
</style>

<script src="https://code.jquery.com/jquery-1.12.4.min.js"></script>

<script type="text/javascript">

$(document).ready(function(){

   $("div").click(function(){

      var color = $(this).css("background-color");

      $("#result").html(color);

   });

});

</script>

</head>

<body>

   <div style="background-color:orange;"></div>

   <div style="background-color:#ee82ee;"></div>

   <div style="background-color:rgb(139,205,50);"></div>

   <div style="background-color:#f00;"></div>

   <p>The computed background-color property value of this DIV element is: <b
id="result"></b></p>

</body>

</html>
```

Set a Single CSS Property and Value

The css() method can also take property names and values as parameters used to set one CSS property for the specified elements. The syntax is:

$(selector).css("propertyName", "value");

In the example below, the CSS background-color property for the specified <div> elements is set to a color value of red when it is clicked on:

```html
<!DOCTYPE html>
<html lang="en">
<head>
<meta charset="utf-8">
<title>jQuery css() Demo</title>
<style type="text/css">
  .box{
    width: 100px;
    height: 100px;
    margin: 10px;
    cursor: pointer;
    border: 1px solid #cdcdcd;
    display: inline-block;
  }
</style>
<script src="https://code.jquery.com/jquery-1.12.4.min.js"></script>
<script type="text/javascript">
$(document).ready(function(){
  $(".box").click(function(){
    $(this).css("background-color", "red");
  });
});
</script>
</head>
<body>
```

```
  <div class="box"></div>

  <div class="box"></div>

  <div class="box"></div>

  <div class="box"></div>

</body>

</html>
```

Set Multiple CSS Properties and Values

Several CSS properties can be set simultaneously using the css() method. The syntax you would use to set multiple properties for elements is:

$(selector).css({"propertyName":"value", "propertyName":"value", ...});

In this next example, the background-color and padding CSS are set for the specified elements simultaneously:

```
<!DOCTYPE html>

<html lang="en">

<head>

<meta charset="utf-8">

<title>jQuery css() Demo</title>

<style type="text/css">

  p{

    font-size: 18px;

    font-family: Arial, sans-serif;

  }

</style>

<script src="https://code.jquery.com/jquery-1.12.4.min.js"></script>

<script type="text/javascript">

$(document).ready(function(){
```

```
$("button").click(function(){
    $("p").css({"background-color": "yellow", "padding": "20px"});
  });
});
</script>
</head>
<body>
  <h1>This is a heading</h1>
  <p style="background-color:orange;">This a paragraph.</p>
  <p style="background-color:#ee82ee;">This is another paragraph.</p>
  <p style="background-color:rgb(139,205,50);">This is none more paragraph.</p>
  <p>This is one last paragraph.</p>
  <button type="button">Add CSS Styles</button>
</body>
</html>
```

jQuery Dimensions

In this section, we will discuss how jQuery can be used to help set or get element box dimensions, i.e. width and height. There are a number of methods in jQuery to get or set element CSS dimensions, such as height(), outerHeight(), innerHeight(), width(), outerWidth(), innerWidth(), etc.

jQuery width() and height() Methods

The width() and height() methods are used to get or set width and height for a specified element. This doesn't include any border, padding, or margins for the element.

This next example shows where the width and the height of a specified <div> element are returned:

```
<script type="text/javascript">

$(document).ready(function(){

  $("button").click(function(){

    var divWidth = $("#box").width();

    var divHeight = $("#box").height();

    $("#result").html("Width: " + divWidth + ", " + "Height: " + divHeight);

  });

});

</script>
```

In the same way, the height and width can be set by passing the value as a parameter inside the width() or height() method. The values may be a string or a number. In the next example, the <div> element width is set to 400 pixels and the height to 300 pixels:

```
<script type="text/javascript">

$(document).ready(function(){

  $("button").click(function(){

    $("#box").width(400).height(300);

  });
```

});

</script>

Note

The width() or height() method can be used if the width or height of the element are to be used in mathematical calculations. This is because the value of the height or width property are returned as pixel values without units, i.e. 400, whereas using the css("width") or css("height") methods would return the value with a unit, i.e. 400px.

jQuery innerWidth() and innerHeight() Methods

To set the inner width or height for an element, we would use the innerWidth() and the innerHeight() methods. These include padding but do not include margins or borders for the elements.

In the next example, the inner width and inner height values for a <div> element are returned when a button is clicked:

<script type="text/javascript">

$(document).ready(function(){

  $("button").click(function(){

    var divWidth = $("#box").innerWidth();

    var divHeight = $("#box").innerHeight();

    $("#result").html("Inner Width: " + divWidth + ", " + "Inner Height: " + divHeight);

  });

});

</script>

In a similar way, the inner width and height can also be set by passing the values as parameters to the innerWidth() and innerHeight() methods. All these methods do is change the width or the height of the content area in an element so it matches with the value specified.

For example, an element is 300 pixels in width and the sum of the right and left padding equals 50 pixels. Once the innerWidth has been set to 400 pixels, the new element width will be 350 pixels, i.e. the New Width is equal to Inner Width less Horizontal Padding. You can do the same to estimate the height change when the inner height is set.

For example:

```
<script type="text/javascript">

$(document).ready(function(){

  $("button").click(function(){

    $("#box").innerWidth(400).innerHeight(300);

  });

});

</script>
```

jQuery outerWidth() and outerHeight() Methods

The outerWidth() and the outerHeight() method are used to set or get the outer height or width of the element. This includes the border and the padding, but not the margin.

In the example below, the outer width and outer height of the <div> element is returned when a button is clicked:

```
<script type="text/javascript">

$(document).ready(function(){

  $("button").click(function(){

    var divWidth = $("#box").outerWidth();

    var divHeight = $("#box").outerHeight();

    $("#result").html("Outer Width: " + divWidth + ", " + "Outer Height: " + divHeight);

  });

});

</script>
```

The outer width and outer height including the border, padding, and the margin can also be obtained. All that is needed is to make sure the true parameter is specified for the outer methods, like outerHeight(true) and outerWidth(true).

For example:

```
<script type="text/javascript">
```

```
$(document).ready(function(){

    $("button").click(function(){

        var divWidth = $("#box").outerWidth(true);

        var divHeight = $("#box").outerHeight(true);

        $("#result").html("Outer Width: " + divWidth + ", " + "Outer Height: " + divHeight);

    });

});

</script>
```

The outer width and outer height can also be set by passing the outerWidth() and outerHeight() methods the value as a parameter. These change the height or width of the content area in the element to match the value specified, like the innerHeight() and innerWidth() methods.

For example, an element is 300 pixels in width and the sum of left and right padding is 50 pixels. The sum of the left and right border width is 20. The new element width, once the outer has been set to 400 pixels, will be 330 pixels, i.e. the new Width is equal to the Outer Width less the (Horizontal Padding plus the Horizontal Border).

For example:

```
<script type="text/javascript">

$(document).ready(function(){

    $("button").click(function(){

        $("#box").outerWidth(400).outerHeight(300);

    });

});

</script>
```

jQuery Traversing

Now we'll move on to look at using jQuery for the purpose of traversing through HTML DOM.

What is Traversing?

The selectors we have discussed have only let us select elements down the DOM tree. However, there will be times when we want a parent or an ancestor element and this is where we can use the traversal methods provided in jQuery. Using these methods, we can move up the tree, down, and all around it in a simple way.

DOM traversal is a foremost jQuery feature and, to get the best out of it, you first need to get to grips with the relationships existing in a DOM tree.

Look at this example:

<body>

  <div class="container">

    <h1>Hello World</h1>

    <p>This is an <em>simple paragraph</em>.</p>

    <ul>

      <li>Item One</li>

      <li>Item Two</li>

    </ul>

  </div>

</body>

We can represent this code with the following:

The <body> element is the <div> element parent and it is an ancestor of all that is in the element.

The <div> element that is enclosed is the parent of the following elements - <p>, <h1>, and <ul>. It is also a <body> element child.

The <p>, <h1>, and <ul> elements are all siblings because they all have the same parent.

The <h1> element is a <div> element child and is also a <body> element descendant. It has no children.

The <p> element is an <em> element parent, a <div> element child, and a <body> element descendant. The containing <em> element is the <p> element child and also a <div> and <body> element descendant.

In much the same way, the <ul> element is the <li> elements parent, the <div> element child, and the <body> element descendant. The containing <li> elements are all <ul> element children, and a descendant of both the <body> element and the <div> element. Besides that, the <li> elements are both siblings.

Note

Where a relationship is a logical one, ancestors are parents, grandparents, great-grandparents, and so on. Descendants are children, grandchildren, great-grandchildren, and so on, while siblings are all those who have the same parent.

Traversing the DOM Tree

Now that you have a better understanding of how the DOM tree elements are related, you can begin to learn how the traversing operations work, like moving sideways, up and down a DOM tree with jQuery.

jQuery Traversing Ancestors

We'll start by traversing up the DOM tree. In a logical relationship, ancestors are parents, grandparents, great-grandparents and so on. With jQuery, we have some methods to traverse up a DOM tree, one level at a time or multiple levels, to det to the element ancestors within the hierarchy quite easily. Some of those methods are parent(), parents(), and parentsUntil().

jQuery parent() Method

The parent() method is used to get the direct parent of a specified element. In the next example, the direct parent element for <li> is highlighted; the parent is <ul> by adding the class called .highlight on document ready:

```html
<!DOCTYPE html>

<html lang="en">

<head>

<meta charset="utf-8">

<title>jQuery parent() Demo</title>

<style type="text/css">

  .highlight{

    background: yellow;

  }

</style>

<script src="https://code.jquery.com/jquery-1.12.4.min.js"></script>

<script type="text/javascript">

$(document).ready(function(){

  $("li").parent().addClass("highlight");

});

</script>
```

```
    </head>
    <body>
        <div class="container">
            <h1>Hello World</h1>
            <p>This is a <em>simple paragraph</em>.</p>
            <ul>
                <li>Item One</li>
                <li>Item Two</li>
            </ul>
        </div>
    </body>
</html>
```

jQuery parents() Method

This method is used to get the specified element's ancestors. In our example, a border is added around the ancestor elements of <li>. Those ancestors are <ul>, <body>, <div>, and <html>.

```
<!DOCTYPE html>
<html lang="en">
<head>
<meta charset="utf-8">
<title>jQuery parents() Demo</title>
<style type="text/css">
    *{
        margin: 10px;
    }
    .frame{
```

```
      border: 2px solid green;
    }
</style>
<script src="https://code.jquery.com/jquery-1.12.4.min.js"></script>
<script type="text/javascript">
$(document).ready(function(){
   $("li").parents().addClass("frame");
});
</script>
</head>
<body>
   <div class="container">
      <h1>Hello World</h1>
      <p>This is a <em>simple paragraph</em>.</p>
      <ul>
         <li>Item One</li>
         <li>Item Two</li>
      </ul>
   </div>
</body>
</html>
```

Optionally, one or more selectors can be included as parameters in the parents() method. This will help filter out the ancestor search. In the next example, the border is applied around the <li> elements that are also elements of <div>:

```
<!DOCTYPE html>

<html lang="en">
```

```
<head>
<meta charset="utf-8">
<title>jQuery parents() Demo</title>
<style type="text/css">
  *{
    margin: 10px;
  }
  .frame{
    border: 2px solid green;
  }
</style>
<script src="https://code.jquery.com/jquery-1.12.4.min.js"></script>
<script type="text/javascript">
$(document).ready(function(){
  var arr = $("li").parents("div").addClass("frame");
});
</script>
</head>
<body>
  <div class="container">
    <h1>Hello World</h1>
    <p>This is a <em>simple paragraph</em>.</p>
    <ul>
      <li>Item One</li>
      <li>Item Two</li>
```

```
    </ul>
  </div>
</body>
</html>
```

jQuery parentsUntil() Method

The parentsUntil() method is used to get the ancestors going up to the element the selector matches, but not including that element. Simply put, the return is every ancestor element in between the two elements specified in the DOM hierarchy.

In our example, a border is added around the ancestor elements of <li> but will not include <html>. In other words, the border is added around the <body>, <div>, and <ul> elements.

```
<!DOCTYPE html>

<html lang="en">

<head>

<meta charset="utf-8">

<title>jQuery parentsUntil() Demo</title>

<style type="text/css">

  *{

    margin: 10px;

  }

  .frame{

    border: 2px solid green;

  }

</style>

<script src="https://code.jquery.com/jquery-1.12.4.min.js"></script>

<script type="text/javascript">

$(document).ready(function(){
```

```
    $("li").parentsUntil("html").addClass("frame");
});
</script>
</head>
<body>
    <div class="container">
        <h1>Hello World</h1>
        <p>This is a <em>simple paragraph</em>.</p>
        <ul>
            <li>Item One</li>
            <li>Item Two</li>
        </ul>
    </div>
</body>
</html>
```

jQuery Traversing Descendants

Next is the traversal down the DOM tree. In the logical relationships, the descendant is the child, grandchild, great-grandchild, and so on. With jQuery, there are a number of methods to traverse down the tree in single levels or multiple. This makes it easier to get to the element descendants and two of the approaches used are find() and children().

jQuery children() Method

This method is used to get the specified element's direct children. In our example, the <ul> element direct child is highlighted; this is the <li> element and we do this by adding the class called .highlight on document ready.

```html
<!DOCTYPE html>

<html lang="en">

<head>

<meta charset="utf-8">

<title>jQuery children() Demo</title>

<style type="text/css">

  .highlight{

    background: yellow;

  }

</style>

<script src="https://code.jquery.com/jquery-1.12.4.min.js"></script>

<script type="text/javascript">

$(document).ready(function(){

  $("ul").children().addClass("highlight");

});

</script>

</head>
```

```
<body>
    <div class="container">
        <h1>Hello World</h1>
        <p>This is a <em>simple paragraph</em>.</p>
        <ul>
            <li>Item One</li>
            <li>Item Two</li>
        </ul>
    </div>
</body>
</html>
```

jQuery find() Method

The jQuery find() method will get the specified element's descendant elements. Both the children() and find() methods are alike, but with one exception; find() will look through several levels, all the way down the tree, until it gets to the final descendant. With children(), only one level is searched.

The example below shows where we add borders around all <li> elements descending from the <div> element:

```
<!DOCTYPE html>

<html lang="en">

<head>

<meta charset="utf-8">

<title>jQuery find() Demo</title>

<style type="text/css">
    *{
        margin: 10px;
    }
```

```
    .frame{
        border: 2px solid green;
    }
</style>
<script src="https://code.jquery.com/jquery-1.12.4.min.js"></script>
<script type="text/javascript">
$(document).ready(function(){
    $("div").find("li").addClass("frame");
});
</script>
</head>
<body>
    <div class="container">
        <h1>Hello World</h1>
        <p>This is a <em>simple paragraph</em>.</p>
        <ul>
            <li>Item One</li>
            <li>Item Two</li>
        </ul>
    </div>
</body>
</html>
```

You can get all descendent elements easily just by using the universal selector. See the example below:

```
<!DOCTYPE html>
<html lang="en">
```

```
<head>
<meta charset="utf-8">
<title>jQuery find() Demo</title>
<style type="text/css">
  *{
    margin: 10px;
  }
  .frame{
    border: 2px solid green;
  }
</style>
<script src="https://code.jquery.com/jquery-1.12.4.min.js"></script>
<script type="text/javascript">
$(document).ready(function(){
  $("div").find("*").addClass("frame");
});
</script>
</head>
<body>
  <div class="container">
    <h1>Hello World</h1>
    <p>This is a <em>simple paragraph</em>.</p>
    <ul>
      <li>Item One</li>
      <li>Item Two</li>
```

```html
        </ul>
      </div>
   </body>
</html>
```

jQuery Traversing Siblings

Next, we look at traversing the DOM tree sideways. In logical relationships, the siblings are all the elements that have the same parent element. jQuery provides quite a few methods to use in sideways traversal, including next(), siblings(), nextAll() nextUntil(), prev(), prevAll() and prevUntil().

jQuery siblings() Method

The jQuery siblings() method is used to get all the specified element's sibling elements. In the example, the <p> element siblings are highlighted; these are the <ul> and <h1> elements and this is done by adding the class called .highlight on document ready:

```
<!DOCTYPE html>

<html lang="en">

<head>

<meta charset="utf-8">

<title>jQuery siblings() Demo</title>

<style type="text/css">

   .highlight{

      background: yellow;

   }

</style>

<script src="https://code.jquery.com/jquery-1.12.4.min.js"></script>

<script type="text/javascript">

$(document).ready(function(){

   $("p").siblings().addClass("highlight");

});

</script>

</head>
```

```
<body>

  <div class="container">

    <h1>Hello World</h1>

    <p>This is a <em>simple paragraph</em>.</p>

    <ul>

      <li>Item One</li>

      <li>Item Two</li>

    </ul>

  </div>

</body>

</html>
```

As an option, you may also, include at least one selector in the siblings() method as a parameter to filter your sibling search. In the next example, the border is only applied around the <p> element siblings that are also elements of <ul>:

```
<!DOCTYPE html>

<html lang="en">

<head>

<meta charset="utf-8">

<title>jQuery siblings() Demo</title>

<style type="text/css">

  .highlight{

    background: yellow;

  }

</style>

<script src="https://code.jquery.com/jquery-1.12.4.min.js"></script>

<script type="text/javascript">
```

```
$(document).ready(function(){
    $("p").siblings("ul").addClass("highlight");
});
</script>
</head>
<body>
    <div class="container">
        <h1>Hello World</h1>
        <p>This is a <em>simple paragraph</em>.</p>
        <ul>
            <li>Item One</li>
            <li>Item Two</li>
        </ul>
    </div>
</body>
</html>
```

jQuery next() Method

The next() method is used to get the sibling that immediately follows, i.e. the next sibling element for the specified element. In the example below, the next <p> element sibling is highlighted; this is the <ul> element:

```
<!DOCTYPE html>
<html lang="en">
<head>
<meta charset="utf-8">
<title>jQuery next() Demo</title>
<style type="text/css">
```

```
    .highlight{
        background: yellow;
    }
</style>
<script src="https://code.jquery.com/jquery-1.12.4.min.js"></script>
<script type="text/javascript">
$(document).ready(function(){
    $("p").next().addClass("highlight");
});
</script>
</head>
<body>
    <div class="container">
        <h1>Hello World</h1>
        <p>This is a <em>simple paragraph</em>.</p>
        <ul>
            <li>Item One</li>
            <li>Item Two</li>
        </ul>
    </div>
</body>
</html>
```

jQuery nextAll() Method

The nextAll() method is used to get the specified element's following element. In the example, all the <p> element siblings that come next are highlighted:

<!DOCTYPE html>

```html
<html lang="en">
<head>
<meta charset="utf-8">
<title>jQuery nextAll() Demo</title>
<style type="text/css">
  .highlight{
    background: yellow;
  }
</style>
<script src="https://code.jquery.com/jquery-1.12.4.min.js"></script>
<script type="text/javascript">
$(document).ready(function(){
  $("p").nextAll().addClass("highlight");
});
</script>
</head>
<body>
  <div class="container">
    <h1>Hello World</h1>
    <p>This is a <em>simple paragraph</em>.</p>
    <p>This is another paragraph.</p>
    <ul>
      <li>Item One</li>
      <li>Item Two</li>
    </ul>
```

```
    </div>

</body>

</html>
```

jQuery nextUntil() Method

The nextUntil() method is used to get the following siblings up to the element the selector matched, but not including that matched element. Simply, it will return every sibling element from in between two specified elements in the DOM hierarchy.

In the example, the following sibling element for <h1> will be highlighted, excluding <ul>. That means both <p> elements are highlighted.

```
<!DOCTYPE html>

<html lang="en">

<head>

<meta charset="utf-8">

<title>jQuery nextUntil() Demo</title>

<style type="text/css">

  .highlight{

    background: yellow;

  }

</style>

<script src="https://code.jquery.com/jquery-1.12.4.min.js"></script>

<script type="text/javascript">

$(document).ready(function(){

  $("h1").nextUntil("ul").addClass("highlight");

});

</script>

</head>

<body>
```

```
<div class="container">

  <h1>Hello World</h1>

  <p>This is a <em>simple paragraph</em>.</p>

  <p>This is another paragraph.</p>

  <ul>

    <li>Item One</li>

    <li>Item Two</li>

  </ul>

</div>

</body>

</html>
```

jQuery prev() Method

The jQuery prev() method is used to get the immediate sibling preceding the selected element. In the following example, the previous <ul> element sibling, which is <p>, is highlighted:

```
<!DOCTYPE html>

<html lang="en">

<head>

<meta charset="utf-8">

<title>jQuery prev() Demo</title>

<style type="text/css">

  .highlight{

    background: yellow;

  }

</style>

<script src="https://code.jquery.com/jquery-1.12.4.min.js"></script>
```

```
<script type="text/javascript">
$(document).ready(function(){
    $("ul").prev().addClass("highlight");
});
</script>
</head>
<body>
    <div class="container">
        <h1>Hello World</h1>
        <p>This is a <em>simple paragraph</em>.</p>
        <p>This is another paragraph.</p>
        <ul>
            <li>Item One</li>
            <li>Item Two</li>
        </ul>
    </div>
</body>
</html>
```

jQuery prevAll() Method

The prevAll() method can be used to get the selected element's preceding siblings. In the next example, the <ul> element siblings that come before it are highlighted:

```
<!DOCTYPE html>
<html lang="en">
<head>
<meta charset="utf-8">
<title>jQuery prevAll() Demo</title>
```

```html
<style type="text/css">
  .highlight{
    background: yellow;
  }
</style>
<script src="https://code.jquery.com/jquery-1.12.4.min.js"></script>
<script type="text/javascript">
$(document).ready(function(){
  $("ul").prevAll().addClass("highlight");
});
</script>
</head>
<body>
  <div class="container">
    <h1>Hello World</h1>
    <p>This is a <em>simple paragraph</em>.</p>
    <p>This is another paragraph.</p>
    <ul>
      <li>Item One</li>
      <li>Item Two</li>
    </ul>
  </div>
</body>
</html>
```

jQuery prevUntil() Method

Lastly, the prevUntil() method is used to get the preceding elements that go up to the element the selector matches but not including the matched element. Simply put, all previous sibling elements are returned from in between two specified elements.

In the next example, the previous sibling elements for the <ul> element are highlighted. Both the <p> elements are highlighted but the <h1> element is not.

```
<!DOCTYPE html>

<html lang="en">

<head>

<meta charset="utf-8">

<title>jQuery prevUntil() Demo</title>

<style type="text/css">

   .highlight{

      background: yellow;

   }

</style>

<script src="https://code.jquery.com/jquery-1.12.4.min.js"></script>

<script type="text/javascript">

$(document).ready(function(){

   $("ul").prevUntil("h1").addClass("highlight");

});

</script>

</head>

<body>

   <div class="container">

      <h1>Hello World</h1>
```

```
    <p>This is a <em>simple paragraph</em>.</p>
    <p>This is another paragraph.</p>
    <ul>
      <li>Item One</li>
      <li>Item Two</li>
    </ul>
  </div>
</body>
</html>
```

jQuery Filtering

Now we'll look at using jQuery to filter the selection of the elements. With jQuery, there are quite a few methods to use to narrow the element search down, including filter(), first(), last(), slice(), eq(), not(), has(), etc.

jQuery first() Method

The first() method is used to filter the matched element set and return the first one. In the next example, only the first <li> element inside the <ul> element is highlighted; to do this, the class called .highlight is added on document ready:

```html
<!DOCTYPE html>

<html lang="en">

<head>

<meta charset="utf-8">

<title>jQuery first() Demo</title>

<style type="text/css">

   .highlight{

     background: yellow;

   }

</style>

<script src="https://code.jquery.com/jquery-1.12.4.min.js"></script>

<script type="text/javascript">

$(document).ready(function(){

   $("ul li").first().addClass("highlight");

});

</script>

</head>

<body>
```

```
<ul>

    <li>First list item</li>

    <li>Second list item</li>

    <li>Third list item</li>

    <li>Last list item</li>

  </ul>

</body>

</html>
```

jQuery last() Method

With the last() method, the matched element set can be filtered and will return the final element. In the next example, only the last <li> element in the <ul> element is highlighted; again, this is done by adding the class called .highlight on document ready:

```
<!DOCTYPE html>

<html lang="en">

<head>

<meta charset="utf-8">

<title>jQuery last() Demo</title>

<style type="text/css">

  .highlight{

    background: yellow;

  }

</style>

<script src="https://code.jquery.com/jquery-1.12.4.min.js"></script>

<script type="text/javascript">

$(document).ready(function(){

  $("ul li").last().addClass("highlight");
```

```
});
</script>
</head>
<body>
  <ul>
    <li>First list item</li>
    <li>Second list item</li>
    <li>Third list item</li>
    <li>Last list item</li>
  </ul>
</body>
</html>
```

jQuery eq() Method

With the eq() method, the matched element set can be filtered to return just one element that has a given index number. In the example, the second <li> element in the <ul> element is highlighted; the .highlight class is added on document ready:

```
<!DOCTYPE html>
<html lang="en">
<head>
<meta charset="utf-8">
<title>jQuery eq() Demo</title>
<style type="text/css">
  .highlight{
    background: yellow;
  }
</style>
```

```
<script src="https://code.jquery.com/jquery-1.12.4.min.js"></script>
<script type="text/javascript">
$(document).ready(function(){
    $("ul li").eq(1).addClass("highlight");
});
</script>
</head>
<body>
    <ul>
        <li>First list item</li>
        <li>Second list item</li>
        <li>Third list item</li>
        <li>Last list item</li>
    </ul>
</body>
</html>
```

Note

The index that is given to the eq() method indicates the element's 0-based position; index 0 is targeting the first element, index 1, the second element and so on. The index is also referring to the element's position inside the jQuery object and not the DOM tree.

Negative index numbers can also be specified; these indicate a position starting at the end and not the beginning of a set. For example, eq(-2) would indicate the element that is second from last in the set.

```
<!DOCTYPE html>
<html lang="en">
<head>
<meta charset="utf-8">
```

```
<title>jQuery eq() Demo</title>
<style type="text/css">
  .highlight{
    background: yellow;
  }
</style>
<script src="https://code.jquery.com/jquery-1.12.4.min.js"></script>
<script type="text/javascript">
$(document).ready(function(){
  $("ul li").eq(-2).addClass("highlight");
});
</script>
</head>
<body>
  <ul>
    <li>First list item</li>
    <li>Second list item</li>
    <li>Third list item</li>
    <li>Fourth list item</li>
  </ul>
</body>
</html>
```

jQuery filter() Method

The filter() method takes a function or the selector as the arguments; it will then filter the matched element set based on given criteria. The selector or the function supplied to the filter() method will be tested against all the elements in the set individually; the result will include all the elements that match the selector or pass the test given by the function.

```html
<!DOCTYPE html>
<html lang="en">
<head>
<meta charset="utf-8">
<title>jQuery filter() Demo</title>
<style type="text/css">
  .highlight{
    background: yellow;
  }
</style>
<script src="https://code.jquery.com/jquery-1.12.4.min.js"></script>
<script type="text/javascript">
$(document).ready(function(){
  $("ul li").filter(":even").addClass("highlight");
});
</script>
</head>
<body>
  <ul>
    <li>First list item</li>
    <li>Second list item</li>
    <li>Third list item</li>
    <li>Fourth list item</li>
  </ul>
```

```
</body>

</html>
```

As mentioned earlier, functions can also be passed to filter() providing specific conditions to filter the element set. In the next example, every <li> element in <ul> is tested and those with odd numbered indexes are highlighted. Only the second and the fourth items will be highlighted because the index is zero-based.

```html
<!DOCTYPE html>

<html lang="en">

<head>

<meta charset="utf-8">

<title>jQuery filter() Demo</title>

<style type="text/css">

  .highlight{

    background: yellow;

  }

</style>

<script src="https://code.jquery.com/jquery-1.12.4.min.js"></script>

<script type="text/javascript">

$(document).ready(function(){

  $("ul li").filter(function(index){

    return index % 2 !== 0;

  }).addClass("highlight");

});

</script>

</head>

<body>
```

```html
<ul>
    <li>First list item</li>
    <li>Second list item</li>
    <li>Third list item</li>
    <li>Last list item</li>
</ul>
</body>
</html>
```

jQuery has() Method

The has() method is used to filter the matched element set and return the elements that have the descendant element specified. In the next example, all the <li> elements with descendent <ul> elements are highlighted:

```
<!DOCTYPE html>

<html lang="en">

<head>

<meta charset="utf-8">

<title>jQuery filter() Demo</title>

<style type="text/css">

   .highlight{

      background: yellow;

   }

</style>

<script src="https://code.jquery.com/jquery-1.12.4.min.js"></script>

<script type="text/javascript">

$(document).ready(function(){

   $("ul li").has("ul").addClass("highlight");

});

</script>

</head>

<body>

   <ul>

      <li>Section 1</li>

      <li>Section 2</li>
```

```
      <li>
        <ul>
          <li>Section 2.1</li>
          <li>Section 2.2</li>
          <li>Section 2.3</li>
        </ul>
      </li>
      <li>Section 4</li>
    </ul>
  </body>
</html>
```

jQuery not() Method

With the not() method, the set of elements can be filtered and return all those elements that do NOT meet the conditions specified. A function or the selector may be passed as the argument to the method.

The function or the selector supplied to not() will be tested against every element in the set of elements individually; all elements that do NOT match the selector or [as the function test are returned in the result.

```
<!DOCTYPE html>

<html lang="en">

<head>

<meta charset="utf-8">

<title>jQuery not() Demo</title>

<style type="text/css">

  .highlight{

    background: yellow;

  }
```

```
</style>
<script src="https://code.jquery.com/jquery-1.12.4.min.js"></script>
<script type="text/javascript">
$(document).ready(function(){
    $("ul li").not(":even").addClass("highlight");
});
</script>
</head>
<body>
    <ul>
        <li>First list item</li>
        <li>Second list item</li>
        <li>Third list item</li>
        <li>Fourth list item</li>
    </ul>
</body>
</html>
```

In a similar way to filter(), the not() method can also take functions as arguments. However, it works in the opposite way to the filter() method, i.e. the elements passing the test from the function will be left out of the results, while everything else is included.

The next example tests each of the <li> elements in the <ul> element individually; all the <li> elements with even indexes are highlighted. Because the index is zero-based, the first and third items are highlighted.

```
<!DOCTYPE html>
<html lang="en">
<head>
<meta charset="utf-8">
```

```
<title>jQuery not() Demo</title>
<style type="text/css">
  .highlight{
    background: yellow;
  }
</style>
<script src="https://code.jquery.com/jquery-1.12.4.min.js"></script>
<script type="text/javascript">
$(document).ready(function(){
  $("ul li").not(function(index){
    return index % 2 !== 0;
  }).addClass("highlight");
});
</script>
</head>
<body>
  <ul>
    <li>First list item</li>
    <li>Second list item</li>
    <li>Third list item</li>
    <li>Fourth list item</li>
  </ul>
</body>
</html>
```

jQuery slice() Method

With the slice() method, a set of matched elements using a specified range of indices can be filtered. The slice() method will accept optional start and end index numbers as the arguments. The start index is specifying what index position the range starts, while end specifies the last one to be included.

In the next example, the first and the second <li> elements inside the <ul> element are highlighted; the class called .highlight is added on document ready:

```
<!DOCTYPE html>

<html lang="en">

<head>

<meta charset="utf-8">

<title>jQuery slice() Demo</title>

<style type="text/css">

   .highlight{

      background: yellow;

   }

</style>

<script src="https://code.jquery.com/jquery-1.12.4.min.js"></script>

<script type="text/javascript">

$(document).ready(function(){

   $("ul li").slice(0, 2).addClass("highlight");

});

</script>

</head>

<body>

   <ul>

      <li>First list item</li>
```

```
    <li>Second list item</li>

    <li>Third list item</li>

    <li>Fourth list item</li>

  </ul>

</body>

</html>
```

It is also possible to specify negative numbers. Negative index numbers start from the end of the matched element set and not the beginning. For example, slice(-2, -1) will highlight the third item; it is the only one within the range of two from the end (-2) and one from the end (-1) – the result does not include the end position.

```
<!DOCTYPE html>

<html lang="en">

<head>

<meta charset="utf-8">

<title>jQuery slice() Demo</title>

<style type="text/css">

  .highlight{

    background: yellow;

  }

</style>

<script src="https://code.jquery.com/jquery-1.12.4.min.js"></script>

<script type="text/javascript">

$(document).ready(function(){

  $("ul li").slice(-2, -1).addClass("highlight");

});

</script>
```

```html
    </head>
    <body>
        <ul>
            <li>First list item</li>
            <li>Second list item</li>
            <li>Third list item</li>
            <li>Fourth list item</li>
        </ul>
    </body>
</html>
```

Part 3: Ajax

We'll start by discussing at what Ajax is and how it works with jQuery before we move on to creating Ajax using regular scripts.

What is Ajax?

Ajax is an acronym for Asynchronous JavaScript and XML. It is nothing more than a way to load data from a server onto a web browser without having to reload the entire page.

In short, Ajax uses the XMLHttpRequest object, which is JavaScript-based, to send information to a web browser and receive it asynchronously. It does this in the background without interfering with or interrupting a user's experience.

Ajax is now incredibly popular and you will find it hard to find an application that hasn't made use of it in some way. Some of the largest online applications driven by Ajax are YouTube, Facebook, Google Docs, Google Maps, Gmail, Flickr and so on.

It is worth noting this is by no means a new technology. In fact, it is safe to say that it isn't a technology; more of a term describing a process in which data is exchanged asynchronously between server and browser, using JavaScript, with no page refresh necessary.

Ajax with jQuery

Every browser will implement Ajax in a different way. If the standard JavaScript method of implementing Ajax is used, it will need a different code for different browsers to make sure it works cross-browser.

With jQuery, those cross-browser differences are taken care of. Using simple methods, like $.set(), $.get() and load(), Ajax works seamlessly regardless of the browser.

Let's have a brief overview of these methods before going more in-depth and use the same methods in context with web design.

Tip

JavaScript code is what triggers the Ajax requests; the code will send the request to a specified URL. When the request has completed, the code then triggers a callback function so the response can be handled. As this is an asynchronous request, the rest of the code carries on executing at the time the request s processing.

jQuery load() Method

The load() method is used to load the data from a server and then put the HTML that is returned into a specified element. This method is a trouble-free way of asynchronously loading data from a server. The basic syntax is:

$(selector).load(URL, data, complete);

The load() method parameters are:

- The URL parameter is required; it will specify the URL of the file you want to be loaded.
- The data parameter is optional; it will specify a set of query strings, for example, a list of key/value pairs, which are sent with the request to the webserver.
- The complete parameter is also optional; it is a callback function that will be executed once the request is complete. It will fire just once for each of the specified elements.

Let's do something practical with this. Create an HTML file (a blank one) and call it 'test-content.html'. Save it on your web server and then add the following code into the file:

<h1>Easy Ajax Demo</h1>

<p id="hint">This is an easy example of Ajax loading.</p>

<p><img src="sky.jpg" alt="Cloudy Sky"></p>

Create another HTML file and call it 'load-demo.html' and save it in the same place on the server as the last one. Add the following code to it:

<!DOCTYPE html>

<html lang="en">

<head>

<meta charset="utf-8">

<title>jQuery load() Demo</title>

<script src="https://code.jquery.com/jquery-1.12.4.min.js"></script>

<script type="text/javascript">

$(document).ready(function(){

```
$("button").click(function(){

    $("#box").load("test-content.html");

  });

});

</script>

</head>

<body>

  <div id="box">

    <h2>Click the button to load the new content inside the DIV box</h2>

  </div>

  <button type="button">Load Content</button>

</body>

</html>
```

Lastly, open the page in your browser and click on the button that says, "load content". The contents of the DIV box are replaced with the HTML content from your 'test-content.html' file.

Tip

For this example to be tested, the HTML files must go on a web server. If you want to set up a local server on your computer, install XAMPP or WampServer. Because Ajax only makes HTTP requests, the demo file must be opened using http://.

Note

You can only make an Ajax request to a file that is on the webserver used to serve the page from which the request is sent. For security reasons, those requests cannot be made to remote or external servers. This is known as the same-origin policy.

The callback function can also have three parameters:

- responseTxt – If the request is successful, this will contain the content that results from it.
- statusTxt – This will contain each request status, like error or success.
- jqXHR – This will contain the XMLHttpRequest object.

Below is a modified version of the last example. This will display the error or success message to a user as per the request status:

```html
<!DOCTYPE html>

<html lang="en">

<head>

<meta charset="utf-8">

<title>jQuery load() Demo</title>

<script src="https://code.jquery.com/jquery-1.12.4.min.js"></script>

<script type="text/javascript">

$(document).ready(function(){

   $("button").click(function(){

      $("#box").load("test-content.html", function(responseTxt, statusTxt, jqXHR){

         if(statusTxt == "success"){

            alert("New content successfully loaded!");

         }

         if(statusTxt == "error"){

            alert("Error: " + jqXHR.status + " " + jqXHR.statusText);

         }

      });

   });

});

</script>

</head>

<body>

   <div id="box">

      <h2>Click the button to load the new content inside the DIV box</h2>
```

```
</div>

    <button type="button">Load Content</button>

</body>

</html>
```

Loading Page Fragments

The load() method can be used to fetch a small part of the document. This is done very simply – the URL parameter is appended with a space and a jQuery selector. The next example should make this clearer:

```
<!DOCTYPE html>

<html lang="en">

<head>

<meta charset="utf-8">

<title>jQuery load() Demo</title>

<script src="https://code.jquery.com/jquery-1.12.4.min.js"></script>

<script type="text/javascript">

$(document).ready(function(){

  $("button").click(function(){

    $("#box").load("test-content.html #hint");

  });

});

</script>

</head>

<body>

  <div id="box">

    <h2>Click the button to load the new content inside the DIV box</h2>

  </div>
```

```
<button type="button">Load Content</button>

</body>

</html>
```

This is a selector called #hint inside the URL parameter. This specifies a part of the 'test-content' file that is wanted to go inside the DIV box. This is an element with the ID attribute and a value hint, for example id-"hint" (see our first example).

jQuery $.get() and $.post() Methods

The GET and POST methods send data to and receive it from a web server using Ajax. Both methods are comparable with one large variance - $.get() uses HTTP GET to makes the Ajax request while $.post() uses HTTP POST.

The syntax of these methods are:

$.get(URL, data, success);

$.post(URL, data, success);

The parameters in these methods are:

- The URL parameter is required; it is used to specify to which URL to send the request.
- The data parameter is optional; it is used to specify query strings sent with the request to the server.
- The success parameter is also optional; it is a callback function that only executes for a successful request and is used to retrieve the returned data.

Using jQuery to Perform GET Request

In the next example, the $.get() method is used to make an Ajax request to the file called "date-time.php"; to do this, the HTTP GET method is used. All it does is retrieve or get the data and time the server returns and shows it in the browser without needing to do a page refresh.

<!DOCTYPE html>

<html lang="en">

<head>

<meta charset="utf-8">

<title>jQuery get() Demo</title>

<script src="https://code.jquery.com/jquery-1.12.4.min.js"></script>

<script type="text/javascript">

$(document).ready(function(){

  $("button").click(function(){

```
    $.get("date-time.php", function(data){
        // Display the returned data in browser
        $("#result").html(data);
    });
  });
});
</script>
</head>
<body>
  <div id="result">
      <h2>Content of the result DIV box is replaced by date and time from the server</h2>
  </div>
  <button type="button">Load Date and Time</button>
</body>
</html>
```

For reference, the "date-time.php" file is this:

```
<?php
// Return current date and time from the server
echo date("F d, Y h:i:s A");
?>
```

The request can also be used to send the server some data. In the next example, the code makes a request to a table called "create-table.php" at the same time as sending extra data to the server:

```
<!DOCTYPE html>
<html lang="en">
```

```html
<head>
<meta charset="utf-8">
<title>jQuery get() Demo</title>
<script src="https://code.jquery.com/jquery-1.12.4.min.js"></script>
<script type="text/javascript">
$(document).ready(function(){
   $("button").click(function(){
      // Get the value from the input element on the page
      var numValue = $("#num").val();

      // Send the input data to the server using get
      $.get("create-table.php", {number: numValue} , function(data){
         // Display the returned data in the browser
         $("#result").html(data);
      });
   });
});
</script>
</head>
<body>
   <label>Enter a Number: <input type="text" id="num"></label>
   <button type="button">Show Multiplication Table</button>
   <div id="result"></div>
</body>
</html>
```

For reference, this is the "create-table.php" file:

```php
<?php
$number = htmlspecialchars($_GET["number"]);
if(is_numeric($number) && $number > 0){
    echo "<table>";
  for($i=0; $i<11; $i++){
    echo "<tr>";
      echo "<td>$number x $i</td>";
      echo "<td>=</td>";
      echo "<td>" . $number * $i . "</td>";
    echo "</tr>";
  }
  echo "</table>";
}
?>
```

Using jQuery to Perform POST Request

The POST requests are quite the same as the GET requests and depend entirely on what your server-side code requires. If you have a lot of data that needs to be transmitted, such as form data, you must use POST because GET is strictly limited on how much data can be transferred.

```html
<!DOCTYPE html>
<html lang="en">
<head>
<meta charset="utf-8">
<title>jQuery post() Demo</title>
<script src="https://code.jquery.com/jquery-1.12.4.min.js"></script>
```

```
<script type="text/javascript">
$(document).ready(function(){
  $("form").submit(function(event){
    // Stop form from submitting normally
    event.preventDefault();

    /* The submitted form control values being sent with the request to the server must be serialized */
    var formValues = $(this).serialize();

    // Send the form data using post
    $.post("display-comment.php", formValues, function(data){
      // Display the returned data in browser
      $("#result").html(data);
    });
  });
});
</script>
</head>
<body>
  <form>
    <label>Name: <input type="text" name="name"></label>
    <label>Comment: <textarea cols="50" name="comment"></textarea></label>
    <input type="submit" value="Send">
  </form>
  <div id="result"></div>
```

```
</body>

</html>
```

For reference, this is the "display-comment.php" file:

```php
<?php

$name = htmlspecialchars($_POST["name"]);

$comment = htmlspecialchars($_POST["comment"]);

echo "Hi, $name. Your comment has been successfully received." . "<br>";

echo "This is the comment you entered: $comment";

?>
```

Now you know how to use basic jQuery methods to do AJAX operations, such as load data, submit forms, and so on asynchronously, we'll move on to the No-Conflict mode.

jQuery No-Conflict Mode

One crucial thing to know is how to evade conflict arising between jQuery and any other JavaScript framework or library. As you already learned, the $ (dollar) sign is used as a short way of saying jQuery. So, if you make use of other libraries that also have that dollar sign for a shortcut on the same page as the jQuery library, you may find they conflict with one another. Once again, jQuery comes to rescue and gives a special method to deal with this.

jQuery noConflict() Method

This technique will return full control of the $ identifier to the other libraries in use. In the next example, line 10 places jQuery into no-conflict more the second it is loaded on the page; a new variable name of $j is assigned in place of $ so no conflicts arise with the prototype framework:

```
<!DOCTYPE html>

<html lang="en">

<head>

<meta charset="utf-8">

<title>jQuery noConflict() Demo</title>

<script src="js/prototype.js"></script>

<script src="js/jquery.js"></script>

<script type="text/javascript">

// Defining the new alias for jQuery

var $j = jQuery.noConflict();

$j(document).ready(function(){

    // Display alert message when element with ID foo is clicked

    $j("#foo").click(function(){

        alert("jQuery is working OK with prototype.");

    });
```

```
});

// Some prototype framework code
document.observe("dom:loaded", function(){
    // Display alert message when element with ID bar is clicked
    $(bar).observe('click', function(event){
        alert("Prototype is working OK with jQuery.");
    });
});
</script>
</head>
<body>
    <button type="button" id="foo">Run jQuery Code</button>
    <button type="button" id="bar">Run Prototype Code</button>
</body>
</html>
```

If you don't want to go down the route of defining new shortcuts for jQuery, perhaps because you don't want your code modified or you find $ simpler to use, there is another way to do it – pass $ to the jQuery(document).ready() function, like the example below:

```
<!DOCTYPE html>
<html lang="en">
<head>
<meta charset="utf-8">
<title>jQuery noConflict() Demo</title>
<script src="js/prototype.js"></script>
<script src="js/jquery.js"></script>
```

```
<script type="text/javascript">
jQuery.noConflict();
jQuery(document).ready(function($){
    // The dollar sign works as a jQuery shortcut
    $("#foo").click(function(){
        alert("jQuery is working OK with prototype.");
    });
});


// Some prototype framework code
document.observe("dom:loaded", function(){
    // The dollar sign in global scope is referring to the prototype
    $(bar).observe('click', function(event){
        alert("Prototype is working OK with jQuery.");
    });
});
</script>
</head>
<body>
    <button type="button" id="foo">Run jQuery Code</button>
    <button type="button" id="bar">Run Prototype Code</button>
</body>
</html>
```

While these solutions will avoid the conflicts, they do rely on prototype.js being loaded before jQuery. Load jQuery first, before any other library, including the full name of jQuery in your code – this will circumvent the clash without the need to call no-conflict(). However, in this, the $ will use the meaning that the other library defines.

```html
<!DOCTYPE html>

<html lang="en">

<head>

<meta charset="utf-8">

<title>jQuery noConflict() Demo</title>

<script src="js/jquery.js"></script>

<script src="js/prototype.js"></script>

<script type="text/javascript">

jQuery(document).ready(function($){

    // Use full jQuery function name to reference jQuery

    jQuery("#foo").click(function(){

        alert("jQuery is working OK with prototype.");

    });

});


// Some prototype framework code

document.observe("dom:loaded", function(){

    // The dollar sign has the meaning defined in prototype

    $(bar).observe('click', function(event){

        alert("Prototype is working OK with jQuery.");

    });

});

</script>

</head>
```

```
<body>

    <button type="button" id="foo">Run jQuery Code</button>

    <button type="button" id="bar">Run Prototype Code</button>

</body>

</html>
```

That's the basics dealt with. It's time to move on to something more complex.

XHR Feature Detection

We will now discuss writing Ajax feature detection using pure JavaScript -this is ONLY to put things into a historical perspective- so you can see how things have changed. This is compulsory above all for those using Internet Explorer 6 or lower – timeworn and not many people use them at the present time. These days, jQuery takes care of feature detection.

Since it was first defined by Jesse James Garret in 2005, Ajax has grown significantly. Not only did it describe a method to create web applications that were more robust, but it also helped make JavaScript an incredibly popular language for web programming and design.

Many developers are still not aware of how Ajax has advanced in jQuery so, to help explain, we'll go back to the early days first.

Until Internet Explorer 7, XHR implementation in Microsoft was unlike all the other browsers. That was because XMLHTTP could not be accessed directly in the browser by using window.XMLHTTP in your code.

Instead, it was placed inside ActiveXObject Microsoft technology. Ajax became very popular at this time but it meant that feature detection code was needed to ensure Ajax code would work across all browsers.

The simple version of that code looked something like this:

// Feature-detect XMLHttpRequest implementation

var xhr;

if (window.XMLHttpRequest) { // Browsers other than IE 6 and lower

* xhr = new XMLHttpRequest();*

} else {

* if (window.ActiveXObject) { // For IE 6 and lower*

*   xhr = new ActiveXObject("Microsoft.XMLHTTP");*

* }*

}

In this example, a variable named xhr is created. It is then checked to make sure that XMLHttpRequest was attached to the window object for the browser. If it did, xhr referenced a new XMLHttpRequest instance directly when Ajax tasks were performed.

The code also checked if ActiveXObject had been attached via the window object to the browser. If yes, xhr would reference as new ActiveXObject directly when Ajax tasks were carried out.

Later, developers discovered that window.ActiveXObject was used in different ways across older Internet Explorer versions and they also realized some of the browsers used by many individuals didn't have support for XHR. The result was an update to the feature detection code:

```
// Feature-detect XMLHttpRequest implementation

// Better detecting of ActiveX

function getXHR() {

 var xhr;

 if (window.XMLHttpRequest) { // Browsers other than IE 6 and lower

  xhr = new XMLHttpRequest();

 } else {

  try { // Browsers with one type of ActiveXObject build

   xhr = new ActiveXObject("Msxml2.XMLHTTP");

  } catch (e) {

   try { // Browsers with a different type of ActiveXObject build

    xhr = new ActiveXObject("Microsoft.XMLHTTP");

   } catch (e) {

    // Browsers that don't support XMLHttpRequest or ActiveXObject

    xhr = false;

   }

  }

 }
```

return xhr;

}

The code was rewritten so that it was a function called getXHR, which could be reused. It checked across the browsers internally for XMLHttpRequest; any new getXHR instance would make use of XHR without having to worry about cross-browser problems.

Also, getXHR looked for XMLHttpRequest as well as looked to see if the browser had one of the two ActiveXObject builds, along with checking if ActiveXObject or XMLHttpRequest actually existed.

To look for all the different ActiveXObject versions, a Javascript try...catch statement was used. If the statement didn't find ActiveXObject or XMLHttpRequest, the xhr variable value was set as false and no Ajax work would be carried out.

At the end of the code, getXHR said to return xhr and this allowed new getXHR instances to be created externally to the function.

Enough of the history, let's move on to using Ajax to load page content.

Load Page Content with Ajax

The process of loading content using XHR takes four steps:

1. A new instance of the XHR object is created.
2. Wait until we have an XHR state of 4.
3. Wait for the server to return a 200 response code.
4. Everything is brought together with "onreadystatechange".

Let's explain these steps one at a time.

Step 1: Creating the new XHR object instance

While there are some instances to include the XHR feature detection, normally this is because the Ajax code requires Internet Explorer 6 or below to run. These browsers don't tend to be used these days so it is sensible to keep it out of the code and go down the route of creating a direct instance of XHR:

var xhr = new XMLHttpRequest();

Step 2: Wait until we have an XHR state of 4

XHR requests come in five different states, each with a number value starting from 0 through to 4. The final request state, 4, is the more important one, but before we move on, let's have a look at a brief description of each state. There are two specifications of XHR states that are widely accepted – WHATWG definition and Microsoft.

The WHATWG definition has five states with number values:

- 0 – everything is in UNSENT state – the code is aware that an xhr instance has been created but nothing is happening.
- 1 – everything is in OPEN state – the open() method is invoked in the code and, if any data needs to be sent to a server, it can be done using the send() method.
- 2 – everything is in the HEADERS_RECEIVED state – when you download headers, the state is set as 2 once they are all downloaded.
- 3 – everything is in the LOADING state – all data is loading.
- 4 – everything is in the DONE state – the data has fully downloaded or an error occurred during the download.

The Microsoft definition is much shorter but also uses numbers:

- 0 – uninitialized
- 1 – loading
- 2 – loaded
- 3 – interactive
- 4 – complete

Step 3 – Wait for the server to return a 200 response code

Web servers will send multiple response codes, each one in numerical format. The most important one for Ajax is 200 OK. When the code sees this response, it will know the server request by XHR has been successful.

Step 4 – Use "onreadystatechange" to bring it all together

This "onreadystatechange" is an event handler used to watch for the point when readystate changes and readystate is always going to have a number value of 0 to 4. Although there are times when you will want to know whenever the state value changes, the most important change with Ajax is to 4 – done.

When readystate equals 4 and onreadystatechange comprehends this, it will recognize all data is successfully downloaded and can be used in the Ajax code. It may also mean the download was not successful, but for the purpose of this section, we'll be writing in a way that our final code is effective.

<!DOCTYPE html>

<html lang="en">

```
<head>
  <meta charset="UTF-8">
  <title>Sample 03</title>
</head>
<body&ht;
  <div id="textTarget"></div>
  <script src="scripts.js"></script>
</body>
</html>
```

Note that we added a div tag into index.html, with a "textTarget" ID. The Ajax code loads data into that element.

```
// sample01/scripts.js
var getArticleInfo = new XMLHttpRequest();


getArticleInfo.onreadystatechange = loadText;
getArticleInfo.open("GET", "articleName.txt");
getArticleInfo.send();


function loadText() {
  var text = document.getElementById("textTarget");
  if (getArticleInfo.readyState === 4) {
   if (getArticleInfo.status === 200) {
    text.innerHTML = getArticleInfo.responseText;
   } else {
    console.log('There was a problem with the request.');
   }
```

}

};

On reviewing the code:

var getArticleInfo = new XMLHttpRequest();

We can see that a new instance of XHR has been created and named getArticleInfo.

getArticleInfo.onreadystatechange = loadText;

getArticleInfo.open("GET", "articleName.txt");

getArticleInfo.send();

For the moment, getArticleInfo.onreadystatechange will run a function named loadText whenever the state changes. What is needed is to write the code ensuring loadText can only run when the state is equal to 4.

Note the open() method used in the above code. This is an XHR method and is an essential part of any Ajax application. Why? Because this is the technique dictating the data that needs to be loaded to the page.

First, getArticleInfo.open() described the method to get the data. The first parameter, GET, took care of this by telling the servers to "get" something.

The second parameter for getArticleInfo.open() described what needed to be retrieved, i.e. the data. In this code, we were looking for a file named articleName.txt.

The data request is sent to the server by getArticleInfo.send(). When we use GET, the default value is null, but if used with POST, a parameter can be passed to send().

function loadText() {

...

};

Start building the loadText() function defined above.

var text = document.getElementById("textTarget");

A variable reference to the <div id= "textTarget"> in index.html is stored

```
if (getArticleInfo.readyState === 4) {

  if (getArticleInfo.status === 200) {

    text.innerHTML = getArticleInfo.responseText;

  } else {

    console.log("There was a problem with the request.");

  }

}
```

In this code, we checked first if getArticleInfo.readyState was beyond doubt equal to 4. If yes, the data would download.

Next, we wanted to check if getArticleInfo.status was equal to 200. If yes, the code has successfully made contact with the server.

The code then locates the <div id= "textTarget"> element on the page referenced by the variable called text, and placed the content of getArticleInfo.responseText inside. This is referring to data that getArticleInfo.open() requested, the articleName.txt file. The copy from the file was placed into <div id= "textTarget">.

If a connection to the server was not made by the code and getArticleInfo.status wasn't equal to 200, a message would have been displayed stating that "There was a problem with the request".

Important Note

The message would only be displayed in the event the getArticleInfo.status wasn't equal to 200. Note that the getArticleInfo.readyState wouldn't have affected the console message appearing or not appearing.

As we said earlier, it is possible to load Ajax in various document types, so instead of loading in a text document, we could tell getArticleInfo.open() to load in an HTML one:

// sample02/scripts.js

// Update the getArticleInfo.open() method only

// Replace articleName.txt with articleName.html in the directory

...

getArticleInfo.open("GET", "articleName.html");

...

Run a Callback Function Using readyStateChange

By this time, we have used readyStateChange to request data using loadText(), a named function. There is also a callback function to request data:

// sample03/scripts.js

var getArticleInfo = new XMLHttpRequest();

getArticleInfo.open("GET", "articleName.txt");

getArticleInfo.send();


```
getArticleInfo.onreadystatechange = function() {
  var text = document.getElementById("textTarget");
  if (getArticleInfo.readyState === 4) {
    if (getArticleInfo.status === 200) {
      text.innerHTML = getArticleInfo.responseText;
    } else {
      console.log('There was a problem with the request.');
    }
  }
};
```

At once, getArticleInfo.onreadystatechange ran the callback function rather than a named function, which makes the code run that little bit faster.

Using && Will Generate Errors

In this section, we'll be looking at how you should NOT do both status and readyState checks. This is purely a demo and has no bearing or effect whatsoever on the examples.

The code we used checked the readyState values first and then it went on to check the status code for the server. Some developers use &&, which is the logical AND operator to check for both values simultaneously.

The code would look something like this:

```
// sample04/scripts.js

// Update the getArticleInfo.onreadystatechange callback function only

...

getArticleInfo.onreadystatechange = function() {

  var text = document.getElementById("textTarget");

  if ((getArticleInfo.readyState === 4) && (getArticleInfo.status === 200)) {

    text.innerHTML = getArticleInfo.responseText;

  } else {

    console.log("There was a problem with the request.");

  }

};
```

XMLHttpRequest would likely have requested the data and displayed it without error, but the error message was displayed on the console anyway. Why? Because the code did just one specific check.

When the logical AND operator is used, the code will only Ajax in the content if the value of getArticleInfo.readyState equaled 4 and the value of getArticleInfo.status equaled 200 at the same time. However, that wasn't all that ensued in our example.

Sometimes, getArticleInfo.readyState was equal to 0 through 3 and there could also have been a time when getArticleInfo.readyState was equal to 2 while getArticleInfo.status was equal to anything but 200 at the same time.

Because no functionality was defined for any other use case, the message was returned on the console. It didn't matter the data was correctly displayed; the error message was returned regardless.

When you use && in this context, it does not do a thorough check of the state of the application, so it is best to avoid it.

Use a Mouse Click to Make an Ajax Request

In our examples so far, we have used Ajax to automatically load data. We can also load data using events and using mouse clicks is a common way of doing this:

...

Load the HTML file

```
<div id="textTarget"></div>
```

What we did here was add a button tag that has an ID getHTMLFile and this was added above <div id="textTarget">. When this button is clicked on, the contents of the specified HTML file are loaded in the div tag.

```
// sample05/scripts.js

function loadHTML() {

  var getInfo = new XMLHttpRequest();


  getInfo.open("GET", "articleName.html");

  getInfo.send();


  getInfo.onreadystatechange = function() {

    var text = document.getElementById("textTarget");

    if (getInfo.readyState === 4) {

      if (getInfo.status === 200) {

        text.innerHTML = getInfo.responseText;

      } else {

        console.log('There was a problem with the request.');

      }

    }

  }
```

}

// Code that loads the data on a button click

document.getElementById("getHTMLFile").addEventListener("click", loadHTML);

The Ajax code was all put into a loadHTML function and new code was added at the bottom to run the function when the button was clicked. The addEventListener method was attached to the button that has the ID getHTMLFile.

Here, that button was inspecting for the specified event, in our case, a button click. When the code detected that click, the loadHTML function was run and the Ajax code processed.

Multiple Buttons with Ajax Functionality

We can also create buttons to load different data using Ajax:

...

Load the HTML file

Load the text file

<div id="textTarget"></div>

A new button tag has been added; it has an ID getTextFile and has been placed right above the <div id= "textTarget">. When this button is clicked on, the contents of the text file in the div tag loads.

// sample06/scripts.js

// Pass a parameter to loadFile and refer to it in getInfo.open()

function loadFile(file) {

  var getInfo = new XMLHttpRequest();

  getInfo.open("GET", file);

    ...

}

...

```
// A new button is added to the bottom of scripts.js

// Each button will run loadFile() to load in a different file

document.getElementById("getHTMLFile").onclick = function() {

  loadFile("articleName.html");

};


document.getElementById("getTextFile").onclick = function() {

  loadFile("articleName.txt");

};
```

Now loadFile will require a parameter; we're calling this "file" and it will define the file that getInfo.open will load on the page.

The button code was also updated. While the loadFile function still ran, to work properly, it required a parameter. The parameter supplied was the name of the file to be loaded on the page.

Our new button was loaded into a text file and the old button was loaded in HTML.

Creating Reusable Code for Multiple Buttons

The last example code is just fine if we have just a few buttons. If we needed to create the onclick functionality for many buttons, things would start to get muddled. The best way around that is to create code to reuse and can be shared by the buttons:

...

Load the HTML file

Load the text file

```
<div id="textTarget"></div>
```

...

The two buttons we already had on our HTML page were updated; we took the ID out of each one, gave them each a class named btn and a data attribute file named data-file.

Each button had a unique value for the data attribute; the values were the name of the file that we wanted Ajax to load:

```
// sample07/scripts.js
// Don't change the loadFile() function
// Remove button code for the two buttons at the bottom
// Add new code
...
var getButtons = document.querySelectorAll(".btn");


for (key in getButtons) {


  var singleButton = getButtons[key];


  singleButton.onclick = function() {
   if(!this.dataset) {
    loadFile(this.getAttribute("data-file"));
   } else {
    loadFile(this.dataset.file);
   }
  }


}
```

We replaced the code for the two buttons with some new code; this found the buttons that had the btn class by using document.querySelectorAll and then stored the buttons in a group inside a variable named getButtons.

A *for...in* loop was run for the total number of buttons in getButtons, and in our case, this was two times. Whenever the loop was run, a variable named singleButton was created. This variable stored references to a single button at a time, with the reference being the line of code with getButtons[key] in it.

Next, every singleButton was told by the code what it needed to do when it was clicked. It looked at each data attribute value and then passed that value to the loadFile function as a parameter to load on the page.

There is no support in Internet Explorer 10 or below for data attributes, so we needed to run a feature detect and then give the relevant browsers some fallback code. We used this.dataset to find the dataset property of the button clicked.

First, we wanted to see the dataset wasn't in the browser and we did it with if(!this.dataset). If it wasn't there, the data attribute value was retrieved using the getAttribute() method.

If dataset was found in the browser, it was used to retrieve the data attribute value by using this.dataset.

Loading JSON with AJAX

Ajax is diverse enough to work with assorted data types but the most used one is JSON. There are several ways JSON can be used with Ajax and below is a basic example:

```
<!DOCTYPE html>

<html lang="en">

 <head>

  <meta charset="UTF-8">

  <title>Sample 08</title>

 </head>

 <body&ht;

  <div id="textTarget"></div>

  <script src="scripts.js"></script>

 </body>

</html>
```

We removed the buttons from the HTML file.

```
// sample08/soccerplayers.json
```

```json
{
    "manchester united": {
        "playerOne": "Paul Pogba",
        "playerTwo": "Marcus Rashford",
        "playerThree": "Romelu Lukaku"
    },
    "Liverpool": {
        "playerOne": "Mohammed Salah",
        "playerTwo": "Virgil van Dijk",
        "playerThree": "Roberto Firmino"
    },
    "Chelsea": {
        "playerOne": "Olivier Giraud",
        "playerTwo": "Eden Hazard",
        "playerThree": "Gonzalo Higuain"
    }
}
```

Rather than loading data from a text or HTML file, it was loaded directly from a JSON file.

```javascript
// sample08/scripts.js
(function(){
    var getPlayerInfo = new XMLHttpRequest();


    getPlayerInfo.open("GET", "soccerplayers.json");
    getPlayerInfo.send();
```

```
getPlayerInfo.onreadystatechange = function() {

  if (getPlayerInfo.readyState === 4) {

    if (getPlayerInfo.status === 200) {

      var players = JSON.parse(getPlayerInfo.responseText),

        text = document.getElementById("textTarget");

      for (i in players) {

        var newDiv = document.createElement("div");

        newDiv.innerHTML = players[i].playerOne;

        text.appendChild(newDiv);

      }

    }

  }

}
})();
```

Let's break this down

```
(function(){

...

})();
```

The biggest change here is that the function ran immediately the pages were loaded rather than having to be invoked somewhere in the code. We did this using an IIFE, or an "immediately invoked function expression".

...

```
var getPlayerInfo = new XMLHttpRequest();

getPlayerInfo.open("GET", "soccerplayers.json");

getPlayerInfo.send();
```

...

The primary variable in the Ajax code was given a new name of getPlayerInfo and the JSON file was fetched using the open() method.

...

```
getPlayerInfo.onreadystatechange = function() {
  if (getPlayerInfo.readyState === 4) {
    if (getPlayerInfo.status === 200) {
      var players = JSON.parse(getPlayerInfo.responseText),
        text = document.getElementById("textTarget");
      for (i in players) {
        var newDiv = document.createElement("div");
        newDiv.innerHTML = players[i].playerOne;
        text.appendChild(newDiv);
      }
    }
  }
};
```

...

As soon as readyState was equal to 4 and the code made a successful connection to the server, two variables were created – text and players. Players used responseText to get the data as it did before and then used JSON parse to turn it into JavaScript object format that is more readable.

The text variable referenced the <div id="textTarget">element on the HTML page. Like before, the data was loaded into that element.

Next, a *for...in* loop was used to loop through the JSON content in the variable called players and, for each loop iteration, three steps were done:

1. A div tag was created by the loop using document.createElement; the tag was then stored in a variable named newDiv.

2. The loop looked at every item inside 'players' and located the property called playerOne. That property was then put in the div tag the newDiv variable was created by accessing the innerHTML property for the div tag.
3. Last, the loop located the variable called text, which was referencing the <div id="textTarget"> element already on the page, and loading the context from newDiv into it.

That really was just a basic illustration but it shows you how Ajax loads JSON content.

Ajax and jQuery

We talked about this at the start of the chapter but now we're going to take things a little further by adding jQuery to our project. But first, jQuery has always had great support for Ajax because it allows us to write Ajax functionalities that are very configurable but uses less code. When jQuery 1.5 was released, it was significant because it brought about a few important changes related to Ajax. First, it made Ajax work a lot quicker in jQuery; it also introduced Promises and Deferreds, which made the asynchronous functionality work better and, lastly, the jqXHR object gave Ajax surplus functionality in jQuery.

Adding jQuery to the project

For the remaining examples in this section, we have added the core jQuery library to index.html using the jQuery CDN. Our index.html file should look like this:

```
<!DOCTYPE html>

<html lang="en">

 <head>

  <meta charset="UTF-8">

  <title>A Sample with the jQuery code attached to it</title>

 </head>

 <body>

  <div id="textTarget"></div>

  <script src="http://code.jquery.com/jquery-1.11.2.min.js"></script>

  <script src="scripts.js"></script>

 </body>

</html>
```

Did you spot that jQuery was in there BEFORE scripts.js and the library version we are using is 1.11.2, not one of the 2.x versions? This means jQuery has been optimized so it works well in all Internet Explorer versions from 6 upward; version 2.x of jQuery is optimized for Internet Explorer 9 and above. So, by using the earlier version, we can easily perform the ActiveXObject feature detection.

Understanding $.ajax

$.ajax is one of the most powerful techniques in jQuery and one of the most configurable. It is the method used to manage all the Ajax calls jQuery makes. There are quite a few ways $.ajax can be configured and we really don't have the time or the space to review them all. What is important is to understand the structure of it.

```
<!DOCTYPE html>

<html lang="en">

 <head>

  <meta charset="UTF-8">

  <title>Sample 09</title>

 </head>

 <body>

  <div id="textTarget"></div>


  <script src="http://code.jquery.com/jquery-1.11.2.min.js"></script>

  <script src="scripts.js"></script>

 </body>

</html>
```

This is the same HTML code we used earlier with an addition – a div that has a D of isLoadedTarget along with the jQuery library.

```
// sample09/scripts.js

$.ajax({

 url: "articleName.html",

 success: isLoaded,

 statusCode: {

  200: function() {

   console.log("Everything is loaded!!!");
```

```
    }

  }

}).done(function(data) {

  $("#textTarget").html(data);

});



function isLoaded() {

  $("#isLoadedTarget").html("The articleName.html file has loaded...check the console
for a message returned by the statusCode property!!!");

}
```

$.ajax can be used with or without any parameters being passed to it. If parameters are passed, you can use a configurable object to pass one or more.

Our configurable object was created with three options set:

1. The first option is 'url' – this was used to define the file that Ajax was to load. In our example, the sample was loaded in a file called articleName.html.
2. The second option was 'success' – this was used to define what should be done if the file request succeeded. In this case, a function named isLoaded would be run.
3. The third option is 'statusCode' – this was used to define what should happen when a given server status code was called. In this instance, a message was shown on the browser console when a 200 status was achieved.

.ajax was chained to the method called .done; this was to ensure it was next to run. We will discuss the .done method in more detail later when we look at Promises and Deferred; for now, it is enough that you understand the method is a callback function that was run once .ajax had completed everything it needed to do.

.done actually has a callback function of its own and we passed 'data' to it as a parameter. That parameter represented every one of the .ajax-configured options, including the 'url' option value.

The html method was used by the callback to load articleName.html into our <div id="textTarget"> just like earlier; this time though, the 'data' parameter was passed to .html and not the file name. The .done method is clever enough to recognize it must look at the value for 'url' to work out the content that needs to be loaded.

jQuery Ajax Shorthand Methods

$.ajax is incredibly powerful, but you don't need it. The latest version of the documentation for $.ajax states the function will underlie every Ajax request that jQuery sends and it isn't always necessary to call the function directly; there are a number of alternatives, such as .load() and $.get(), that are higher-level and undemanding to use. If, however, you need the less common options, $.ajax() is quite flexible.

We tend to refer to the high-level functions in jQuery as shorthand methods and each of them internally uses the core .ajax method. There are five shorthand methods in Ajax:

- .load
- jQuery.get
- jQuery.getJSON
- jQuery.getScript
- jQuery.post

jQuery.post is used to deal with interactions with the server; we won't discuss it here because it isn't within the scope of this book.

.load

.load is by far the easiest way to use Ajax in jQuery. Although we discussed this formerly, we'll look at it again in context with our current examples. The .load function is the jQuery equivalent of <a href="#readystatechange," which we talked about earlier in the onreadystatechange section.

```
<!DOCTYPE html>

<html lang="en">

 <head>

  <meta charset="UTF-8">

  <title>Sample 10</title>

 </head>

 <body&ht;

  <div id="textTarget"></div>

  <script src="http://code.jquery.com/jquery-1.11.2.min.js"></script>
```

```
<script src="scripts.js"></script>

</body>

</html>
```

This is an HTML page much like we have used in prior examples and it has the <div id="textTarget"> where the content is loaded when the page loads.

// sample10/scripts.js

```
$("#textTarget").load("articleName.html");
```

In this, jQuery is searching for <div id="textTarget"> on the page. When it was found, it was run against the .load function, which then used Ajax to load the content in the div tag. The content was defined in the .load parameter as articleName.html.

Using .load to Make Ajax Requests with a Mouse Click

In an earlier case in point, a mouse click was used to load Ajax in content, so, let's look at the jQuery version:

…

Load the HTML file

```
<div id="textTarget"></div>
```

A button tag was affixed with getHTMLFile as an ID and it was added above the <div id="textTarget"> tag. When this button is clicked, the contents of an HTML file are loaded in the div tag.

// sample11/scripts.js

```
$("#getHTMLFile").click(function(){

  $("#textTarget").load("articleName.html");

});
```

The jQuery .click method was bound to the newly added button and when clicked, a callback function was run, which then ran the .load code from the last example.

Using .load to Create Reusable Code for Multiple Buttons

Plain JavaScript was used to create separate buttons that allowed different content to be ajaxed in. But it is far more efficient to use plain JavaScript to create shared functions to load in the content.

...

Load the HTML file

Load the text file

<div id="textTarget"></div>

...

Two buttons were created, each having the btn class and the data-file data attribute. The name of the file that we want Ajax to load is stored in the data-file attribute.

// sample12/scripts.js

$(".btn").click(function(){

  var getData = $(this).data("file");

  $("#textTarget").load(getData);

});

As we did before, all the buttons that had the btn class shared a .click function to allow content to be loaded in. The buttons performed a pair of tasks at the same time – searching the data-file attribute to find the file and loading it into <div id="textTarget"> element.

To get to the file in the data-file attribute, $(this).data() was used. Note that the '*this*' keyword from JavaScript is still used, but it has been wrapped in a jQuery object; it can be reused by other Query objects.

The data attribute names that we are looking for has been passed as a parameter to the method called .data. We were searching for the attribute called date-file, so all we needed to name the parameter was "file".

All of it was stored in the getData variable and because that variable is referencing the value of the data attribute for the clicked button, it can be passed to .load as a parameter so the method can load the files into <div id="textTarget">.

Using .load to Load Fragments

We can also use the .load method to load parts of data, i.e. fragments, instead of an entire HTML document.

...

<div id="textTarget"></div>

...

We use a page that just has the <div id="textTarget"> element on it:

Ajax Tutorial for Beginners

By John Jay Smith

Next, we create a new page named article.html; this has two numeric elements on it - <div id+"title"> and <div id="author">

// sample13/scripts.js

$("#textTarget").load("articleName.html #author");

The .load method is used to load Ajax into the file called article.html but, rather than the whole file, we just load the content from the <div id="author"> element.

<a href="http://api.jquery.com/load/" target="blank" "title"=Read more about jQuery's '.load' method>Read more about jQuery's ".load()" method</a>.

Use jQuery.get

There are a few differences between .get and .load:

- .load is a method while .get is a global function. This means if you want to start a jQuery code block, you use .get but .load is used as a chainable method within the block.
- It makes perfect sense to use the .load method to Ajax in only the HTML documents; .get is used for all document types.
- .get will only manage the Get server requests; .load can manage GET and POST requests.

Keeping with the HTML file we used in the last example, we can bring content on via Ajax using .get like this:

// sample14/scripts.js

$.get("articleName.html", function(data) {

  $("#textTarget").html(data);

});

.get was used to start the code block and then .load was used as a chainable method inside the block. The first parameter defined what content would be loaded onto the page, in this case, articleName.html.

The second parameter, a callback function, was used to define the location for the content to be loaded. A parameter called data was passed to the function and this was representative of the content loaded to the page.

The internals of the function loads the content in the textTarget element using the .html method from jQuery.

We passed the parameter called data to the .html method, thus telling the method exactly what it needed to load. The function parameter can be whatever you want it to be, but it is common practice to call it 'data'.

jQuery.getJSON

The get.JSON method can be used to load JSON content as we did with the plain JavaScript. This is our JSON file:

```
// sample15/soccerplayers.json
{
  "manchester united": {
    "playerOne": "Paul Pogba",
    "playerTwo": "Marcus Rashford",
    "playerThree": "Romelu Lukaku"
  },
  "liverpool": {
    "playerOne": "Mohammed Salah",
    "playerTwo": "Virgil van Dijk",
    "playerThree": "Roberto Firmino"
  },
  "chelsea": {
    "playerOne": "Olivier Giraud",
```

"playerTwo": "Eden Hazard",

"playerThree": "Gonzalo Higuain"

}

}

And the file called scripts.js looks like:

```
// sample15/scripts.js

$.getJSON("soccerplayers.json", function(players) {

  $.each(players, function(i) {

    var newDiv =  "<p>"  + players[i].playerOne +  "</p>" ;

    $("#textTarget").append(newDiv);

  })

});
```

.getJSON has two parameters – the first was the name of the JSON file we want loaded on the page and the second is a callback function that actually loads the data.

The callback function was passed a parameter called player and this is referencing the JSON file. Next, the .each method from jQuery was used to do what our *for...loop* handled earlier – to look in the JSON data for the properties.

.each also had two parameters. The first was called players and this, like the previous one, defined where the JSON data was. The second was yet another callback function to load the data, both onto the page and onto specified page elements.

Inside the function, a variable named newDiv was created. This created a new div tag using jQuery. Then, the .append method from jQuery looked on the JSON object items for playerOne properties, moving them to the new div tag.

At that point, the div tag had content; we took the content and loaded it into the existing textTarget element using the .append method.

jQuery.getScript

The .getScript method is used to load single JavaScript files using Ajax. A callback function is a common practice to execute the code inside the loaded file.

Index.html looks as it has, but now we have added a file named loadFile.js while we update scripts.js.

...

<div id="textTarget"></div>

...

This is quite the same HTML structure we have used untill now.

// sample16/loadFile.js

function getHtmlFile() {

  $("#textTarget").load("articleName.html");

};

function setText() {

  $("#textTarget").css({

    "color": "red",

    "font-weight": "bold"

  });

};

Two functions were created in loadFile.js – setText and getHtmlFile. articleName.html is loaded into the <div id="textTarget"> element using getHtmlFile(), just like in previous examples and setText() was used to change the <div id="textTarget"> copy, turn it red and make it bold.

// sample16/scripts.js

$.getScript("loadFile.js", function() {

getHtmlFile();

$("#textTarget").click(function(){

  setText();

 });

});

Inside scripts.js, the method called getScript loaded loadFile.js. A callback function was run, which then ran getHtmlFile immediately, loading articleName.html in, and when <div id="textTarget"> was clicked, the function also ran setText.

If you used a decent developer tool, such as Chrome Developer Tools, or Firebug, for example, to view index.html in a browser, make sure to open the Network Panel. You will see the loadFile.js filename has a timestamp appended:

// this looks different every time the page is reloaded

loadFile.js?=1421161342213

This happens because .getScript will "cache-bust" any script it loads, thus forcing the browser into downloading a newer version of the file rather than finding the cached version. You can avoid this by letting caching through .ajaxSetup:

// sample17/scripts.js

$.ajaxSetup({

  cache: true

 });

$.getScript("loadFile.js", function() {

  getHtmlFile();

```
$("#textTarget").click(function(){

  setText();

});


});
```

If you looked in Network Panels now, there is no time stamp on the filename.

jqHXR and Promises

A few of the shorthand methods and $.ajax will return the object called XMLHttpRequest, more commonly called the jqHXR. One method that doesn't return this is the .load method.

All jqHXR is, is the XMLHttpRequest object wrapped in a jQuery API. The documentation for jQuery states the jqHXR is a superset of the HRR.

One of the most important parts of the API is Promises. These are a part of the Deferred object in jQuery; for the rest of this section though, we will focus on Promises.

What is a Promise?

Promises are not new technology but they are quite new to JavaScript and are fast becoming imperative. While we don't have the space to discuss them in their entirety, we can give you a basic understanding.

A promise is representative of the result of an operation carried out asynchronously. The main interaction method with a promise is the *then* method; this registers the callbacks to receive the eventual value of the promise or a reason why the promise can't be completed.

In more basic terms:

- A promise will wait until your code has finished everything it needs to do.
- A promise will allow you to run callbacks to do things after the code has done all that needs to be done.
- A promise must have a then() method to return a promise; this method is used to manage callbacks.
- A promise has special event handling for times when a part of the code may fail.

An important note about jQuery Promises

If Promises are not available in your browser, you can add libraries to your project to make them work. Note that jQuery is not one of those libraries because there are two ways in which it doesn't conform to the spec for Promises:

- The Promises specs declare the Promise and, when implemented, must be its own object. Promises are wrapped in the Deferred object (jQuery).
- The Promises spec states Promises must use specific ways to manage errors. jQuery currently doesn't do this.

Use Deferred methods with jqXHR

jqXHR is part of the Deferreds in jQuery, which means it can access every Deferred method. There are four commonly used methods:

- done
- fail
- always
- then

Promises allow callbacks to be implemented in a neater way and it is considered to be best practice in jQuery.

The .done method

This method sets the callback for what is meant to happen once the code has finished running.

```
<!DOCTYPE html>

<html lang="en">

 <head>

  <meta charset="UTF-8">

  <title>Sample 18</title>

 </head>

 <body>

  <div id="textTarget"></div>

  <script src="http://code.jquery.com/jquery-1.11.2.min.js"></script>

  <script src="scripts.js"></script>

 </body>

</html>
```

This is the HTML code needed for this example:

```
// sample18/scripts.js

$.get("article.html").done(function(data) {

 $("#textTarget").html(data);
```

console.log("The file has loaded!");

});

Here, article.html was requested by .get and a .done method was chained to it. Once the request was successfully completed, the .done method ran the callback function.

We could do this using the .get method because the jqXHR method was returned. Just to remind you, the .load method is not able to return jqXHR.

While the HTML stayed the same, the JavaScript was updated.

// sample19/scripts.js

$("#textTarget").load("article.html")

  .done(function(data) {

    // Won't run because "load" doesn't understand "done"

    // "done" will return as an undefined function

    console.log("The file has loaded!");

});

The file was loaded but there was no console message. Because .load doesn't return jqXHR, .done will not work in the code.

The .fail method

The fail method is used to set callback functions to define what transpires if the code is rejected or if it fails. While index.html stays the same, article.html was deleted from the directory. Our script.js file looks like this:

// sample20/scripts.js

$.get("article.html")

  .done(function(data) {

    $("#textTarget").html(data);

  })

  .fail(function() {

    $("#textTarget").html("The file didn't load!");

});

Because article.html was deleted out of the directory, our code did not work. As a result, the .fail method was called and a message loaded into textTarget to confirm the failure.

The .always method

We use the .always method to set callback functions to define what occurs if the code is rejected or resolves itself.

...

<div id="textTarget"></div>

...

We added a div tag, giving it an ID of textTarget02 underneath the textTarget div tag.

// sample21/scripts.js

// Try & load "article.html" into "<div id="textTarget">"

$.get("article.html")

  .done(function(data) {

    $("#textTarget").html(data);

  })

  .fail(function() {

    $("#textTarget").html("The file didn't load!");

  })

  .always(function(){

    console.log("The 'article.html' file either did or didn't load!");

  });

// Try & load "article02.html" into "<div id="textTarget02">"

$.get("article02.html")

431

```
.done(function(data) {

  $("#textTarget02").html(data);

})

.fail(function() {

  $("#textTarget02").html("The 'article02.html' file didn't load!");

})

.always(function(){

  console.log("The 'article02.html' file either did or didn't load!");

});
```

We have two functions here – one loading the existing article.html and one loading the non-existent article02.html. Each method chains the other three methods - .done, .fail, .always.

Because the first method is loading the existing article.html file. The chained .done method runs, as will the .always method. As the second function is loading the nonexistent article02.html, the chained .fail method runs along with the .always method.

The .then method

Finally, the .then method is used to set a callback function for what happens if the code is in progress, resolves, or is rejected.

<!-- sample22/index.html -->

<!-- Remove <div id="textTarget02"> from our last example -->

...

<div id="textTarget"></div>

...

We deleted the <div id="textTarget02"> element out of index.html.

```
$.getJSON("soccerplayers.json").then(

function(data) {

  $.each(data, function(i) {
```

```
    var newDiv = "<p>" + data[i].playerOne + "</p>";

    $("#textTarget").append(newDiv);

    })

  }, function(){

    $("#textTarget").html("The data failed to load.");

  },

  function(){

    $("#textTarget").html("The data is loading...");

  }

);
```

.getJSON was used to get the JSON and parse it as we did previously. This time, the .then method manages our callback functions. The callbacks are passed as parameters to the functions of which there are three:

- The first describes what happens if the Promise is resolved.
- The second describes what happens if the Promise is rejected.
- The third describes what happens if the Promise is still in progress.

Because the file called soccerplayers.json exists, the Promise resolves itself but if the file could not be found, it would reject. If we removed that .json file, the function inside the second parameter would display the following message on the page:

The data failed to load.

With such a small amount of JSON data, it isn't easy to demonstrate the third progress function but it is vital to understand that a message would be shown stating "the data is loading" should the Promise be rejected or resolved.

That concludes our brief look at Ajax. It should become second nature as you work your way through JavaScript and jQuery. Having a good grasp of how it works and how to use it with jQuery is essential, so hopefully, this tutorial has given you a decent basis from which to start.

Part 4: Web Design and Mobile Applications

Building Your First Web Page

Before we delve into what makes up a web page in terms of design, we'll take a brief look at a few basics first. This is a hands-on tutorial that will walk you through the process from start to finish, but first:

Three ways to build a web page

1. Use a pre-made template

Web design templates are design templates someone else has already created. You can customize these templates to match what you want to achieve with your website and you can find them in numerous formats, such as HTML and Photoshop. Most of the time, the templates are fully compatible with the HTML editors like Dreamweaver, FrontPage, and GoLive.

Utilizing website templates isn't a cheats way of doing things; even experienced web designers employ them to get their website creation off the ground quickly. They are also an efficient way to fashion a website with trivial knowledge of web design or HTML.

2. Use an HTML Editor

HTML editors are designed in such a way that building your web page can feel very much like creating a Microsoft Word document – quite stress-free. There is a downside though; you don't have so much control and, in many cases, you can find yourself becoming more dependent on the editor.

3. Using a Text Editor to Write Your Own HTML Code

Doing it this way, you learn much faster how to build a web page and you have far more control over everything you do. This is the method we will be using.

Let's get to our first web page.

HTML Tags

First, you need to understand what HTML tags are. A tag is a piece of text that acts as a marker for the web browser to read; the browser will then interpret the meaning of the tag. The HTML tags are used to tell web browsers what is to be displayed on a web page and how. Tags are placed around and in text and images you want to be shown on your page.

There are quite a few HTML tags to build your web page and each has a specific structure so the browser can distinguish them from standard text.

Tags tend to be abbreviations or words placed within a set of angled brackets. For example, if you wanted the text bold, you would use a bold tag that looks something like this:

**** this text will be made bold****

The paragraph tag is also used a great deal:

<p> this is a paragraph>/p>

HTML tags tend to be in pairs. There is an opening tag (<name of tag>) and a closing tag (</name of tag>) and the only difference between the two is that there is a forward slash contained in the closing tag.

Look at these to see if they make things any clearer:

****Makes the text bold****

*<i>*Makes the text italic*</i>*

<h1>Tells the browser this is important text and the browser will usually make it much larger</h1>

<table>Creates an HTML table - much like a standard spreadsheet</table>

HTML tags aren't just for the placement of text or formatting; they can also be used to include video, animations, audio, flash, and multimedia programs.

How HTML Pages Are Structured

HTML pages tend to be divided into two main sections:

The Head

The <head> section of a page is where you will find the page information you don't see displayed on the web page, with the exception of the page title. While you may not see this information, it does play a big part in how the page will be displayed,

The Body

The <body> section contains everything you see on the finished web page when you open it in your web browser. This is the text, the flash movies, images, videos, anything you included on the web page that a visitor can see. This means all the tags we use to format everything will also be in there.

Note that both sections are marked on an HTML page with their tags - <head> </head>) and <body> </body>).

If a body tag is used to create an HTML page body and the head creates the head of the page, how do we actually create an HTML page? Quite simply, we use the HTML tags:

<html></html>

This is the granddaddy of all the tags and, like all the rest, it must have an opening and a closing tag. All web pages, without exception, must have an opening and closing HTML tag otherwise there is no way for the web browser to display the page. You must also have the head tag and the body tag but all the others are optional.

So, as an absolute basic requirement, every page must show these tags in this order:

<html>

   <head>

      <title>Title of your page</title>

   </head>

   <body>

   </body>

</html>

Building Your First HTML Page

We could continue with the theory but you would soon get bored so we can move on and start to learn properly by building a web page. Don't fret if you don't comprehend this yet; as you get to work, it will all become clearer.

Step 1 – writing code

Open a text editor, something like Notepad on Windows. Type in the following code:

<html>

   <head>

      <title>Your first hand-written HTML page</title>

   </head>

   <body>

<h2>Hand coding web pages is easy! </h2>

<p>I would like to thank all those who helped me create

this page.</p>

</body>

</html>

Step 2 – Save it

Save your file to your desktop as an HTML file; use the Save As function in your text editor and call it webpage.html, or anything else, but follow these rules when you do:

- Web page names cannot have spaces in them; for example, web page.html wouldn't be accepted.
- End your file with .html or with .htm. This way, the computer will know it is dealing with a web page and use the web page browser to look at it.
- Never include symbols such as $, ^, %, or & in the name, only standard numbers and letters.
- If you are using Notepad, save the file as UTF-8.

Step Three – View Your Page

At this stage, you can double-click the page to open it or open your web browser, click on File menu, choose Open File and then find your file. The page will open so you can see exactly what it looks like. If you don't see anything, go back and make sure you typed the code correctly.

That's your very first page built; now we can move on to building a complete website.

What is a Website?

A website is nothing more than a load of HTML pages, like you just built, all grouped together and connected using links. There is a <link> tag to do this and, at its most basic, it looks like this:

<a href="...''></a>

This is a link tag with a destination, i.e. website name added in:

<a href=" http://www.killersites.com ">Go to killersites.com</a>

Everyone has used links when they browse the internet. Links are what take you from one page to another by means of the link tag and this is one of the most important tags in HTML because it links and interconnects everything together including the entire internet.

In our earlier example, the link tag pointed to a website called www.killersites.com and you can see the text on the web page would say "Go to killersites.com". You could use a link to any website you wanted – just replace killersites.com with any web address.

Like other tags, a link tag has an opening and the closing tag but they are more complex than the ones we have looked at so far – not so intricate that you can't get the hang of them, though!

You may also have noticed the link tag contains text before the website address. That text is:

http://

This tells the browser the link goes to a web page; links can point to whatever and the browser needs to know what it is.

Absolute vs Relative URL

When you link one web page on your website to another you can use one of two types of addresses – an absolute address which is complete, or a relative address, which is partial. An absolute URL (address) is the entire web address of the web page that can be found from anywhere on the internet. For example, let's say you have a page named contact.html and it is at the root of your website. For this, we'll assume your website is called www.myStore.com. The absolute URL would read:

'http://www.myStore.com/contact.html'

Let's step back and look at what the root is. The root of any website is the base - the level from where the site begins. All the files, which are the images, the pages, etc., that make your website are organized, saved into folders, just as you do with other files on your computer. The web host provides you with space on the server to save all your files so they are kept together. This space is called the root of the website.

As far as the internet goes, all the files in that space, regardless of what they are, can be accessed by your domain name and the item name. Let's say, for example, you have two files saved on your root space:

Index.html

Contact.html

You have a folder named 'products' and, in this folder, are a lot of pages; one of those is called 'bookcases.html'. You made the decision to place all 'product' HTML pages into your 'products' folder as a way of keeping things organized.

What would the absolute URL be for the bookcases.html web page? If your domain name were ....myStore.com, it would be:

http://www.myStore.com/products/bookcases.html

Take some time to contemplate this and it will make sense.

Relative URL

These are partial addresses relative to the page where the link has been placed. If you were, for example, linking from index.html to bookcases.html, the relative address would be:

products/bookcases.html

And the link tag would look like:

<a href="products/bookcases.html">Look at our bookcases!</a>

All you are doing is telling the browser that you want to link to an HTML page that is in a folder called 'products'.

Take some time to play around with folders and links on your website and it will fall into place and be clear. It is necessary you get this right because, if you don't, things won't load.

Let's do one more example; we'll link from index.html to contact.html:

<a href="contact.html">Contact us</a>

Because both pages are on the same root level, we only had to add the html file name.

Ten Steps to Build a Website

That's the basic theory out of the way. Don't worry, we are a long way from finished! Before we move on, we'll look at the 10 steps you need to take to build your website and bring it to life.

1. **Define what your website purpose is**

When you begin developing a website, you need to understand your objectives and those of the website. Those goals will affect the choices you make and they will, ultimately, determine if it succeeds or fails.

Yes, this may sound obvious, but you would be surprised at the number of websites put together without any goals. The result? A messy web store that has no structure and is virtually impossible to maintain.

Let's say you want to build an e-commerce website to sell products; as a web designer, consider things, such as: Do you need a shopping cart system for orders? Do you need to include payment processing? How many products will be on your website, at least to start?

This is a single example; the point is that you need to define the purpose of your website so you prepare it and build it with the correct tools and people.

2. **Draw a simple diagram of your website structure**

One of the best ways to "see" your website is to draw a simple diagram. You don't need anything special; a simple box diagram with one box for each page connected by lines to show how they will be linked. Usually, a diagram like this follows a pyramid scheme showing the website from the top down.

3. **Write out the website text**

Before you even begin to think about writing the HTML, use a word processing program, like MS Office, to write the text to be included. This can help you make the design process spot on.

Make sure all the text is finished before it makes its way to the web page – it is tricky to correct things on an HTML page!

4. **Choose the basic layout – one layout, all pages**

Once you have a diagram and the text, now choose the basic layout. You could go wild and choose something funky, but more often than not, a standard layout works best.

5. **Pick your colors and fonts**

Next, think about the basic colors and the fonts you will use. Try to keep it fitting with the style and tone of your website. For example, if you have a hardware store, you don't really want pink and black – that may do well for a florist! Establish your style before you begin to create the pages, otherwise, you could be redoing them.

Later, we'll look into CSS, the way to make styling a website uncomplicated.

6. **Build your website**

Now, you are ready to create your web pages. Take everything you did in the first five steps and link all the web pages together. You can get some practice to try to build your own small website with a few pages.

Practice makes perfect!

7. **Pick a domain name**

When your website is built, the next step is getting it onto the internet, and to do that, you need a domain name. Every website must have one of these and the name you choose can determine how easily your website can be found. Here are a few pointers on choosing a good domain name:

- The name should give a clue as to what the website is about. Search engines love these and visitors will find you much easier too. For example, if you were building a hardware site, you wouldn't want a name along the lines of "prettypinkUnicorn". It doesn't tell you what the website is about whereas a name like "discountHardware" does.
- Search engines look at lots of different parts of a website to determine what it's about. The domain name is a key one and search engines look for keywords in the name to help the search bot to put your website into a category.
- Your name does not have to include your business name – it just has to be clear and easy to remember.

8. **Registering your domain name**

This isn't a simple task because most of the good names are taken. Forget about having a single word name because they were the first to be chosen. Think of several names; the chances are, you will need to go through a few to find one that hasn't already been used.

In the past, you only had .com or .co.uk domains because the likes of .org and .net were reserved for special use. That's all changed, and now there are lots of domain extensions to choose from.

As far as the search engines go, it makes no difference whatsoever what extension your domain name has.

Some folks say you should register your domain name first and then build the site, but that only counts if the name has an impact on the design. How you do it is up to you.

The quickest way of determining if your chosen domain has been taken or not is to type it into a search engine and see what comes up. Failing that, go to your chosen domain registrar and see what's available.

9. Find your hosting company

These days, website hosting is not expensive. Fepending on your requirements you can get hosting that costs little to nothing right up to expensive packages – it's your choice.

There are a number of things that go into the pricing of website hosting:

- **Traffic** – the more traffic your website gets, the more it will cost you per month but you need to have a popular website if this were to have any effect, especially as you are a newbie to all this.
- **Extra Services and Features** – hosting providers offer all sorts of features and services and you just won't need many of them. Be careful what you decide on – you can always upgrade in the future.

Choose what suits your website the best, no matter what the cost.

10. Upload your website

Your website is created, you paid for and registered your domain name, and you have a hosting plan in place. Now it's time to upload your website to your chosen host server. Your provider will give you all the help you need.

Quick Tips

- Keep your web pages small.
- Keep your <h2> header tags clear and precise
- Keep your text paragraphs short.
- Keep all your contact information together in the same spot on all your pages.
- Keep each page consistent in structure and look.
- Make sure your website has a Home button to get your users back to the start easily.
- Always underline your links and never use CSS to remove the underlining – most people presume that all underlined text is a link.
- Have your website logo on all pages and link it to the home page.

Now you know what building the website is all about, let's get down to it and start learning CSS. Cascading Style Sheets are the best way to make your web design look professional.

Learn CSS

Cascading Style Sheets, or CSS, is a sister language to HTML, a key tool in web design that makes styling web pages so much easier. Previously, we looked at the HTML tag to make some words on our web page bold:

\<b\> make text bold **\</b\>**

This is fine and it works well, but what if you bolded many words on your web page and now you want to make all of them underlined? You would need to go to every separate part of the page and change the tags for each one.

There is another disadvantage. If you wanted to make the text above bold, change the font to Verdana style, and change the color to red, you would need to wrap a lot of code around your text:

\<font color="#FF0000" face="Verdana, Arial, Helvetica, sans-serif"\>

\<b\>This is text\</b\>\</font\>

This is far too wordy and all it does is makes your HTML code look messy. When you use CSS, you can create custom styles somewhere else, set all the necessary properties, name it, and tag it in your HTML to apply the properties:

\<p class="myNewStyle"\>My CSS styled text\</p\>

Between your opening and closing head tags, right at the top of the page, is the CSS code that defines your new style:

\<style type="text/css"\>

\<!--

> *.myNewStyle {*

>> *font-family: Verdana, Arial, Helvetica, sans-serif;*

>> *font-weight: bold;*

>> *color: #FF0000;*

> *}*

-->

\</style\>

What we did here was include a style sheet code in the page and this works just great for small projects or when you only need to use your defined styles on one page.

What if you want to apply those styles across the complete web page? This is commonplace. Having to copy and paste the code onto every page is nothing short of a hassle. Quite apart from the fact that you will be using duplicate code on each page, you will find you have multiple pages to edit individually if you ever need to make a change to the style.

So what's the answer?

As with JavaScript, we can define CSS styles and create them in separate files and link them to pages where the code needs to be applied:

<link href="myFirstStyleSheet.css" rel="stylesheet" type="text/css">

This code line links your CSS style sheet, called myFirstStyleSheet.css to the HTML document. The code goes between the opening and closing head tags on the page.

How do you create the external style sheet?

It's as simple as creating a text document and then changing it to .css from .txt. The extension is what tells your computer the type of file it is dealing with and allows it to determine what to do when you try to open it or handle it in some other way.

All that means is a CSS file is a text file formatted in a specific way. The file itself is nothing special, it's just the content that makes it into a CSS document.

When you work with external CSS documents, keep a couple of things in mind:

- The following tags do NOT get added into the CS document or page as they would the CSS code were embedded in the HTML:

<style type="text/css"></style>

The link on your web page connecting the CSS and HTML pages together already states that the link goes to a CSS page, and there is no need to declare your code as CSS. That is what the tags above are doing; all you need to do instead is add the code straight to the page:

.myNewStyle {

    font-family: Verdana, Arial, Helvetica, sans-serif;

    font-weight: bold;

    color: #FF0000;

```
}
```

```
.my2ndNewStyle {

    font-family: Verdana, Arial, Helvetica, sans-serif;

    font-weight: bold;

    color: #FF0000;

}
```

```
.my3rdNewStyle {

    font-family: Verdana, Arial, Helvetica, sans-serif;

    font-weight: bold;

    font-size: 12pt;

    color: #FF0000;


}
```

In this example, a sequence of CSS classes was created and these can be applied to any of the HTML tags, like this:

`<p class="myNewStyle">My CSS styled text</p>`

Or

`<h2 class="my3rdNewStyle">My CSS styled text</h2>`

Notice that we gave an <h2> tag a CSS style; the tag is setting the text size so it wraps to a preset size (preset in browser). When a CSS class is applied to it, the CSS will override the preset size normally applied to <h2> tags and replace it with the size you specified in the CSS class.

This shows you how to override HTML tag behavior with CSS!

What we have in these examples is CSS code that defines CSS classes and then applies those classes to elements on the web page. You could also apply CSS in another way, and that is by globally redefining HTML tags so they look a specific way:

h1 { font-family: Garamond, "Times New Roman", serif; font-size: 200%; }

This code sets the font size and style of every <h1> tag on the page in one go. Doing it this way means you don't have to apply CSS classes to any of the <h1> tags like you did earlier because the new style rule affects all of them.

Here's another example, this time making all the margins on a page larger:

body { margin-left: 15%; margin-right: 15%; }

So you see, it is easy enough to redefine HTML tags and change how they look and this is some potent stuff:

div {

   background: rgb(204,204,255);

   padding: 0.5em;

   border: 1px solid #000000;

}

Now, using this code, any <div></div> tag is going to have a background color rgb(204,205,255) and padding of 0.5em with a 1 pixel border in a solid black color.

Let's just go over a couple of things about this:

There are three ways to express color in CSS:

- Using Hex, i.e. #000000 which is black and #FF0000 which is red
- In rgb, i.e. rgb(204,205,255) which is a light purple-blue
- By using actual color names, like blue or red

Hex is the most commonly used method. By using the actual color words, we could have written our last example like this:

div {

   background: green;

   padding: 0.5em;

   border: 1px solid #FF0000;

}

RGB stands for Red Green Blue and when you use this or Hex, you can get the exact color that you want to use, so long as you know what your codes are. Many programs provide color pickers now, so there is no need to memorize all the codes anymore.

One more example; in this one we'll look a cool piece of CSS code that lets us create the link roll-over effects without using images:

:link { color: rgb(0, 0, 153) } / for unvisited links */*

:visited { color: rgb(153, 0, 153) } / for visited links */*

:hover { color: rgb(0, 96, 255) } / when mouse is over the link */*

:active { color: rgb(255, 0, 102) } / when the link is clicked */*

This CSS code causes the link to change color when the relevant action is carried out, providing instant rollover without images. An important thing to note with this code is that style declarations must be in the correct order – link, visited, hover, active – otherwise some browsers may not be able to handle it and the code will break.

CSS is an incredibly powerful tool that lets you do things standard HTML just doesn't allow. All of today's modern browsers support it and it's the one tool all web designers must learn.

The examples we have used here are just a tiny sample of what CSS can be used for. It's enough to get you started but, as with a lot of technologies, there is far more to CSS than many people know exists, let alone use. Don't fall into the trap of thinking just because a feature exists, it is imperative you use it – it's simply not true.

Building a CSS Web Page

Now that we have described a few of the basics, we can start our three-part tutorial on building a web page from pure CSS. That's right; we're not just going to use CSS styling, but CSS positioning as well, and that means we don't need to use any tables.

Once you have completed the tutorial, you will be able to create CSS pages in ways that allow your web sites to be viewed on all devices and screen types. Later, we'll delve deeper into responsive web design. For now, let's go through the tutorial because it will take less effort to create a website and your pages will load faster, be easier to update, and stress-free to print.

CSS Templates

In this first part of the tutorial, we will concentrate on looking at the key CSS components to produce some nice web pages. We can only go so far with this tutorial;

once you're finished with it, hopefully, you will have more than enough information and be tempted to go further.

For now, let's get started.

We'll begin by discussing the tags we will use. Because CSS is so authoritative, we can cut the number of HTML tags significantly while still being able to create fabulous looking pages with just 6 different HTML tag types.

To layout the content, we will use these tags:

<h.> Heading tags go from <h1></h1> to <h6></h6> and these will be used for tagging the page headings. The most important one is the <h1> and the least important is the <h6>. An example of one of the headings for this section is:

CSS Templates

This tells the browser and search engine this is page is mostly about CSS Templates.

Every browser has its own default size for the <h> tags, usually a different size for each one, and this dictates how the text between the tags is rendered. A lot of the defaults are not usable, like the <h1> because they are just too big. But that's where CSS comes into play and helps to make the text the way we want it.

<p>. We use the paragraph tag to mark out specific bits of the page as paragraphs. These are block elements that act as blocks where spaces are inserted automatically before each <p> tag air and at the end too. You've seen it in previous examples and you will also see more of it in future ones.

<ul> and <ol>. These are list tags and we use these to create menus. The <ul> tag is for unordered lists creating lists with bullet points or other icons that are not used to specify an order. The <ol> tag, on the other hand, is the ordered list tag creating a list marked with numbers or letters that denote an order. You will see this in later examples.

<div> and <div>. We use div tags to demark part of a page we want to do things with. Basically, we put the page section into a container so we can do all sorts of things, such as animation, styling, make it invisible, visible, and more. We will be using the div tags to separate our page – the navigational menu will be held in one div tag while our main page is held in another.

<a href>. The href tag is the most important of all HTML tags because it is the link or hyperlink tag. This is how we make portions of text into hypertext; when we click it, another page loads or we activate some other piece of JavaScript, known as ECMA script.

<img>. The image tag lets us add links to images so visitors can see them on our web page. With HTML, we don't embed images into the page; we use the<img> tag to point to where the image is stored so the browser can load it when a visitor arrives on the web page.

This just about covers the HTML tags we will use for our layout. We won't be using tables, br, or font tags.

Before we go any further, we need to create a practice HTML page, so let's do that right now.

From your desktop, right-click and select New>Text Document. This creates a blank document you can name practiceHTML.htm and save to your desktop. The window will show you a warning message asking if you want the file extension changed. Click Yes and then right-click the file. Choose Open With and then click Notepad. Paste the template code below into the file:

My Practice HTML Page<meta http-equiv="Content-Type" content="text/html; charset=iso-8859-1" />

This is the basic structure for every HTML page. Now copy code sample form between these tags:

<!--Insert code here! -->

A note here; between the opening and closing body tags you can see a 'comment'. These are useful because you can add notes, perhaps to explain a piece of code not seen in the browser. Anything between these tag characters is a comment:

<!-- and -->

Comments are great because later down the line either you will forget what a piece of code did or somebody else will read your code and the comments explain things nicely.

Building Up The CSS

Now you have your template page. Create a new folder and name it myCSSwebsite. Put your HTML page in this folder. Create a text document in this folder and name it myCSS.css. Now open that new document and copy this code:

/ Generic Selectors */*

body {

> *font-family: Georgia, "Times New Roman", Times, serif;*

```
        font-size: 14px;

        color: #333333;

        background-color: #F9F9F9;

}


p {

        width: 80%;

}


li {

        list-style-type: none;

        line-height: 150%;

        list-style-image: url(../images/arrowSmall.gif);

}


h1 {

        font-family: Georgia, "Times New Roman", Times, serif;

        font-size: 18px;

        font-weight: bold;

        color: #000000;

}


h2 {

        font-family: Georgia, "Times New Roman", Times, serif;

        font-size: 16px;
```

```css
        font-weight: bold;

        color: #000000;

        border-bottom: 1px solid #C6EC8C;

}


/*************** Pseudo classes ***************/
a:link {

        color: #00CC00;

        text-decoration: underline;

        font-weight: bold;

}


li a:link {

        color: #00CC00;

        text-decoration: none;

        font-weight: bold;

}


a:visited {

        color: #00CC00;

        text-decoration: underline;

        font-weight: bold;

}


li a:visited {
```

```css
        color: #00CC00;

        text-decoration: none;

        font-weight: bold;

}


a:hover {

        color: rgb(0, 96, 255);

        padding-bottom: 5px;

        font-weight: bold;

        text-decoration: underline;

}


li a:hover {

        display: block;

        color: rgb(0, 96, 255);

        padding-bottom: 5px;

        font-weight: bold;

        border-bottom-width: 1px;

        border-bottom-style: solid;

        border-bottom-color: #C6EC8C;

}


a:active {

        color: rgb(255, 0, 102);

        font-weight: bold;
```

```
}


/*********************** ID's ***********************/


#navigation {

        position: absolute;

        z-index: 10;

        width: 210px;

        height: 600px;

        margin: 0;

        border-right: 1px solid #C6EC8C;

        font-weight: normal;

}

#centerDoc {

        position: absolute;

        z-index: 15;

        padding: 0 0 20px; /*top right bottom left*/

        margin-top: 50px;

        margin-left: 235px;

}
```

Save it.

Don't worry about this code; you don't need to understand it at this stage and we'll go over the important stuff soon so you see how easy it is. Before we finish, we're going to add some code to the HTML page.

Open it and find the opening and closing <body> tags. Place this code in between them:

<div id="navigation">

```
    <h2>The Main navigation</h2>

</div>

<div id="centerDoc">

    <h1>The Main Heading</h1>

    <p>

        Go to the home page for the Web Designers Killer Handbook and get the HTML
        practice page we'll be using. Look under where it says, "To create the practice
        HTML page, do this" and follow the guide on creating a page.

    </p>

</div>
```

Next, find the head tags and place this code in between them:

```
<title>First CSS Tutorial</title>

<meta http-equiv="Content-Type" content="text/html; charset=iso-8859-1" />

<link href="myCSS.css" rel="stylesheet" type="text/css" />
```

Now we are ready to begin styling the page – although, if you took a peek you would see we already began to do this.

The HTML Code

In the first part, we created a layout that has two columns using left-side navigation, and we mostly used CSS for this with a few HTML tags. We looked at the tags so now we will look at the HTML code we already used plus the CSS.

So far, we have a simple page. You already know we use HTML code in body tags to display text, images, etc., on the web page. In our case, this is what we have:

```
<body>

        <div id="navigation">

                <h2>The Main navigation</h2>

        </div>

        <div id="centerDoc">
```

```
        <h1>The Main Heading</h1>

            <p>

        </p>

    </div>

</body>
```

Note:

Use your HTML practice page to play along and build this page up.

In this example, we have two sections, each is inside a separate <div> tag. The div tags place parts of the page into containers so we can work on them. In our case, we have two of these containers and each has a unique ID:

<div id="navigation">

...

<div id="centerDoc">

Note that all the page contents are in these two containers. So, your first questions should be – What are the rules surrounding IDs in HTML pages and why do we need IDs and assign them like div tags to elements?

1. An ID can be assigned to any HTML tag, regardless of what it is.
2. You should only use an ID once on a page. One ID cannot be used for more than one element because the ID is meant to be a unique identifier for a page element. So, in the last example, we have just one-page element with an ID of 'navigation' and one-page element with the ID of 'centerDoc'. It is better to use IDs to identify the element clearly so you know exactly what is going on.
3. HTML page element or tag IDs are also used in CSS. The ID can be targeted in CSS code to change position, appearance, and behavior of the specified element and this is done by a reference to the element ID.

Header tags <h1> and <h2> are used in our <div> tags for setting the headers, and lastly, we also used some <p> tags, adding text between them to make this page.

Now, we can look at the CSS file affixed to our HTML page. This is attached using this line of code between the head tags:

<head>

　<link href="myCSS.css" rel="stylesheet" type="text/css">

</head>

Like any normal link, this has an href attribute pointing to a CSS document containing all the CSS code that affects the page it is linked to. In the link above, the CSS file is named like this: href-"myCSS.css and the browser are told we are linking to a CSS page that has the attribute of type="text/css". Most important is that the link points at the named CSS file.

We have a style sheet we linked to our document. Now we can look at some CSS code and this first snippet is what we use to style our IDs:

#navigation {

> *position: absolute;*
>
> *z-index: 10;*
>
> *width: 210px;*
>
> *height: 600px;*
>
> *margin: 0;*
>
> *margin-top: 0px;*
>
> *border-right: 1px solid #C6EC8C;*
>
> *font-weight: normal;*

}

#centerDoc {

> *position: absolute;*
>
> *z-index: 15;*
>
> *padding: 0 0 20px; /*top right bottom left*/*
>
> *margin-top: 50px;*
>
> *margin-left: 235px;*

}

There is quite a bit going on, so for the time being, we'll concentrate on a couple of elements. The example above has two selectors - #navigation and #centerDoc. One selector for one ID and note that each one has a set of curly brackets after it. In between the brackets, the properties we are using to specify the style for the selectors are lists. So, let's remove those properties for now; this is what the code will look like:

```
#navigation {

        /*Look, no CSS rules!*/

}

#centerDoc {

        /*Look, no CSS rules!*/

}
```

Where it says, "Look, no CSS rules!", this is to indicate where the code would normally be. Anything in between the set of curly brackets is part of a package or group known as a property in CSS.

In the instances above, there is text before our curly bracket and that text names the selector. In our case, we have two selectors and two selector names - #navigation and #centerDoc. Now another question; why do we use # in front of the name?

As is it is in HTML and in most programming languages, specific text placed in particular areas is telling the system it must do a required task. In our case, when we use the # symbol at the front of a selector name, we are stating the selector is a special selector type called an ID selector. Why are these special? Because an ID selector can only be applied to a single element in an HTML page.

Thus, we have one CSS ID selector for each div that has an ID and the names correspond with one another. The CSS selector called #centerDoc applies to the <div id="centerDoc"> div and so on. Whatever rules or styles that you want to code into the ID selector will also change the code in the corresponding div tag. So, for our navigation div, these are the rules we have:

```
#navigation {

        position: absolute;

        z-index: 10;

        width: 210px;

        height: 600px;

        margin: 0;
```

margin-top: 0px;

border-right: 1px solid #C6EC8C;

font-weight: normal;

}

Note we gave font-weight a property of 'normal', thus saying all text will have that font-weight:

font-weight: normal;

It would have been just as easy to say all the text in the navigation div tag should appear bold, using this property:

font-weight: bold;

It is effortless to change all the styles at once.

Back to our page. Our navigation div sits to the left and it has a border – why is this? Because that's what we set it as in our code with a 1-pixel wide light green border:

border-right: 1px solid #C6EC8C;

Pay around; change the border color and see what it looks like. Playing around is how you learn, so don't be afraid to experiment.

Now, why is navigation on the left of our page and centerDoc on the right of the page? To explain, first look at the following line in your navigation selector:

position: absolute;

This line is telling the browser this div should be placed on the page exactly as it is. That is an oversimplified explanation but, for now, it will do.

Where the real magic happens is in the centerDoc CSS code:

#centerDoc {

position: absolute;

z-index: 15;

padding: 0 0 20px; /*top right bottom left*/

margin-top: 50px;

margin-left: 235px;

}

This line

margin-left: 235px;

is telling your browser it should insert a margin of 235 pixels on the left of the centerDoc div. The result of this will be the div being pushed over, providing more room for the div navigation to take its place. In our case, all it does is creates a left-hand column.

Before we even thought about what the margins should be, we set our padding first. Padding just creates space wrapped around the tag.

In CSS, this feature goes with the box model concept; this is nothing more than a box wrapped around the HTML tags and that box is made up of padding, borders, margins, and our content. Using this lets us put borders around elements, and space the elements relative to others. Looking from the inside out, it is in this order:

content -> padding -> border -> margin

In our code, anything between the div tags is our content and is followed by the padding. Then we have the border and, lastly, the margins. Padding and margins may seem like they are the same, but think about it – can you see how you make your layout look great by having control over the space that comes before the border (the padding) and the space that comes after the border (the margin)?

Notice the navigation div is higher up our page than the centerDoc div is. This has nothing to do with the order they are in the HTML; if you were not using CSS then this would matter but, with CSS, it comes down to how we set the margins for the selectors. For centerDoc, the upper margin was set as 50 pixels:

margin-top: 50px;

and the navigation div upper margin was set as:

margin-top: 0px;

We set our top margin for navigation to 0 pixels and that makes it 50 pixels above the centerDoc div. Move the navigation div position to beneath the centerDoc div and see what changes. Notice the position of the div in the HTML code is irrelevant to how it shows to a user because CSS positioning has been used.

Note there is also quite a bit more HTML before the initial <body> tag; this is important to our page but has no direct bearing on what appears to a user on the page so we won't be discussing it here.

OK, we learned what the major HTML sections on our page are and we know how to use div tags with IDs to establish some degree of separation:

<div id="navigation"> ... </div>

<div id="centerDoc"> ... </div>

Using the div tag to position the main sections of the page is the alternative to what is used most commonly – tables. One method doesn't necessarily work any better than the other but CSS is considered to be the official way of positioning elements on the page while tables should only be used to store tabular data.

That said, there may well be times when it is easier to use a table and CSS just doesn't suffice. With the layout here with navigation left or right, CSS is perfect and simpler to use.

From here, things get a good deal easier. We have our main document, all the main sections are in their right places, and all that's left is to add text and images to the page.

Breaking the Page Down

What we have on the page so far is unpretentious:

We have one heading:

<h1>The Main Heading</h1>

And we have one paragraph:

<p>

Go to the home page for the Web Designers Killer Handbook and get the HTML practice page we'll be using. Look under where it says, "To create the practice HTML page, do this" and follow the guide on creating a page.</p>

We decided how we wanted our headings and paragraphs to look and we defined it in CSS code:

p {

> *width: 80%;*

}

h1 {

> *font-family: Georgia, "Times New Roman", Times, serif;*

font-size: 18px;

font-weight: bold;

color: #000000;

}

Thus far, things are easy enough to understand. What should be mentioned is the <p> tag widths were set to 80%, which allows us more control over the width of all the text, and in one place that is simple to edit.

What is missing from this page is navigation and the easiest way to add this is to make use of <li> tags (list tags). That makes sense because a navigation menu is nothing more than a list of the pages on the website.

The list item tags were styled using this CSS:

li {

list-style-type: none;

line-height: 150%;

list-style-image: url(../images/arrowSmall.gif);

}

This code makes use of a small image in place of each bullet point and increases the space in between each listed item to 1 ½ time more than usual. You don't need to use images if you don't want to; just remove the attribute below to get rid of them:

list-style-image: url(../images/arrowSmall.gif);

You can also make use of one of the options built-in – square, circle, or disc.

Next, we need to place a <ul></ul> or unordered list between the div tags for navigation, and beneath the heading of Main Navigation on the HTML page:

<h2>The Main Navigation</h2>

<ul>

<li><a href="cssTutorialPage1.php">Page One</a></li>

<li><a href="cssTutorialPage2.php">Page Two</a></li>

</ul>

We could make things easier and include a built-in bullet by changing the CSS code that affects our <li> tags:

li {

    list-style-type: disc;

    line-height: 150%;

}

And now our page has navigation!

That covers this basic tutorial on building a CSS web page but we really have only scratched the surface. We've got a nice page built using a few HTML tags and, while there isn't a great deal of text there right now, you can see how easily you can add more. In fact, it is simple to pad this out into a fully-fledged website, adding more pages, without really touching too much on HTML.

Take some time now to play around and see what you can come up with. At the end of the day, building your website from here is a simple process of building several pages like this and linking them all together.

In the next section, we'll take a look at HTML tags and everything else you need to know to build websites.

HTML Tags For Web Designers

HTML is not a difficult technology and it is easy to acquire. Once you have a basic understanding, you can dive right into the website design without too much thought. Most web designers don't take enough advantage of what CSS and HTML offer and this doesn't just waste time, it makes life more challenging.

One of the fundamental HTML concepts that can make things so much easier for any web designer is the difference between logical tags and physical tags. So, let's take a look.

Logical Tags

HTML has both logical and physical tags and the logical ones are used to tell a browser what the text enclosed in the tags means. As an example, the <strong></strong> tag is a logical tag. When you put text inside these tags, the browser knows the text is important.

By default, a browser will bold any text inside the strong tags so it stands out and that is what the strong tag does – relays the importance of the content to the browser. This gives the search engines more to look at when ranking your page as they take tags into consideration when working out what your web page is about.

There are a few logical tags, including:

- **Strong -** <strong> - relays the importance of the text in the tag
- **Emphasize -** <em> - renders the text so a webpage visitor sees it in italics
- **Neutral inline container -** <span> - discussed later
- **Neutral block element -** <div> - discussed later

Logical tags always have a default rendering method, i.e. the way the browser interprets them to display them on the page. However, it should be understood we use CSS to style these how we want them to look.

Physical Tags

By contrast, a physical tag provides the browser with specific details on how the text should be displayed. Some of the more common physical tags include:

- **Bold -** <b> - makes the enclosed text bold
- **Big -** <big> - makes the text at least one size larger than the surrounding text
- **Font -** <font> - applies a specified font face, such as Helvetica, Georgia, Arial, etc. and a color for the font as well
- **Italics -** <i> - makes the text italic

These are far more straightforward than the logical tags as you can see from the descriptions - what you see is what you get!

So, why would you use one over the other?

In simple terms, the physical tags were designed to add style to an HTML pages because, at that time, we didn't have the style sheets. That said, at the time, HTML wasn't designed to have physical tags because they are somewhat tedious and, for the most part, far more trouble than they are worth.

That's where CSS comes in, and rather than using physical tags, you should be using style sheets.

Block-Level vs Inline Tags

Do we really need the "inline" description in the tag categories? In HTML, a tag is one of two things – block-level or inline.

Block-Level HTML Tags

A block-level tag exists inside a virtual box and will always be followed with a line-break – much like pressing the enter key after you type a sentence. Simply, block-level tags break up the flow of the text and the other elements, thus putting itself inside a virtual box.

Inline-HTML Tags

An inline tag is a part of the text flow in which they are inserted; they do not have a box, virtual or otherwise, around them and there is no line break after them either.

One example of a block tag is the <p> tag and an inline tag example is the <b> tag. Try both tags and see what transpires when you use them one after the other- you will understand it better.

So why should we care?

You should care because learning the differences, and that isn't difficult if you give yourself the time, and once you learn that CSS can be used to change tags from block to inline and vice versa, you will have so much more authority when it comes to laying out and styling your webpages.

The Web Designer's Checklist

Every website should have these elements:

- A structure that is clean, easy to read, and easy to update

- The design should be usable.
- You should have light pages that are fast to load.
- Use technology intelligently. For example, if you don't need Flash on your page, don't use it just because you think it's cool.
- Your website should convey its meaning immediately.

Let's break this down:

1. **A Clean Structure**

Not so long ago, pretty much every webpage you opened had funky animations; while it might have seemed like fun, these days, designers are starting to use the design principles and create sleek, minimal websites. Where things get difficult is that design isn't nearly as flexible as it should be. Because websites are constantly changing and if it's going to take a huge amount of work to add a navigation button, reconsider your design. Elements should be easy to add and remove freely, with no trouble.

2. **A Usable Design**

Usability may be one of the latest buzzwords but it is also important as far as web design goes. It means a visitor should be able to navigate your website without difficulty and not hunt for things. If they can't, it's the result of poor design.

3. **Light Pages that Load Fast**

This is one of the oldest rules and one you must abide by. If your web page takes too long to load - more than a couple of seconds - people will leave it and look elsewhere. This isn't an issue with high-speed internet but with the speed of loading and always something to keep in mind on all internet speeds.

4. **Using Technology Intelligently**

This is common sense to most people. Just because the technology is there, doesn't mean you need it all on the webpage. Design is about being clever and expending only what you need to produce the page you want, not what's in fashion at the time.

5. **Get your Meaning Across Immediately**

There is nothing worse than opening a webpage and trying to figure out what it's about. The design may be fantastic, but it's a waste of time if it's ambiguous.

Use content that clearly explains your message and secure those tags to make it stand out where it needs to.

What you Need to Start Web Design

There is no special hardware needed for web design; a normal computer with an internet connection is more than sufficient. Of course, if you want to splash out a few thousand dollars on a new OC you can, but before you do, understand that:

- An HTML page is nothing more than a text document

Web design is more about creating HTML Pages than fancy animations and designs. HTML is a text document with keywords or tags in it. These are very simple to create, easy to use, and easy to manipulate. Even smaller mobile devices can see them! And that goes for some of the older handhelds like PDAs that have a tiny fraction of the computing power a standard desktop has.

OK, so I can hear the shouts now – web design is more than text and HTML. What about images? These have to be created and then added in and manipulating images can take quite a bit of computing power. This is true but only in print work – images need to be heavier for that. For web design, the images are much lighter so they download onto the page quickly.

Web design isn't tough; as long as you learn the basics of CSS and HTML, you can do whatever you want and produce a basic website in a short time. Nonetheless, what about mobile app development? We'll look at that next.

Mobile App Development

The Ins and Outs of Mobile Web App Development

Today, there are more than 7.7 billion people in the world and more than 5 billion of them own a cell-phone. The highest majority own a smartphone of some sort, and according to the Pew Research Center, in the last 5 years, the number of people using smartphones to access the internet has more than doubled and so has the number of people using mobile applications.

Mobile computing is now widespread and, frankly, it's fantastic. Never has the world been more connected than it is now; never have we had so much information, quite literally, at our fingertips.

What is the number one complaint from mobile users?

Badly designed mobile applications.

The biggest issues faced by mobile app developers is the work needed to get their app to work on a huge range of different devices, each with its own set of unique problems. As a designer, it doesn't matter whether you opt to design a native app, a mobile app, or a hybrid app; it must work on all those devices and on all browsers - be they web or mobile, and on all platforms.

And that's a tough call.

Every web developer has to agonize about providing support for mobile devices but, with these devices fast taking over as our main way of accessing the internet, if your website doesn't support mobiles now, it will need to in the near future.

Mobile vs. Native vs. Hybrid

There isn't such a thing as a one-size-fits-all approach, especially when it comes to developing web apps for mobile devices. Sure, there are plenty of best practices you could consider and not all of them are technical. First, what audience are you targeting? Do they want a mobile version of the app or a native mobile app? What is the difference between hybrid and native apps? What resources do you have at your disposal for development? What mobile technologies are most people most familiar with? Have you envisioned a licensing and sales model? What is it?

The list can go on but, in general terms, with one or two exceptions, mobile web apps are the fastest and the cheapest route, more so than native mobile apps, particularly when your major objective is to build support for as many different devices as possible. On the other side of the coin, there may be things like movement sensors and other capabilities native to mobiles, totally essential to the app but which can only be accessed through a native app – that would make mobile web apps a non-starter.

If we go beyond the web vs. native apps subject, we have the hybrid app. This could be the answer you are looking for, depending on what your requirements are and what constraints you have on your resources. Like a native mobile app, a hybrid app will run on the mobile device and not in a browser but will be built using CSS, HTML5, and JavaScript web technologies. Typically, they are underpinned by hybrid frameworks and run in a native container. At the same time, they use the power of the browser engine on the device but not the browser for rendering HTML and locally processing JavaScript. The addition of an abstraction layer enables device capabilities that cannot otherwise be accessed in a mobile web app to be used for things like local storage, the accelerometer, the camera, and so on.

It doesn't matter whether you choose a mobile web app, a native mobile app, or a hybrid; make sure you research thoroughly and confirm the stats before you even start. Let's say you opt to develop an e-commerce app - a native mobile one - to sell your products. According to HubSpot, over 70% of those who use their mobile device for shopping, do so through a mobile web app and not a native app, so yours would probably fail at the first hurdle. Research is key.

Next, you have to take the practical considerations into account – time and money. There's an old saying – "faster, better, cheaper…pick any two". Time to market and financial constraints are imperative in developing web applications but it is vital you don't make a compromise on quality. If someone who uses your app has a bad experience the first time, don't expect to get them back and put in a good word for you!

Indeed, all three – the native, mobile web, and hybrid app – are different and each comes with its own set to challenges and, ultimately, benefits. Rather than developing an app from start to finish, we shall concentrate on the tools and the methods to employ, and avoid as you develop mobile web apps that are intuitive, easy, and functional.

Mobile App Development = Detailed Planning

The first step and one of a long line of best practices is to identify the requirements of the target audience for the app. Careful research is key; look at the capabilities you are targeting to work out if they can be achieved with your app. It's not productive to get halfway there and realize one essential client function has no support. You've already invested your time and resources into designing the infrastructure and interface and now you have to start over – all because you didn't do your homework.

Another mistake is to assume you are going to use web-based code designed for desktop browsers in your mobile web app without a problem. It doesn't work that way. There are significant dissimilarities and if you don't know what they are, you could get bitten – badly.

For example, the autoplay function for the HTML5 <video> tag won't work on any mobile browser and, in the same way, the CSS properties called opacity and transition are not consistently supported in most of the browsers used on mobile devices. In addition, some of the web API methods will give you trouble on mobile platforms – the SoundCloud music streaming API, for example, needs Adobe Flash, which has no support on most mobiles.

One factor can cause a lot of complication when developing mobile web apps; mobile devices don't have as long a lifespan as a desktop display. Add to this a constant slew of new mobile devices hitting the market and new technologies, and you can see how tough it is for the app developers. The landscape never stops changing. You have to keep up with every single change. If your app works in a browser, some of this is alleviated because the more device-specific problems are not an issue; however, you still need to have a view that works in a browser, but also supports multiple screen resolutions and can adjust correctly for both portrait and landscape orientation.

Put serious thought into being able to support the Retina displays on the Apple devices. These are a liquid crystal with a much higher pixel density, which means the human eye cannot pick out individual pixels at a normal distance of viewing. For mobile web apps, it is vital the Retina display can turn low-res images fuzzy and pixelated. The best solution in terms of development is to ensure the server recognizes the request for an image comes from a Retina display and provides the user with a higher resolution image.

To make use of some of the great functionality provided by HTML5, verify ahead of time that the functionality is supported on the device landscape most likely to be used by your audience. For example, the navigator getUserMedia functionality is not supported on iOS 6 or higher because the camera can only be accessed via native apps.

You can also make use of CSS3 media queries to provide each device with properly customized content. Take a look at the example below where we capture some of the difference characteristics on a device, such as screen resolutions, pixel density, and orientation:

/ For resolutions of 700px or lower*/*

@media (max-width: 700px) { ... }

/ the same but with orientation set to landscape*/*

```
@media (max-width: 700px) and (orientation: landscape) { ... }

/* Adding orientation and width, we can add a clause for a media type, like   'tv' */

@media tv and (min-width: 700px) and (orientation: landscape) { ... }

/* for the lower resolution displays with a background-image */

.image {

    background-image: url(/path/to/my/image.png);

    background-size: 200px 300px;

    height: 300px;

    width: 200px;

}

/* for the higher resolution or Retina displays with a background-image */

@media only screen and (min--moz-device-pixel-ratio: 2),

only screen and (-o-min-device-pixel-ratio: 2/1),

only screen and (-webkit-min-device-pixel-ratio: 2),

only screen and (min-device-pixel-ratio: 2) {

  -repeat;

    background-size: 200px 400px;

  /* rest of your styles... */

  }

}
```

Mobile Web App Optimization for Performance

As a mobile app developer, the absolute last words you want to hear is, "why is this so slow?!" In order to never hear those words, carefully deliberate how each byte is reduced and optimized, how you must do the same to each server transfer so the user isn't left hanging. It isn't realistic to expect all transfers to happen over Wi-Fi networks; many users prefer to use mobile data or only have that option. It's also worth bearing in mind that more than 60% of those who use mobile web apps expect the site to load on their device in under 3 seconds. By the same token, Google research indicated that for every extra 5 seconds an app or website takes to load, the traffic drops by around 20%. Loading times are also used by search engines in their calculations of page quality scores.

Here are some tips to optimize your mobile web app performance and keep latency at an absolute minimum:

- **Image Optimization** – Loading time of in-app images is one of the biggest issues that affects loading times on a mobile device. You can use online optimizers, like smushit.com to help you optimize your images.
- **Code Compression** – Compressing the CSS and JavaScript files can significantly improve performance.
- **Database Queries** – Not all mobile devices accept the same number of cookies as a desktop browser and this can result in more database queries being needed. Ensure server-side caching is in place for mobile web app clients. Also, remember to use the right filters to keep SQL injection out as this can compromise your server and site security.
- **CDN** – If you intend to have a high number of videos, audio files, images, and other media types on your app, consider using a content delivery network. Some of the best commercial ones include Microsoft Windows Axure, Amazon S3, and MaxCDN and the benefits are tremendous, such as:
  - *Better download performance* – *When you use the resources offered by a CDN, you can distribute your web app loading, use less bandwidth, and get much better performance. The higher-end CDN's offer a superior level of availability, lower packet loss and lower latency over the networks and many of them have global data centers that allow users to download from the server nearest to them.*
  - *Concurrent downloads* – *Usually, a browser limits how many concurrent connections are allowed on one domain, after which, any other download is blocked. Try downloading a number of large files from one website and you will likely see this in action. Every additional CDN, on different domains, allows for many more concurrent downloads.*
  - *Bette analytics* – *Some of the commercial CDNs offer usage reports in addition to website analytics.*

Mobile Web App Development Tools

Another old saying is, "the right tools for the right job", and this is so true in the case of mobile web app development. Choosing the best tools to develop your app puts you halfway to getting the job done. We'll look at some of them here but don't limit yourself – there are plenty of other tools to use.

The Right JavaScript Mobile Web App Framework

Developing mobile web apps creates similar challenges, such as inconsistency across mobile browsers for both CSS and HTML, compatibility across browsers, and so on. Frameworks have been developed to help get around these problems as easily as possible on the widest conceivable range of mobile devices. Most of the mobile frameworks are relatively lightweight, which means they are stress-free to provide the fastest experience for browsing the web without compromising how your application both looks and feels to a user.

The most popular JavaScript framework, if we step beyond just mobile apps, is jQuery. We talked about the desktop version, but there is also a mobile version called jQuery Mobile. In it, you will find a widget library that turns semantic markups into more gesture-friendly formats, which makes carrying out some operations on a touchscreen much easier. The newest version has a codebase that is incredibly lightweight but packs a mighty punch offering a ton of graphical elements to turn user interface from boring into something remarkable.

Sencha Touch is another alternative that is gaining ground; it offers fabulous performance and helps developers create an interface that looks and feels like a native one. It also has a fully-featured widget library based on the ExtJS JavaScript library.

Comparing jQuery with Sencha Touch, we can see there are a couple of fundamental differences:

- **Look and feel** – In general, Sencha Touch apps have an exclusive look and feel to the jQuery Mobile apps but reactions like this are subjective.
- **Extensibility** – jQuery Mobile provides a large number of 3rd party extensions and is highly extensible; Sencha Touch, on the other hand, is a more closed framework.
- **Device support** – jQuery Mobile supports more mobile devices than Sencha Touch.
- **HTML vs JavaScript** – jQuery is more HTML, mostly used for manipulation and extension of HTML code in JavaScript. Sencha Touch is based entirely on JavaScript – remember, you need to consider your developmental resources. When you pick your team, think about things like this.
- **External dependencies** – jQuery Mobile needs jQuery and the jQuery UI for the manipulation of DOM whereas Sencha has no external dependencies.
- **Learning curve** – For most developers, jQuery is quicker to learn than Sencha Touch perhaps because many developers are already familiar with the many jQuery libraries.

Responsive Frameworks and Mobile Web Applications

More and more responsive frameworks have begun appearing in recent times and the two popular ones are called Foundation and Bootstrap. Responsive frameworks make responsive UI design for web apps much simpler and far more streamlined, which makes them easier to implement. Much of this is because they bring in many of the UI paradigms and common layouts to a framework that can be reused and is optimized for performance. Most frameworks are based on JavaScript and CSS and they are open-source. This makes them free to download and use and they can effortlessly be customized to your requirements; unless your conditions are off the scale, then at least one of the available frameworks is likely to help you reduce the effort of designing your mobile web app.

Some of the fundamental differences between Foundation and Bootstrap are:

- **Targeted platforms** – Bootstrap does offer support for tablet, smartphone, and desktop but its focus is on desktop use, whereas Foundation was designed for almost all types and sizes of the screens.
- **Browser compatibility** – Bootstrap offers support for IE7 and above, and Foundation is limited to IE9 and above.
- **Layouts and components** – Bootstrap offers more UI element collections than Foundation does.
- **Auto-resizing** – In Foundation, the grid will stretch or shrink as per the height and width of the browser; Bootstrap has only support for a set of pre-defined grid size based on a standard subset of different screen sizes.

Debugging and Testing Mobile Web Apps

When it comes to debugging, with mobile apps, the whole process can be frustrating. Even more so if you need to find several different types and sizes of the devices to test things on, or SDK's need to be installed for emulating targeted platforms – and these are usually a long way from being perfect too!

In this context, there is a clear advantage to developing mobile web apps as opposed to native apps – standard developer tools that are browser-based can be used for debugging. Remote debugging is a common form and one of the best tools is Chrome's popular DevTools. You could also use Firebug in Firefox and Dragonfly in Opera.

Chrome DevTools is the most prevalent because:

- **Mobile Emulator** – This is the main reason why DevTools is the preferred option among developers. It is a great way of debugging mobile web apps. Some of its best features include touch event emulation, throttling of network

bandwidth, user agent spoofing, geolocation, and device orientation overrides, CSS media Type emulation, and more.
- **Interactive editor** – You can edit CSS and JavaScript as you go.
- **JavaScript debugger** – This is one of the very best. This debugger permits you to profile JavaScript at execution time and allows DOM breakpoints.
- **JSON and XML Viewers** – This means there is no need to use plugins to inspect server responses.
- **ADB Protocol Support over USB** – The Android Debug Bridge makes it easy to instantiate a remote session to debug.
- **Dynamic resource inspection** – You can inspect the local data sources for your app, including the Web SQL and IndexedDB databases, cookies, local storage, session storage, and the application cache resources. In addition, you get quick access to the visual resources for your apps, such as the fonts, images, and style sheets so you can easily see if there are any problems

There are also plenty of online tools to test cross-browser compatibility and layout of your mobile web application. One such tool is called BrowserStack; just type your application URL, choose your browser, operating system, and so on, and you will be given an emulated view including loading speeds of your app in the specified environment.

With more people joining the mobile revolution, and the quantity and diversity of the mobile devices coming onto the market, there is a greater need for high-quality, user-friendly, responsive mobile web apps these days, and that will continue to grow. If you can develop your mobile apps efficiently and intelligently, you will continue having an assured place in the market.

There are several factors to consider when you make a decision on the type of mobile app to develop – native, web, or hybrid – and each comes with its own advantages. Mobile web apps are, more often than not, the most efficient to develop and get to market and this tends to be the route most developers take.

A Last-Minute Overview

What is a mobile web app?

These are web applications that have been optimized to work on mobile devices too. They are not actually mobile applications; rather, they are websites that have been written using CSS and HTML and run in browsers. They are designed to feel and look like a mobile app but they actually have little in common.

What is a native app?

A native app is an application that has been written for a specified platform using APIs specifically for that platform.

What is a hybrid app?

Hybrid apps are those written with web technology, like CSS and HTML, but given a thin native web browser to wrap them in. These can be ported easily and quickly to several platforms where they work using the same codebase.

Is there an impact on the user experience between the native and mobile web app?

Mobile web apps are websites that have been optimized to work on mobile devices and, if done properly, the user experience is akin to that of a hybrid or a native application.

Why are native apps superior when it comes to performance?

They are superior because they are developed for a specific platform using specific APIs. Hybrid apps tend to be slower with more bugs because they have to go through numerous containers and jump through hoops to work.

It was outside the scope of this book to actually develop a mobile application, mainly because it isn't a case of one-size-fits-all. There are too many variants, too many platforms to take into account, and it really deserves a lot more space than we could give it here. Hopefully, you have an idea of how to go about developing a mobile web app now and so we will move on to responsive design.

Responsive Web Design

The internet has taken off far quicker than anyone would ever have thought and now mobile growth is catching up fast. Internet usage via mobile devices has grown so fast that it is now approaching desktop internet usage levels.

These days, it's not so easy to find a person who doesn't have at least one mobile device connected to the net and, in the UK alone, there are more mobile devices than actual persons in the country; if these trends continue, internet usage via a mobile device will outstrip desktop use within the next 12 months.

With this massive growth comes one question: How do you build a website that suits all kinds of users? The answer to that is something called RWD, or Responsive Web Design.

RWD is the art of building websites that work flawlessly on all types of devices, be they desktop or mobile, and on all screen sizes. It is focused on building intuitive user experience to benefit both desktop users and mobile device users. This allows you to view your favorite websites on whatever device you want, to use web apps on your mobile instead of having to download the mobile app version.

Responsive vs. Adaptive vs. Mobile

The term, "responsive" is not new to some while others are more familiar with the terms, "adaptive" or "mobile". That probably leaves you asking the question: What, if anything, is the difference between these three?

Adaptive and responsive design are close to one another and you often see both terms used for the same thing. In general, responsive means a quick and positive reaction to change and adaptive means easily changed or modified for a new situation, like a change. A website that has been responsively designed will change continuously in a fluid way based on all sorts of factors, and the website built adaptively is constructed using a set of predefined factors. The ideal situation would be a website created using both practices because that would give us the perfect mix for a fully functional website. Hence, there isn't enough difference to worry about which term you use.

Mobile, on the other hand, it's a different story. A mobile website is built specifically for mobile users and, in general, only work on those devices. This can be useful at times, but with responsive web design, it isn't necessary and not a good idea anyway. Mobile websites tend to be lightweight but they come with baggage – the potential for browser sniffing and the dependencies that go with a new code base – two big obstacles, not just for the developer but the end-user too.

Responsive web design is currently the most popular option among developers because the design will adapt to various device and browser viewports, changing the content and the layout to suit. RWD is actually a perfect combination of all three – responsive, mobile, and adaptive – and it has the benefits of all three.

Flexible Layouts

We can break responsive web design into three core parts and the first part is a flexible layout. This is the practice that revolves around building a website layout using a flexible grid. This grid is dynamic resizing to the required width at the time it is needed. To build a flexible grid we need relative length units, usually an em unit or a percentage. These declare the values for the common grid properties, like padding, margin, or width.

Relative Viewport Lengths

With CSS3, we have a few new relative length units that were related specifically to device or browser viewport size. Those units include vw, vh, vmin, and vmax. Right now, support for these units isn't skillful but it is increasing all the time, and eventually, they will play a big role in responsive website building.

- vw – viewports width
- vh – viewports height
- vmin – viewport height and width minimum
- vmax – viewport height and width maximum

With the flexible layout, you should not use units of fixed measurement, like inches, or pixels. Why? Because the height and the width of the viewport are constantly changing depending on the device being used. All website layouts need to adapt easily to this kind of change and the fixed values are far too constraining. Nonetheless, there is one easy formula to identify what the flexible layout proportions are using the relative values.

The formula takes the element width and divides it by the parent element width, thus giving the target element's relative width:

target ÷ context = result

Flexible Grid

Let's try using this on a layout with two columns. In the example below, we have a division with the parent element with the class called container wrapping around the elements called aside and section. What we want to achieve is to have the section element on the left and the aside element on the right, and equal margins in between them. Usually, the styles and the markup for this kind of layout would look like the following in HTML and CSS:

HTML

```html
<div class="container">
  <section>...</section>
  <aside>...</aside>
</div>
```

CSS

```css
.container {
  width: 538px;
}
section,
aside {
  margin: 10px;
}
section {
  float: left;
  width: 340px;
}
aside {
  float: right;
  width: 158px;
}
```

Fixed Grid Demo

If we use that formula, we can convert the fixed-length units into relative units. In the next example, we make use of the percentage unit, but you could do exactly the same if you used the em unit. Notice – it doesn't matter what the width of the parent container is; the margins and the widths for both aside and section will scale proportionately:

section,

aside {

  margin: 1.858736059%; /* 10px ÷ 538px = .018587361 */

}

section {

  float: left;

  width: 63.197026%;   /* 340px ÷ 538px = .63197026 */

}

aside {

  float: right;

  width: 29.3680297%; /* 158px ÷ 538px = .293680297 */

}

Flexible Grid Demo

We can also take the concept and the formula for the flexible layout and reapply it to different parts of a grid. The result of this will be a website that is totally dynamic and scale easily to meet all sizes of the viewport. You can take things further and get even more control using the flexible layout by leveraging a number of properties, namely:

- min-width
- max-width
- min-height
- max-height

On the other hand, using this layout on its own simply isn't adequate. There will be times when a browser's viewport width is too small for proportional scaling to work and you will end with minuscule columns that can't display the content correctly. If a layout is too small or even too large, the text becomes unreadable, and there is also the chance the layout will break down. In this case, we can build better using media queries.

Media Queries

Originally, media queries were built as extensions to the media types found when styles were targeted and included. The queries provide us with the ability to choose a sundry style for each different circumstance of browser and device, such as the orientation of the device or the viewport width, for example. When you can apply styles that are uniquely targeted, you open up a whole new world of leverage and opportunity as far as responsive web design goes.

Initializing Media Queries

There's more than one way to use a media query:

- Use the @media rule in a style sheet that already exists
- Use the @import rule to import a brand new style sheet
- Linking to a style sheet from the HTML document

The most common method is the first one as this will avoid making more HTTP requests:

HTML

<!-- Separate CSS File -->

<link href="styles.css" rel="stylesheet" media="all and (max-width: 1024px)">

CSS

/ @media Rule */*

@media all and (max-width: 1024px) {...}

/ @import Rule */*

@import url(styles.css) all and (max-width: 1024px) {...}

Each query may have a media type with at least one expression following it. The more common media types include:

- All
- Screen
- Print
- Tv
- Braille

Included in the HTML5 specifications are new types, and that includes 3D glasses. If a media type does not get specified, the query will go to the media default which is screen.

The expression in the media query may have media features and their values, and these values will evaluate as true or false. When features and value are evaluated true, the specified styles will be applied; if it is false, they won't be applied.

Using Logical Operators in Media Queries

You can use logical operators in your media queries to build some powerful expressions. There are three you can use:

- And
- Not
- Only

The logical and operator will allow you to add an extra condition to the media query to ensure the device or browser does a, b, c, and so on. You can separate several individual media queries by commas, which then becomes an unspoken logical or operator. The next example gets all the media types between a width of 800 and 1024 pixels:

@media all and (min-width: 800px) and (max-width: 1024px) {...}

The logical not operator will negate a query specifying any except the identified one. In the next example, the expression will apply to all devices without a color screen, for example having a monochrome or black and white screen:

@media not screen and (color) {...}

The logical only operator is new and, so far, isn't recognized by the HTML4 algorithm. This means the styles are hidden from any browser or device that doesn't have support for media queries. In the example below, the expression will only select those screens in portrait orientation and with an agent that has the capability to render a media query:

@media only screen and (orientation: portrait) {...}

Omitting Media Types

When you make use of the only or the not logical operator, you can omit the media type. In this situation, the media type would go to the default of all.

Media Features in Media Queries

One of the best ways to be introduced to media queries is by learning the syntax and how the logical operators come into play. The real work though comes with the media features. These identify the properties or attributes the media query expression will target.

Height and Width

One of the more universal features is centered on determining the width or the height for a browser or device viewport. We can find the width or height using the related media features and each of those features could also have a prefix of a min or a max qualifier, thus building up a feature like max-width, min-height and so on.

The width and height features are based on the width and height of the rendering area for the viewport, such as the browser window. The height and width feature values may be a relative or an absolute length unit.

@media all and (min-width: 320px) and (max-width: 780px) {...}

When it comes to responsive design, the features used the most are things like min-width and max-width. These are worthwhile to build websites that are responsive and work flawlessly on mobile devices and desktops with none of the confusion over the features on the devices.

Minimum and Maximum Prefixes

We can use min and max prefixes on a fair number of media features. The min prefix indicates values greater than or equal to, and the max prefix indicates values that are less than or equal to. When we use these prefixes we can avoid getting into conflict with the HTML syntax; specifically not using the < > symbols.

The Orientation Media Feature

This feature is used to determine which orientation mode a device is in – landscape or portrait. Landscape mode will be triggered when the display is wider than it is tall and portrait when the device is taller than it is wide. This is an important feature for mobile devices:

@media all and (orientation: landscape) {...}

Aspect Ratio Media Features

These media features include the aspect ratio and the device aspect ratio features and they are used to specify the height and width pixel ratio of the output device or the rendering area that was targeted. We can also use the min and max prefixes with these aspect features to identify ratios below or above the stated ratio.

The aspect ratio feature value is made up of a pair of positive integers separated by a forward slash. The first one identifies what the pixel width is while the second one identifies the pixel height.

@media all and (min-device-aspect-ratio: 16/9) {...}

Pixel Ratio Media Features

Along with the aspect ratio features, we also have pixel-ratio features. As well as the min prefix and the max prefix, these features have the device-pixel ratio feature too. This pixel-ration feature is a great tool for identifying devices that have high-definition displays and that includes the Retina displays. To do this, a media query looks like this:

@media only screen and (-webkit-min-device-pixel-ratio: 1.3), only screen and (min-device-pixel-ratio: 1.3) {...}

Resolution Media Feature

We use the resolution media feature to specify what the output device resolution is in pixel density, also called DPI or dots-per-inch. This feature will accept both the min and max features and it will also accept dots-per-pixel (1.3dppx), dots-per-centimeter (118dpcm), and many other resolution values based on length.

@media print and (min-resolution: 300dpi) {...}

Other Media Features

There are other media features including the identification of the output colors available using the color, monochrome and color-index features, the identification of bitmap devices using the grid feature and identification of the scanning process of television using the scan feature. These are not ordinary features but are helpful at times.

Media Query Browser Support

The media features do not work with IE8 or lower nor do they work with other legacy browsers. However, there are some suitable JavaScript alternatives.

First is respond.js which is a light-weight alternative. This will only look for the media types with min or max-width, which is ideal if those are the only media types in use. Second is CSS3-MediaQueries.js, which is a somewhat heavier and better developer, offering support for a bigger range of the more complex queries.

Keep in mind that alternatives tend to be worse in performance and can slow your website so make sure the tradeoff is worth it.

Media Queries Demo

Let's get practical and use media queries to write our previous flexible layout again. One of the biggest problems with the demo at the moment is, at times, the width of aside becomes too small in the smaller viewports and becomes useless. By including a media query that targets viewports under a width of 420 pixels, the floats are turned off and the widths of both aside and section are changed:

@media all and (max-width: 420px) {

```
section, aside {

  float: none;

  width: auto;

  }

}
```

Identifying Breakpoints

Instinct might tell you to write a breakpoint around the more common sizes of viewport, as it is determined by the different resolutions – 320px, 768px, 1224px, etc. This is NOT a good idea.

When you build responsive websites, they should automatically adjust to fit all viewport sizes, irrespective of the device. You should only introduce a breakpoint when websites start to look a bit odd, break down, or the user experience is poor.

Plus, bear in mind new devices with different resolutions are being brought out continually and keeping up with everything is a never-ending job.

Mobile First

One of the most popular techniques in use with media queries is a technique called mobile-first. This approach makes use of styles targeted at the small viewports and sets these as the default styles for the website; media queries use them to add new style as the size of the viewport becomes larger.

The main belief behind the design of mobile-first is when a user is on a smartphone or a tablet with a much smaller viewport, they should not have to first load the desktop styles and then have it overwritten by the mobile styles later. This is a complete waste of time and precious bandwidth – an important factor for anyone looking for a fast website.

This approach also says we should design with the mobile user in mind first, taking their constraints into account before those of a desktop user. To be honest, it won't be long before mobile internet access exceeds desktop usage by a significant majority. Plan for this and develop those mobile experiences:

The mobile-first media queries could look something like this:

/* Default styles first followed by media queries */

@media screen and (min-width: 400px) {...}

@media screen and (min-width: 600px) {...}

@media screen and (min-width: 1000px) {...}

@media screen and (min-width: 1400px) {...}

You can also use media queries to reduce the need to download unnecessary media assets. Avoid CSS3 gradients, shadows, animations, and transforms in the mobile styles because when these are overused, they cause significant delays and can affect the battery life of the device.

/ Default media */*

body {

  background: #ddd;

}

/ Media for the larger devices */*

@media screen and (min-width: 800px) {

  body {

    background-image: url("bg.png") 50% 50% no-repeat;

  }

}

When we add some media queries to our last example, some of the styles were overwritten to provide a better layout on the smaller device viewports, those under a width of 420 pixels. If we were to rewrite it using the mobile styles first and then add the media queries for the large device screens (over 420 pixels wide), it would look like this:

section,

aside {

  margin: 1.858736059%;

}

@media all and (min-width: 420px) {

  .container {

    max-width: 538px;

  }

```
  section {

   float: left;

    width: 63.197026%;

  }

  aside {

   float: right;

    width: 29.3680297%;

  }

}
```

Note this is not more code than we had before. There is one exception – mobile devices only need to render a single CSS declaration. All other styles are deferred and will only load on the bigger viewports without the initial styles being overwritten.

Viewports

Today's mobile devices do a great job of displaying nearly any website, but it's fair to say they could do with a little help on occasion, especially when it comes to identifying scale, viewport size, and resolution. Apple came up with a "cure" for this – the viewport metatag.

Viewport Height and Width

When you use the viewport metatag together with the width or the height values, the viewport width or height is defined. Each of the values will accept a keyword or a positive value. For height, the property will take a keyword device-height value and for width, the property will take the keyword device-width value. When you use these keywords, the default width and height values for the device are inherited.

To get the best results and to ensure your website looks the absolute best, use the device defaults. This is done by applying the device-width and device-height values.

```
<meta name="viewport" content="width=device-width">
```

Viewport Scale

If you want more control over scaling your website on a mobile device and on how your users can scale it, use these properties:

- Minimum-scale
- Maximum-scale
- Initial-scale
- User-scalable

At the outset, the website scale should be set at 1 because this will define the ratio between device-height in portrait and the size of the viewport. If the device happens to be in landscape mode, the ratio would be between the width of the device and the size of the viewport. Initial-scale values must always be a positive integer somewhere between 0 and 10.

<meta name="viewport" content="initial-scale=2">

The values for minimum-scale and maximum-scale should determine the minimum and maximum scaling of a viewport. When you use the minimum-scale, you should have a positive integer as the value less than or equal to the initial-scale value. By the same token, maximum-scale should have a value of a positive integer greater than or equal to the initial-scale. Both of those values should be between 0 and 10.

<meta name="viewport" content="minimum-scale=0">

In general, you should not have these values set as the same value the initial-scale. Why? Because zooming would be disabled. That is better accomplished by using the user-scalable value instead. When you set the user-scalable value as no, zooming is disabled while, conversely, setting the value to yes enables the zooming.

Never disable zooming ability on a website because you impair usability and accessibility and that prevents some people from being able to see your website.

<meta name="viewport" content="user-scalable=yes">

Viewport Resolution

Allowing the browser to determine how a website should be scaled, based on the scale values for the viewport is good. If you need more control where the device resolution is concerned, use the target-densitydpi value. This viewport will accept several values, including:

- Device-dpi
- High-dpi

- Medium-dpi
- Low-dpi
- A DPI number

It is erratic you would need to use the target-densitydpi value but pixel-by-pixel control could be effective.

`<meta name="viewport" content="target-densitydpi=device-dpi">`

Combining Viewport Values

You can provide the viewport meta tag with both individual and multiple values to set several viewport properties simultaneously. To do this, each value must be comma-separated within the value of the content attribute. You can see a recommended outline for a viewport value below that makes use of both the initial-scale and the width properties.

`<meta name="viewport" content="width=device-width, initial-scale=1">`

CSS Viewport Rule

Because the viewport meta tag is centered on setting the styles controlling how a website is rendered, the recommended use is to take the viewport from a meta tag that has HTML and put it in a @ rule in the CSS. By doing this, the style is kept separate from the content and gives a better and cleaner approach.

Some browsers already have the @viewport rule implemented but it doesn't go across the board just yet. The viewport meta tag that was recommended would look like this CSS @viewport rule:

@viewport {

* width: device-width;*

* zoom: 1;*

}

Flexible Media

The last but no less important aspect of RWD revolves around the subject of flexible media. As the size of the viewports changes, it doesn't always chart that the media will follow. Videos, images, and any type of media on a website must be scalable and must change size as the viewport size changes.

One of the quickest ways to make your media scalable is by using the property of max-width and giving it a value of 100%. By doing this, as the size of the viewport shrinks, the media scales down as per the width value is given to its container:

img, video, canvas {

  max-width: 100%;

}

Flexible Embedded Media

Regrettably, the max-width property will not work properly on all media instances. It doesn't, for example, do well on embedded media or iFrames and this is a bitter letdown for those third-party websites, like YouTube that uses the iframe for the embedded media. As with anything though, there is a workaround.

If you want your embedded media to be completely responsive, the element that has been embedded must have an absolute position in a parent element. That parent must have a width set as 100% so the scaling will be based on the viewport width. Plus, the parent must also have a height set as 0 in order for the hasLayout mechanism to be triggered in the browser, in this case, Internet Explorer.

We then add padding at the bottom of the parent and set the value to the same aspect ratio as the embedded video is set. Doing this means the parent element height will be in proportion to the width.

Remember what the RWD formula is – if your embedded video has a 16:9 aspect ratio, dividing 9 by 16 equals .5625; that means the padding at the bottom should be 56.25%. We use bottom padding rather than top padding to ensure earlier versions of IE cannot break and the parent element is treated as absolutely positioned.

HTML

<figure>

  <iframe src="https://www.youtube.com/embed/4Fqg43ozz7A"></iframe>

</figure>

CSS

figure {

  height: 0;

  padding-bottom: 56.25%; /* 16:9 */

```
  position: relative;

  width: 100%;

}

iframe {

  height: 100%;

  left: 0;

  position: absolute;

  top: 0;

  width: 100%;

}
```

Again, a complete tutorial on responsive web design is outside the scope of this book but this gives you an idea on the basics, specifically how it applies to scaling for different size devices.

To finish this book, we'll take a detailed look at scripts in the next section, followed by some best practice on user experience, or UX as it is known.

Part 5: Scripting

JavaScript is one of the easiest ways of giving your website all kinds of elements, including some dynamic ones. Unless you are experienced in programming, JavaScript will be a new concept, but it is the simplest scripting language.

It was invented with the explicit purpose of making websites more dynamic. By itself, HTML can output pages that are static. Once loaded, your view will change very little unless you click on something, like a link that takes you to another page. When you add JavaScript to the code, your document looks completely different – changing the text font, the text color, the options that you might have in a drop-down menu and so on.

JavaScript is classed as a client-side language; the action ensues on the client's or user's side of things. JavaScript will work seamlessly without visiting a server, which is great because a server would slow things down dramatically.

In addition, JavaScript operations tend to be performed at once, and you find the language used for performing those operations that would, in any other way, weigh the server down, such as validation of form input. Distributing the work like this, by using the much-quicker client-side, makes things speedier.

The browsing environment is where JavaScript tends to be integrated and can acquire information about the HTML page and the browser. This data can be modified, and this is how things are changed on your screen. Being able to access this information means JavaScript is far more powerful and gives you more control over the browsing experience, in providing quick reactions when a user clicks the mouse or points at a specific element on the page and other events.

More importantly, JavaScript is very easy to learn and use. It has a technical side but very shortly, you will soon be scripting with the best of them.

The Java Connection

It isn't a revelation the connection between Java and JavaScript is misunderstood, but it is important to note they are not the same.

Java was created by Sun Microsystems and it is a computer programming language used to write large-scale programs. JavaScript was created by Netscape and is based, to a certain extent, on Java. The code syntax is similar but JavaScript isn't utilized for anything external to a web browser. It was meant to be called Live Script, but with Java growing in popularity, Netscape chose to call it JavaScript.

Scripting languages are often thought as lightweight languages, a language that doesn't need to be compiled before a browser can interpret it. All a script is, when you break it down, is a series of commands, a way of telling the browser what it needs to do.

Java and JavaScript share other similarities. The most significant one is they are OOP or object-oriented programming. This means you are working with objects; smaller objects grouped together to form a larger one – more about that later.

You might have heard of applets – Java used side-by-side with HTML. Applets are applications on a tiny scale and they are embedded into web pages providing some advanced effects. However, they aren't practical because of larger file sizes and limited utility. In contrast, JavaScript can be extremely useful.

JavaScript Versions

Like every tool used to create a website, JavaScript has more than one version. Each version brings new features and new compatibilities. V1.0 was the first one, arriving in Netscape Navigator2 and subsequent updates went through v1.1, 1.2, and 1.3. With Internet Explorer 3, Microsoft tried to provide support for JS 1.0 but it was too buggy and unreliable. The latest browsers all fully support v1.3.

All the issues and incompatibilities lead to a new and standardized version being released, sometimes known as ECMAScript. All the modern browsers like Safari, IE8 and above, Firefox and more, offer great support for ECMAScript to make sure all modern browsers operate on the same DOM.

Document Object Model

The Document Object Model, or the DOM, is the framework JavaScript needs to work on. Remember we mentioned about JavaScript being object-oriented? The OOP concept considers all the elements that make up a web page as objects. A document is also an object and it is made up of several other objects, such as images, forms, and tables.

Form objects themselves are made up of other objects, such as submit buttons and text boxes.

Every one of these objects has its own properties and those properties have values defining length, color, and so on. JavaScript has the ability to read and modify these properties or react to things occurring to objects, changing the object in an instant in the browser window. Scripts are able to work by themselves or respond to user interaction.

Every action a script performs on or with an object is called a method. A method is a function built into an object. The way user-controlled events, such as mouse movement, clicks, etc. are dealt with through event handlers, which are also commanded. Put together, all of these concepts are what JavaScript programming is based on.

The DOM gives you the ability to access all of the different page objects. There was quite a situation where the two biggest browsers had support for different DOM versions. The Netscape DOM wouldn't work properly with the Microsoft DOM and Dynamic HTML pages written for one browser wouldn't work in another. In recent times, the model was standardized, thus the DOM level 1 was created. More about this later but, for now, don't fret unless you intend on creating huge sites fueled by JavaScript.

Implementation

Therefore, how do we get this JavaScript onto a webpage? We write JavaScript the same way as we write HTML – using a text editor. Implementing JavaScript is done the same way we implement CSS – outside files can be linked to using the .js file extension, code blocks can be written into HTML scripts using <script> tags, and so on. The usual criteria for choosing are the same – link to external files if you want the same script on multiple pages, otherwise, embed it.

The first example is an embedded script and this will print a text line on the page:

<script type="text/javascript">

<!--

document. Write("<i>Hello World!</i>");

//-->

</script>

When this goes in the code, you will see the text, Hello World, on your screen, like this:

Hello World!

Breaking this down, the script tag is used to enclose the script code you want to be used. We used a type attribute to let the browser know what script type it will be dealing with to make it easier to interpret the code.

Comments with that code are used so the older browsers that can't understand the tag won't try to display text on the page. Any browser capable of reading JavaScript will understand and ignore the comments. Note as well, we commented out the comment with a JavaScript comment of a pair of forward slashes; this is for the benefit of Netscape (now owned by Mozilla) and stops errors in the older versions.

External Scripts

If we want to import a script from an external JavaScript file, the code must be saved with the .js extension in a text file, but the comments and tag scripts must be removed first. The code would literally be the part that says document.write("Hello World!"). This will do very little by itself, so we link the document using the code below in the web page <head> tag:

<script type="text/javascript"

src="simplemethods.js"></script>

Now, every variable and method in the file can be used on the web page. We'll look into that later on.

Consider the end-tag; the usual benefits of abstraction apply. That script file can be updated and all your pages will change appropriately. The script file is cached, and it won't need downloading again for any page that needs it.

Includes should always go in the page <head> tag; this way, when the user calls for a script, the browser can execute them immediately. If a script was called for that the browser didn't know existed, an error message would be thrown.

A Simple Script

Along these lines, what did the code do? Look at it again:

<script type="text/javascript">

<!--

document.write("<i>Hello World!</i>");

//-->

</script>

To start, we take control over the document object and make use of the write() method so some text can be output to the document. The text enclosed in a set of double quote marks is a string and this will be added to the web page. Sounds simple? Using the methods or the properties of the object, we write the name of the object followed by a dot, and then the name of the property or the method. Each of the lines of code in the script is finished with a semicolon. This is important – there is no give in JavaScript; if a line is written wrong an error code will be thrown, so be careful.

One more example before we end this part. The new script creates HTML and text.

<script type="text/javascript">

<!--

document.write("<h1>Main Title</h1>");

document.write("<p align='right'>Body</p>");

//-->

</script>

Note: when attribute values are quoted, single quote marks must be used. If you used double quotes, the write() method will reason the string prematurely ended and an error would be thrown.

<noscript>

The <noscript> tag is a method of providing a browser with alternate content when the browser has no support for JavaScript or if JavaScript has been disabled in a modern browser. It works in a simple way – the older browsers don't understand this tag, so it is ignored, displaying what's inside whereas the modern browsers will understand the tag and will skip over it. It can be used like this:

<noscript>
<p>Sorry, your browser has no support for JavaScript.</p>
</noscript>

You could also provide something comparable to what the script produces. In some cases where there is no fluent equivalent and that means <noscript> tags are irrelevant. That said, try to use the tag wherever you can because it ensures your content is always accessible.

On to the next section.

Event Handlers

Now onto the dynamic parts of JavaScript. An event is an occurrence triggered by a user when they interact with the web page. That occurrence could be as simple as moving the mouse around the page or clicking on something. By the time we get to the end of this section, you will have all sorts of interactions going on.

Basic Events

When an event is triggered by a user, the browser will do something to respond. Click on a link and the page in the href for the link will load. When a form filed is clicked on, it receives the focus of the browser. These event handlers are the defaults for each of the objects on an HTML page. Event handlers are written directly into the HTML code so the browser knows exactly which element is being addressed and lets new commands be added above the default actions already there. An event handler is not actually a script but it will, more often than not, use methods, variables, and functions from a script to do what it needs to do.

There are loads of proprietary and standard events that can happen on a web page, but we'll begin with a few of the more common ones – Load, mouseOver, and Click.

Browser Compatibility

Events are not new, they've been in existence since JavaScript started. Basic events have support in all browsers but the newer is less supported.

Assigning Handlers

The first thing is to give an event handler to the object that it will work with. This is by way of an attribute that goes with the HTML tag and we add it into a link. The code we would use is this:

<a href="http://www.yourhtmlsource.com" onMouseOver="window.status='Go back to the Homepage';
return true">Home</a>

This creates Home. When you hover on the link in your browser, look at your status bar at the bottom of the browser window. The handler will wait; when the event it reacts to occurs, it proceeds when the mouse is placed on the link and the text changes to what was placed in the code. Be aware Firefox will not allow changes to be made to the status bar content by JavaScript so the effect won't show. You can, however, change this in the Options panel for Firefox.

Thus, what happened here?

First, onMouseOver is nothing more than an attribute with one exception – the value in the attribute is JavaScript code. In our case, the status property for the window object, which contains everything that is on the page (including Document), is used to change it to a string of "Go back to the Homepage". Don't forget to separate objects and methods or properties with a dot. Also note that the text is enclosed in single quotes and this is followed by a semicolon, indicating the command is finished.

At the end is the command of return true. This means the default action must also happen – if a user clicks on a link, that link is followed. This value is a Boolean and it takes one of two values – true or false. If you set this command to false, the default action will not happen, so you could set a click event to return false to disable the link.

There is one exception to the return rule – text is written into the status bar. You could be forgiven for thinking that setting it to false would stop the default of the href being displayed, but it isn't true. In order for the handler to perform, it has to return true.

If you were to make use of the handler on your web page you would most likely perceive when the status bar has been set, it doesn't change. This isn't all good; we need to set something as the default text to remain in the status bar even after the mouse has moved away from the link. Luckily, there is a property in the window we can use. It's called defaultStatus and it can have a value assigned to it.

Using the event called onload, this is triggered once the page has fully loaded. Make a change to your <body> tag so it looks like this:

<body onLoad="window.defaultStatus='Welcome to my site'">

The loading event is going to be useful when we want our script to become active only when the whole page has loaded along with all its arrays and images. The window has plenty of properties as do most objects – we'll talk more about those later.

onClick is another basic event handler; we'll use it to set up a button that, once clicked, will trigger an alert. The code is:

<button onClick="alert('Boo!'); return false;">Click me</button>

And this creates

Click me

That's quite simple. Our alert object is beneath the window in the hierarchy for the object but we can leave window out; after all, the other objects are contained inside it. In our case, we could use window.alert, but we don't need to reference the window specifically unless more than one is open. In fact, if you wanted to, the above examples could be recoded using nothing more than status=".

An event may also be fired by the window when unloading starts. This will happen when links are followed or the window is closed. It is worthwhile to have more windows open when a user leaves your site.

Form Events

The events that usually transpire when users interact with forms are onFocus, onBlur, onSelect, and onChange.

onFocus will happen when the browser focus is on an object, when a user is interacting with the object. Click on a form and the focus is on it. When the focus leaves that element, it is known as 'blurred'. onBlur will come in when the object in focus is clicked away from, thus losing the focus.

onChange happens when a text box or area value is changed; when you move away from the input box, that change is registered. To create a text box, we use this code:

```
<input type="text" value="Change me" onchange="alert('You\'ve changed, man');">
```

Note that an apostrophe is used in the alert text. You can't normally do this because it would finish the text string early, so we used a backslash to escape the character. This happens a lot in programming and the backslash never shows in the alert – it is used purely so an apostrophe can be used.

onSelect happens when the text is selected in a field but we'll talk more specifically about this later.

Every form has events called reset and submit – they are self-explanatory. These are useful for form validation; by using onSubmit, you can make sure the form has been properly completed before the data is sent.

Modern Events

Most modern browsers allow you to assign any HTML element with an event handler, a change from the early days when it was only forms and links. A few all-new events have been added to the abilities of the browser to increase how much interaction may be achieved.

Along with click, mouseOver, and mouseOut, we can add an event called dblClick, which means -you guessed it- double-click. Plus, using mouseUp and mouseDown provides better control over the click event. These events correspond to a mouse button being clicked (mouseDown) and then released (mouseUp). And you have mouseMove, which you can also react to. You already know how to create an event for these – just add the word 'on' to the name of the event.

In later browsers, events were added relating to the keyboard actions. Both keyUp and keyDown will fire when you expect them to and, if you hold a key down, the keypress will continuously fire. You can also find out which of the keys is being pressed but we'll go onto that in the near future.

Writing Scripts

Now we know how to trigger off a script, so what comes next? Having them actually do something. We covered all this in the opening part of this book but here's an overview of the JavaScript programming basics.

Variables

Variables are a part of almost all programming languages and we covered them earlier as a part of the JavaScript language. Variables can be defined as a bit of text or a number and the value of the variable may then be used in a script. JavaScript does not require declaring what the variable type is, i.e. whether it is text or number, only the name of it and its value. This makes it incredibly easy to switch from one type to another:

var age = 18;

var introText = "Many years ago...";

You can think of a variable as a box or a container with a name and can be used for strong values. When you learn how to access a page object, you can also create a variable using the form field values.

The name of a variable must begin with a letter but it may have numbers in it. Convention states the first is a lowercase letter and any subsequent word in the name will start with a capital letter, as in introText.

Variables may then be used like this:

document.write(introText + " I was " + age);

For the text below to be created, put the name of the variable inside the right parentheses without using the quotes. If you used the quote, the browser would mistake the names as strings. They are then joined with quoted strings using the + sign.

Many years ago... I was 18.

Variables can also be defined with no value and automatically be given the empty value of undefined. We do this using code line such as var textLength and provide the value down the line.

Arrays

An array is a specific type of variable that may have more than one value. Each value will have an index, which is the position number in the array. Don't forget that JavaScript is zero-indexed, which means the first number is 0. For example:

var months = new Array();

months[0] = "January";

months[1] = "February";

If you were to use document.write(months[1]), February would be printed. All you do is add the index inside a set of square brackets at the end of the variable name and you get access to the value of that index. Arrays can have more than one entry and when you create arrays this way, you create an array object. This object will have its own properties, such as length, etc.

Strings

A String variable plays a vital part in JavaScript and they are used a lot. A string variable is a group of characters, a sentence, a word, a url for example. They also have many properties and an array of methods.

You saw strings in use earlier – the text in the alert for example. A string is always delimited using quote marks; you can use single or double; as long as the opening and closing quotes match.

Look at these examples. You can do this:

var a =   "Welcome to JavaScript"

and this

var b =   'Let\ ' s get busy '

But you can't do this

var a =   'Welcome to JavaScript"

And remember; the only way to include an apostrophe in a string is to escape it using the backslash. The same rule applies when you use double quote marks inside a string that is double-quoted.

If you want to join a pair of strings, otherwise known as concatenation, you use a + sign:

document.write(a + b);

This would produce "Welcome to JavaScript. Let's get busy".

Note we did not include any quotation marks around a+b because those quotes would make the letters into a string and that isn't what we want. Instead, we want a space added, so we would modify it to read a + " + b. A single-space string is appended, so the strings are split up.

Something which tends to cause a problem in other languages is very simple in JavaScript – bringing words and numbers together. All you need is to write something like:

document.write(a + ' ' + 3 + 2);

The browser would simply assume everything is a string and you would get a result of Welcome to JavaScript 32. If you wanted the numbers added, you would use parentheses to first perform the addition, and then the concatenation like this:

document.write(a + (3 + 2));

The result would be Welcome to JavaScript5. You can use any other arithmetic operations without needing the parentheses.

String Methods

If you wanted to find out what the length of a string was, use the length property. For example, a.length would result in 21, the number of characters in the string including spaces. This is common for all types of strings in JavaScript.

The toString method is used to convert numbers to strings:

*var c = 8/2 + (9*4) + 1;*

var d = c.toString();

The indexOf method is used to search a string for a specified character. This will find the index, which is the position the character holds in the string and then return it. Every character has an index beginning at 0. For example:

document.write(b.indexOf('y'));

A value of 13 is returned because this is the index accompanying the initial instance of 'y' in the variable b, recalling indexes start at 0. You can search for multiple characters, in the same way, finding the first instance of each one.

You can also look for the first instance of a specified character that comes after a certain index.

Finally, it is possible to find the first instance of a character after a certain index.

document.write(b.indexOf('s', 3));

If the letter isn't found in the parameters provided, a value of -1 is returned. This is useful later to check if a specific character appears in a string, using an if()statement.

Some more methods:

- string.**lastIndexOf**('x') - This provides the index of the final instance of the character on the string.
- string.**charAt**(0) – This provides the character at the given index.
- string.**substring**(0, 10) – This will create a new string using the original one; starts at the first and ends at the second number but not including it. If the second number is omitted, the string prints to the end.
- string.**substr**(4, 6) -This is like the substring but the second character indicates how many characters should be taken, rather than the ending index.
- string.**toLowerCase**() – This converts every character in the string to lowercase. toUppercase would do the opposite.

One of the most helpful methods is split(), allowing you to split a long string into several smaller strings. You need to state which character the string is split at using the parentheses for the parameter. A new array must be created for the parts of the string to go into:

var b =   'Let\ ' s get busy ' ;

var frags = new Array();

frags = b.split(' ');

b will be split into pieces at each of the spaces and you should get an array like this one:

frags[0] = "Let\ ' s";   frags[1] = "get";   frags[2] = "busy";

All the spaces are now gone.

Statements

A statement is a construct that makes up every script and there are two important ones in JavaScript, both control statements – *if()* and *for()* loop. These are very common, but you need to understand Boolean logic before we can move onto them:

Boolean Logic

We use Boolean logic to find out the answer to several conditional statements. Boolean values are true or false; they cannot be any other value. In computer programming, we usually compare two or more values to see if they are equal or not and which is bigger or smaller. For example, x == 1 would evaluate true if x were equal to 1; otherwise, it would evaluate false. We can also use > for greater than, < for less than, >== for greater than or equal to and <== for less than or equal to. There are also three evaluation operators in JavaScript:

- AND - && - This will evaluate true if all of the elements are true. For example,(x == 2 && y <= 18)
- OR - || - This will evaluate true if one or more of the elements are true. For example, (x == 4) || (y > 0)
- NOT - != - This evaluates true if the element is false. For example, (X != 0) && (y !=0) || !(x < 0)

Boolean variables can be declared, for example, var x = true. When you place an exclamation mark in front of a variable or an equal sign, you change the Boolean value. In that case !x is false.

if() Statement

We use the *if()* statement as a way to test for equality. Code will only be executed when or if a given condition is met. Provided the statement placed inside the parentheses is true, the code inside the curly brackets will be executed. If it is false, the code won't be executed.

Multiple evaluations may be tested at once and when you use the parentheses, specific parts of the code can be evaluated first. The equalities in the parentheses are always evaluated before anything else.

var x = 0;   var y = 2;   var z = 10;

if ((x != 0) || ((y >= 2) && !(z > 15)))

{

document.write("It is true.");

}

Look at this and decide – will the It Is True string be printed or not? Yes, it will.

We can take this further and use else to test for more conditions. If the first of the if statements evaluates false, the browser will go on and execute the code inside the else block:

```
if (x > 0) {

        do something

} else {

        do something else

}
```

Another if statement can be included inside the else, ensuring it is executed only if the initial statement evaluates false and the following statement is true. You can cover multiple conditions using else statements:

```
if (x <= 0) {

        do something

} else if (x == 2) {

        do something else

}
```

If the initial condition evaluates true, the else statements corresponding to it will not be executed regardless of whether they are true or not. And, as you can see, we can now skip an entire code block if, for example, x was 1.

And we can compare strings the same way – if (a == "Welcome to HTML"){}

for() Loop

When you use a *for()* loop, one code block can be executed a given number of times. For example, the next code will print "JavaScript" along with a rising number five times:

```
for (var i=0; i<5; i++) {

        document.write("JavaScript" + i);

}
```

First, we define the variable called i like 0. The loop is then saying that while i<5, the code block will be executed. Whenever the loop is run, i will be incremented by 1. After 5 iterations of the loop, it will stop. Each time, i is printed and it will increase by 1 each time, from 0 to 4.

A custom in computer programming is for the counter variable to be i. You cannot use the variable outside a loop otherwise problems will occur. And, if logic dictates, the variable can be decremented with i== until it reaches less than 0.

All the elements inside an array can be revised by setting the continue condition of i< =theArray.lenght-1. Using this, the array goes through one index at a time and the array may be populated with values, or an action may be performed on each index, for example. When the array is gone through, it will stop at the final index which is, if you remember, lower than 1.

Functions

A function is a method to set up to work for you. Whatever you want JavaScript to do, you can create a function for it. Functions are time-savers as the output will depend entirely on what the inputs are and you give the function those inputs. To that end, you can use one function to do several things.

Basic Function Structure

We learned about variables, event handlers, and statements and how they fit into scripting, so now it's time to bring it all together to create some functions. These are the real workhorses and a basic function will look something like this:

function addNumbers(a,b)

{

    var c = a+b;

    return c;

}

This function adds two numbers we provide and then returns the sum of those numbers. The first thing is to define a function and then name it. Inside the parentheses, we place the arguments for the function; in our case, those arguments are a and b. These variables are special; they can take any values you provide; this means any numbers and it will add them. The function can be called from any part of the web page and when it is called, any code inside the set of curly braces is executed and the arguments passed to it are substituted in.

Calling a Function

Functions will only operate when they are called, not like normal code lines that operate regardless. The function can be called during a standard embedded script, in this way:

document.write("Two plus Three is " + addNumbers(2,3));

This function call takes a2 and b3, adds them together, and the output is c. This output is returned to the page; the function call is replaced by the return value in the same way the name of a variable is replaced by the value. This function can also be used to add values to an event.

Functions can have one or more arguments -as many as needed- and those arguments may be strings or numbers. To add more, just increase the argument variable to the function definition, not forgetting to use commas to separate each argument. If a function is called with the incorrect number of arguments -more or less than the function is being defined to use- an error is thrown.

Functions can be defined without a return value or an argument:

function popup()

{

      alert('You clicked on this page');

}

These function types will always do the same whenever you use them.

Return

When a function returns, it will no longer execute even if there are other code lines inside the definition following the return statement. Strings and Boolean variables can also be returned. For example, when you validate a form, you can make sure it has been correctly completed with a function and will return either true or false to determine if the form should be submitted or not.

As well, a return can be used to stop a script before it runs. The Internet Explorer object that contains the page elements is called document.all and it is the proprietary DOM structure for Microsoft. If we were to write a script containing this IE DOM, we should confirm no other browser can execute the script code – if they did, all sorts of errors would be thrown. To do this, we need to test to see if there is support for document.all. If not, the script is ended and, if it is, the browser carries on until the real return value is reached:

if (!document.all) {

      return;

}

// Internet Explorer-specific DHTML starts here

We'll look at more support detection later on.

Fixing Errors

No doubt, while you have been going through the examples, you have come up against one or two JavaScript errors. They appear when you least expect them and even the programmers who have years of experience still get them. Most are relatively easy to find and there are customarily a few ways of solving whatever the problem is. We'll take a look at some of the more common errors you are likely to come across.

Errors in scripts tend to show up in the status bar. Provided your browser has been correctly configured, you may also have alerts pop up when an error happens; these alerts should tell you what the error is and where in your code it takes place.

JavaScript errors fall into two categories – syntax and runtime. Syntax errors are usually easy to pick up as they tend to appear when the page loads and they regularly end up being a spelling mistake or a variable you forgot to define. Use the error messages to find these and eliminate them. With a runtime error, you don't usually see these until the script is executed. They are tough to find because they may not always be apparent; testing may be needed to expose them.

Two things commonly cause errors:

- Using a text editor that automatically puts a margin to the side of your code. To work properly, JavaScript commands must be right at the very left of the code.
- A line break in the middle of the code. Command has to be on one line or an error will be thrown. Try using an Editor with word-wrapping ability; not only will you not have to scroll through code horizontally, but it will also add in virtual line breaks without severing the code.

To find a line with an error, count from the first line of the document down. A blank line is a line and must be included. Look at the example below, where line 6 has an error:

```
<html>
<head><title>Page 1</title></head>
<body>

<script type="text/javascript">
document.write("Welcome to my page"
);
</script>

</body></html>
```

Can you see what it is? The command ends on a different line than the one it started on. Once you locate the error, check for misspelled words, phantom line breaks, the function and variable names are capitalized correctly, variables are defined, proper quotes have been used, apostrophes in strings have been properly escaped, and so on.

If you get several errors at the same time, don't worry. More often than not, they are caused by the same one or two errors early in the script. Always start at the top and, once you find and fix an error, run the script again. Each time, the error count should drop until it's perfect.

Always build time in to find and correct errors. If a script doesn't work, it shouldn't be included on your web page. Put yourself in the shoes of your users; there is nothing worse than a buggy, error-ridden web page. They don't like it and you don't look very proficient, especially as most are simple to fix.

Objects and Properties

It's all great knowing how to do things, but we need something to do these things on. That's where the DOM comes in, so let's see how we can take control of the objects we use on our pages.

DOM Revisited

The DOM or Document Object Model is the way the objects on a page connect together to work. The DOM can be used to access the properties and the methods for each object and modify them.

Over the years, there have been several DOMs, starting with Level 0 in Netscape 2. Level 0 DOM is supported in all the browsers, and when it first came out it allowed us to access the form fields and objects on the page. Since then, it has been given an extensive scope and now contains other elements; it is the model used for writing JavaScript scripts.

As time went on, the war between browsers escalated. Netscape and Microsoft refused to collaborate on a standard model, and, as a result, we were given two new DOMs, both absolutely incompatible. This brought about a lot of confusion and the threat that it would be too difficult to get DHTML working across the browsers.

Lastly, and the most recent, there was DOM Level 1 after W3C made the model standard. The latest model is supported by all major and modern browsers, and while Netscape opted to drop their model in favor of working with the standardized one, Microsoft chose to maintain support for theirs so that scripts already written in it would continue to be functional.

The Object Hierarchy

Lesson over, let's move on. We already looked at how the document is held by the window and we already know the document contains each individual page element:

Window

    Document

    Image   Image

    Form

Field   Field

Submit Button

This gives you an idea of how the DOM works. In basic browsers, you would only be able to access the elements above, but with the latest browsers, you can access any HTML element. Where an object is nested, a dot is used to indicate this, for example, document.form.field or window.document.image.

Accessing Objects

Once the document loads properly, the browser will create arrays for the forms, images, links, anchors, and everything else. All the objects are sorted into type and placed into the arrays; they are indexed exactly as they were in the source code. For example, the first image on a page is referenced as document.images[0] and the fourth would be document.images[3].

You can also use the name attribute to give each element a textual reference. Let's say your source code has <img src="cat.gif" name="cat1">; access to this would be via document.images[:cat1"] making things a bit easier – just don't forget to add the quote marks around the name. In the more recent browsers, you can also forget the array notation, and refer to it as document.cat1 instead.

In the array called forms[], each entry will contain another array called elements[]. Each of the indexes is the buttons and the forms the page is made up from. So there is an additional level of nesting. Using our basic diagram above, if you wanted to gain access to the first field, you would use document.forms[0].elements[0], or you could use document.forms["form"].elements["field"] or you could even use document.form.field. All work the same and mean the same thing.

Maybe there is no need to say this, but pay attention to the order of the objects. Nesting must always go down the hierarchy, starting from the document and ending at the element you want.

Common Methods and Properties

We looked at a document object write() method; in fact, we've been using it all along. Every method name will allow the same convention with a set of parentheses containing parameters or arguments of the method. In the case of the write() method, it was given a string as a parameter and that string is what is printed on the page.

Two of the most common properties are the values for the form fields and src for the images. Getting or setting text strings inside a text input box requires referencing like this:

document.myform.myfield.**value**

Set it as equal to a string in quotes or to a variable, or you can print it. You should already know how to do that by now, so let's look at a partial example:

```
<form name="inputform">
<input type="text" value="First the value is this...">
<button onClick="document.inputform.elements[0].value='Then it is this!'; return false;">Click to change</button>
</form>
```

This creates a form with a box into which we can input text. And the all-important 'src' is a vital component behind the rollover effects – these are accessed as you would expect; using something along the lines of document.images[2].src.

Form Validation

One of the main reasons for JavaScript was to check if values that users entered into page forms were correct or not. This avoids the need to use a long-winded CGI program to do the checks for you. In this section, we'll look at the methods to validate the form input, by using an event handler called onSubmit.

Validating Form Input

When a form goes to a CGI program on the server, it is commonly programmed with its own error checks. If any are found, the page goes back to the user who enters the correct data before resubmitting the form. JavaScript checks are incredibly useful because they save users a lot of time by rejecting an incorrect form.

CGI scripts will always be more reliable because they work whether JavaScript has been enabled or not on the client-side, and this is a great safety net to have in place. Your page becomes easier and friendlier to navigate and the user no longer has to repeatedly submit a form. It is more precise since the exact form field where the problem lies is pointed out.

Implementing the Check

What we're going to do is use a function to check a form. This function is activated by the form event called to submit, which means we use an event handler called onSubmit. An attribute like the one below would be added on the form you want to be validated:

<form action="script.cgi" onSubmit="return checkform()">

checkForm is the name for the function we will create and we will get a Boolean value in return – a true or a false. The default action for the submit event is to submit data but, provided you give onSubmit a value of returning false, the data won't be submitted.

There is no definitive script because all forms are diverse; they are structured differently and they all have altered values. Nonetheless, we can give a basic script layout which you could change as per your form requirements. It would look like this:

function checkform()

{

    if (value of first field is or isn't this)

       {

```
        // something is wrong

        alert('There is a problem with the first field');

        return false;

    }

    else if (value of next field is or isn't this)

    {

        // something else is wrong

        alert('There is a problem with...');

        return false;

    }

    // If the script gets to this stage without any

    // problems, you can go ahead and submit the form


    return true;

}
```

If you have a complex form, the script will be longer, but the basics are the same for all instances – if and else statements are used to go through each form field to check that the inputs are not blank. The script moves to the next field when the current one has passed the tests.

If a field has a problem, the script returns false and stops; it won't go on to return true unless and until all fields are correct. Your error messages will need to be tailored to each field and could offer solutions to any common errors.

Accessing Values

By now you should know how to find the form element values by using the DOM. We'll use that notation to access the elements, rather than numbered indexes, leaving you free to navigate the fields on the page without rewriting the script every time. A simple form would look something like this:

<form name="feedback" action="script.cgi" method="post" onSubmit="return checkform()">

```
<input type="text" name="name">
<input type="text" name="email">
<textarea name="comments"></textarea>
</form>
```

It would be easier to validate this form than one that had, say, select boxes or radio buttons, but you can access any form element.

Below, we can see the ways the value could be retrieved from all different form element types and, in almost every case, the form is named feedback and the element is named field:

Text Boxes, <textarea>s and hiddens

These are the simplest elements to get into and the code is:

document.feedback.field.value

Normally you would be checking if this value is blank, for example:

if (document.feedback.field.value == '') {

return false;

}

That's how to check the equality of the value with a null string, or a set of single quotes with nothing in between.

Select Boxes

These are a little harder. In a drop-down box, each individual element has its own index inside the array. You find the element value from that index like this:

document.feedback.field.options

[document.feedback.field.selectedIndex].value

You can use JavaScript to change the given index; if you set it to the first option, this would be executed:

document.feedback.field.selectedIndex = 0;

Check Boxes

The checkbox is different from the other elements because its value is always on. You would need to check the Boolean checked value to see whether it is true or false:

if (!document.feedback.field.checked) {

> *// box is not checked*

> *return false;*

}

To check a box, do this:

document.feedback.field.checked = true;

Radio Buttons

Lastly, radio buttons. You'll be disappointed to discover there is no easy way to find out which radio button from a group of them is selected. You have to go through each element with the Boolean AND operators. In the example below, we check to see if none of the buttons have been selected:

if (!document.feedback.field[0].checked &&

!document.feedback.field[1].checked &&

!document.feedback.field[2].checked) {

> *// no radio button is selected*

> *return false;*

}

Radio buttons are checked the same way as to check boxes.

Advanced DOMs

We looked at the Level 0 DOM to have access to the properties and objects on a page but if you want your scripts to be properly dynamic, you need to have more than the form elements, links and images – you need access to every single page element. We're going to look at three advanced DOMs, which are all useful.

A New DOM

While the Level 0 DOM gets the job done, it has constraints; we can only access images, anchors, links, and form fields. Every browser that supports JavaScript will support this DOM, but if we want to access more, such as tables, specific paragraphs, or headings, it just won't do the job.

When DHTML (more about this later) appeared on the scene, we gained an instant requirement to access the style properties of all HTML elements on a page, regardless of what they were. Subsequently, both Microsoft and Netscape came up with their own DOMs, both of which work differently and neither has common support. We got the document.all model from Microsoft, which is not bad, and the document.layers model from Netscape, which is pretty complicated and was soon dropped when the Level 1 DOM came into play.

The Level 1 DOM

The Level 1 DOM is supported on all the major browsers and this is the one we will use for the foreseeable future. It isn't difficult to access elements in it, either. In fact, it is rather straightforward.

First, you use an attribute ID to provide the HTML element you want to access:

<p id="introduction">
<i>Once, many years ago...</i>
</p>

There is a restriction with the ID attribute because only one element on a page may have each of the specified values. The browser will always know which of the elements you refer to. If we used the above example, there could not be another element on that page with "Introduction" as the ID value.

Using the Level 1 DOM, we can pass the ID to the method called "get element by id" to access it:

document.getElementById('introduction')

See, it isn't difficult to get access to an element; we are using its id, which makes it stress-free.

document.all

The document.all DOM from Microsoft was designed for IE 4 and there were a lot of webmasters who wrote scripts specifically for this DOM. They didn't include any code that could be used by other DOMs, so developers for other browsers added the support instead. Later versions of IE still support it to provide backward compatibility.

The IE DOM is somewhat like the Level 1 DOM. We get access by using the id values with the only changes being the method keyword and brackets instead of parentheses.

document.all['introduction'].style.color = 'red';

There are several interesting methods in this DOM but much of it is undiscovered because there is little documentation. Then again, with Level 1 still being developed, much of that functionality will likely make its way into later levels.

document.layers

While this is a clumsily structured DOM with poor implementation and support, there are still project managers who insist on having compatibility for Netscape 4 in their websites, even today. Yes, we are likely to see this decrease over time and, eventually, it will only be mentioned in conversations about the 'bad old days'.

For the sake of comparison, you'll learn about it anyway. Netscape introduced a new element called <layer> which was designed to create 'layers' but this deprecated hastily. This effect was created using <div> and it must have been given a property called position style along with the id attribute.

To access a page element, you need to access the layer element that contains the element – nested documents. This extra layer is not required in other DOMs and makes things more complex.

Let's say we want access to a paragraph contained in a <div>. In turn, the <div> is contained in another <div> which has been given an absolute position on the page. Your HTML would look like:

<div id="header">

<div id="masthead"><p id="hello">Welcome</p></div>
</div>

In Netscape, the DOM call would be:

window.document.header.document.masthead.document.hello

Seriously. For each of the 'notational' layers, another document level is needed to access anything underneath it. It is an intricate method other browsers seem to manage oh, so easily.

Code Branching

With three separate scriptwriting methods, it's not surprising there's a problem with compatibility. Try making DOM call to a browser that isn't supported and all you get is errors. What we need is a way to check the browser to see what DOM it supports and then branch the code in three directions. We use an object detect for this, and, for proper compatibility, this has to be done for every advanced script.

First, we look to see if DHTML is supported and then the relevant code is passed to each of the browser types:

```
if (document.getElementById || document.all || document.layers) {

  if (document.getElementById) {

    // Level 1 DOM code

  }

  else if (document.all) {

    // Microsoft DOM code

  }

  else if (document.layers) {

    // Netscape DOM code

  }

}
```

To ensure your sanity stays intact, use a JavaScript library, like jQuery or prototype to reference the elements; just place the function inside an external script file included so every page can make use of it.

Support Detection

Before you can go ahead and execute most of your functions in JavaScript, see if a specific method or object has support in the user's browser. You could rush in with your brilliantly written advanced script and find most of your users have nothing but error messages to read. We can do support detection in two ways, one far better than the other.

Object Detection

No matter in what capacity you use JavaScript, it won't take you long to realize some features don't have support in certain browsers. That means your advanced scripts will die in older browser versions and even some of the modern ones. It probably seems logical to check which browser the users have by means of the navigator object and then base your script on that.

This way has many obstacles to be of any real use but it's where object detection comes in. All you need to do is write an *if()* statement that checks if a specified object, array, method, or property you require has support. If not, the advanced script is not given to the browser.

On another note, object detection was originally designed to use the script tag's attribute tag. When you have this:

<script language="JavaScript 1.2" type="text/JavaScript">

If a browser doesn't have support for the JavaScript 1.2 methods, the whole code block was supposed to have been bypassed. However, with the browser war between Netscape and Microsoft, this is a useless detection method; in a rush to provide support for things, neither browser gave a thought to supporting the same things. JavaScript 1.2, for example, does not refer to a specific standard. Either omit the language attribute or set it as "JavaScript".

This is how it should be done:

Let's assume we want to set up a script for an image-flip. If it is going to work properly, the document.images array needs to be included. This array is used to access each individual image on a page, so we first need to check if the array exists:

if (document.images) {

    // it exists, so the script can be continued using the array

}

If there is no browser support for the array, the code inside the *if()* statement will never be executed because the condition will always evaluate as false.

Checking a JavaScript method exists requires the name of it to be checked without using the parentheses. For example, before the browser focus is placed on a window, we would write:

if (window.focus) {

  // window.focus is supported

}

If the parentheses were included, you would not be checking for support; instead, you would be executing the command. Check first to see if the method has the support and THEN you can execute it:

if (window.focus) window.focus();

There is no need to check a method in advance of focus placed on a form field because these have support in all JavaScript-enabled browsers. The inconsistencies tend to arise at window-level.

Detecting DHTML Support

Later we'll look at DHTML, but for now, it's enough to know that since the version 4 browsers brought out their own DOMs, it is difficult to accomplish. You also have to contend with the Level 1 DOM, so for true compatibility, you would need to do a check on everything for DHTML support. Then, depending on what DOM is supported by the browser, your code would need to be branched.

First, we have the DHTML check to ensure at least one advanced model has support:

if (document.getElementById || document.all || document.layers)

{

    // browser can do DHTML

}

Note the use of the Boolean OR operator (||); this checks if there is support for at least one DOM. Now you can give the DHTML code; each of the DHTML scripts will need more of the *if()* statements before they can actually do anything to provide the right commands to browsers with different support. We mentioned this earlier under the code branching section.

Browser Detection

Shortly after the web started, browser detection was the thing and it was seen as an easy way to code one script that would work on every browser. Developers would go down the route of coding two versions of one page and sending users what they thought, and hoped it was the right one based on what the browser detect came up with. The script was and remains unreliable.

In most cases, the browser detects would work as expected. For example, a message might appear on the screen saying

You are using Internet Explorer 9 on Windows.

The actual result is based entirely on a browser identification string, which is a code the browser shows your webpage so it knows what browser and version it is. A browser identification string looks something like this:

navigator.userAgent= Mozilla/5.0 (Windows NT 10.0; Win64; x64) AppleWebKit/537.36 (KHTML, like Gecko) Chrome/72.0.3626.96 Safari/537.36

However, there are no guarantees because some of the smaller browsers provide information that isn't strictly true, identifying themselves as a much larger browser. They do this so scripts coded to only run on one of the big browsers will run on the smaller one.

All this does is makes the script wholly unreliable because you would have incompatible browsers trying to work a page that simply doesn't have a chance. Accordingly, it's clear browser detection is old hat and is only worsening over time, especially as new browsers are being released.

What does work every time is object detection, so that should always be the first port of call.

Popup Windows

One of the most popular ways to allow a user to see extra information without needing to leave the webpage is by opening a popup window. JavaScript allows you to specify the position, the dimensions, and which toolbars are visible for the popup window. You can also write your code straight into it, and get both windows working together.

Opening a New Window

With plain HTML, it is easy to open a new window; just use the target attribute on the links, like this:

<a href="example.html" target="_blank">link text</a>

This causes a new page to open in a popup window and this suits most people. However, to gain more control over the popup, you need a bit of JavaScript code. To get a basic popup window via a link, you would need this code and link:

var newwindow;

function poptastic(url)

{

    newwindow=window.open(url,'name','height=400,width=200');

    if (window.focus) {newwindow.focus()}

}

<a href="javascript:poptastic('poppedexample.html');">Pop it</a>

All we've done here is define a new function and this can be passed on to a different URL each time it is used. The URL will open in a popup window, smaller than the original with dimensions stated inside the function.

The link's HTML did nothing more than call the function; the URL for the page we want to open in a separate window is passed as an argument. It looks like:

<a href="javascript:poptastic('/examples/poppedexample.html');">Pop it</a>

The new window was created using the window.open() method and is loaded into a variable. The method will take three arguments – the page address, the window name, and a third argument which holds optional window attributes, such as the dimensions.

When we call the function, the URL is passed to it; that means the function may be used for all different popups, which is fine if you want the same dimension, position, etc. all the time. If you don't, you will need to modify the function each time so it takes more arguments. There are browsers that don't allow pages to be opened on different servers and this is for security purposes. For this reason, test your script. The name specified will be used to open more pages in the new popup window.

The Arguments

For the third argument, there are several options. When any are defined, all the remaining Boolean values, which may be set as:

- True or false
- Yes or no
- 1 or 0

are set as false, no, 0. Whatever you choose, every option will go into one quoted string, each value separated with a comma and no spaces.

- height – This is used to define the window height in pixels – don't use percentages, they won't work.
- width – This is used to define the window width, again in pixels.
- left – This is used to set the distance the window appears to be set from the left side of the screen in pixels. Supported on version 4 or higher browsers.
- top – This is used to push the window of the screen at the top.
- resizable – This is set as true or false and can give the user the option of resizing the window themselves.
- scrollbars – This is a Boolean value and is used for giving the window scrollbars. This should be set to yes if you have more content to display than fits the dimensions of the window.
- toolbar – This will specify whether the toolbar allows users to go back and forward a page should be displayed. Set to yes if your page has links.
- menubar – This specifies if the main window toolbar is shown.
- location – This is used to specify if the address bar is shown.
- status – This is used to specify if there will be a status bar on the window- set this as yes.
- directories – This is used to specify whether the directories or links toolbar is on display.
- fullscreen – This is a Boolean attribute for IE windows; it may allow the window to open in full screen, but as this is incredibly annoying; avoid using it.
- dependent – This is a Netscape 4 attribute that sets the popup window to be dependent on what the main window status is. For example, if you close the main window, the popup will close too.

- screen & screen – These are the old Netscape attributes used for defining the position of the window on the page (left and top should be used instead).

newwindow=window.open(url,'name','height=500,width=400,left=100,

top=100,resizable=yes,scrollbars=yes,toolbar=yes,status=yes');

Focus and Close

There are two important little tricks to ensure your popups are more usable. First, in the function we generated at the start of this section, the code below was executed when the window was created:

if (window.focus) {newwindow.focus()}

First, we want to know if the focus() method has support – this is essential because it stops JavaScript errors. If the focus() method is supported, the browser focus is set on the new window; as soon as it happens, the new window will appear at the front of the display. Browsers always put the focus on a new window when they are initially formed, but when another page is sent to the open window, it does not refocus on it. By leaving this method out, your new window could stay behind the main window and hidden from view, although that depends on what is happening at the same time.

It is good practice to add the option to close the window and it should always be on your popups. We write this from the main window:

<a href="javascript:if (newwindow) newwindow.close()">Close</a> the popup.

First, we check if the popup is open and this is done when the *if()* statement looks to see if there is a value on the variable. Then the close method is used.

From inside the popup, this would be the code:

<a href="javascript:window.close()">Close</a> this popup.

Linking to Windows

Once a window has popped up, other links can be directed into it and this is done with the target attribute. If, for example, the name was defined as 'popsome', the links could be made to open in the window like this:

<a href="page.html" target="popsome">Link</a>

If the popup was already shut down, the browser would then open a normal-sized window and call it as whatever the target value was specified.

Accessible Popups

So far, through all these examples, we used the javascript: link style This is one of the easiest ways to execute functions in Java, rather than using event handlers and linking to dummy anchors:

<a href="#" onClick="poptastic('page.html');">Pop it</a>

For the more modern browsers, we would write:

<a href="javascript:poptastic('page.html');">Pop it</a>

This is one of the best ways to show how popups work, but it isn't the best practice way of doing them. There are two reasons why you should NOT use the javascript: mechanism to create popups:

1. If a user is running a browser that has no support for JavaScript or has disabled it, they will not be able to follow the links and they will miss some valuable information showing up in the popup windows.
2. Most browsers allow a user to right-click on a link and open it in either a new tab or a new window. Without proper href values with these links, all they will do is open a blank window and there is nothing more irritating than this.

There is a better way to link to a popup window and this way lets the links work both ways. In an ideal world, the link would look like this:

<a href="page.html" onClick="poptastic(this.href); return false;">Pop it</a>

This creates a link that will open up in the popup as a standard page in a browser that has no JavaScript support. This is suppressed on modern browsers and the page will pop up exactly as you want it. The URL to be opened has been set as this.href and lets JavaScript know it needs to look at the current link's href value and use it. This means there is no need for the same URL to be written more than once.

Writing to the Window

There are distinct advantages to being able to generate a brand new page using the code for the page that already exists. For starters, you don't have to creatr new pages for each popup window, and the content in the popup is loaded as soon as the main page opens.

First we'll generate a page:

function dirtypop()

{

```
var generator=window.open('','name','height=400,width=500');


generator.document.write('<html><head><title>Popup</title>');

generator.document.write('<link rel="stylesheet" href="style.css">');

generator.document.write('</head><body>');

generator.document.write('<p>This page was generated by

  the main window.</p>');

generator.document.write('<p><a href="javascript:self.close()">

  Close</a> the popup.</p>');

generator.document.write('</body></html>');

generator.document.close();

}

<a href="javascript:dirtypop();">Generate!</a>
```

You can see that a new window has been created as a variable, the name of which is then used instead of window (this usually comes before document) in order to write into it. The document.close() method you see at the end is NOT the equivalent of window.close(). In our case, we use it to signify that we are no longer writing to the window. Be aware; if you have any style sheet info on the main window, it will not be carried forward onto the popup – for this, you need to add the style information into the code for the popup window.

There are a few problems when it comes to generating windows in this way. First, the page URL is down to the browser. Some developers leave it as 'blank' or 'undefined' and others will provide the main window URL, but this causes more problems. Looking at the window above, you can see a view URL link – use this to check what the browser thinks the URL is.

Luckily, while some browsers consider the popup to be part of the same page, using self.close() ensures that only the popup is closed, not the main window.

DHTML Explained

We've mentioned DHTML a few times now so we better look at it a bit closer. When the version 4 browsers came out, web design saw something of a revolution, albeit a small one. While they had poor support for the newer standards like CSS, they had their own great promise. DHTML became a new buzzword at the time and it stood, and still does stand, for Dynamic HTML. This was touted as a way to put an end to the static and somewhat boring websites of the day.

What is DHTML?

What exactly is DHTML? To be honest, many web designers don't know or only have a slight idea of what it means. This is one of the consequences of having no official definition or specifications. The explanation that is widely accepted is that it uses JavaScript to change the HTML style declarations.

When changes to element style declarations are executed, you will see the change immediately in your browser window. And the webpage doesn't even need refreshing. A user can interact with one page, show elements, hide them, move things about, change the color, just generally changing things and they would never need more files or new pages to be loaded.

Before DHTML, we only had the option of static HTML. When a page was loaded, apart from the occasional javascript rollover, the view appearance never changed until the next page was opened. Elements went on the page in a natural way, according to the order they take in the source HTML code. Because DHTML is dynamic, you can interrupt the flow, remove elements for the page, and have them show elsewhere just through user interaction. Clicking on a button or a link can open the way for all kinds of things to take place, and when you use absolute positioning, the order the elements are placed in the source script become irrelevant.

Why, if DHTML is so fantastic, does it get so little use in mainstream websites? Why does it get relegated to the personal sites that designers use to experiment? The answer lies in its past and it wasn't always squeaky clean. When it was announced with the version 4 browsers, there was quite a lot of commotion; people feared this would be the end of the web pages with images and text that were static.

The problems of DHTML as technology started was there was no support in the version 3 browsers and these still had a very large part of the market. This made it impractical to use on commercial sites and, on top of this, because neither Microsoft nor Netscape had the objective of working together on a standard DHTML method, a script that worked in one browser could not, therefore, work in the other.

The Netscape DHTML implementation was nothing compared to IE 4, but because it was released a little bit earlier and because the documentation was more complete, it was taken on as the DHTML standard. Still, it didn't take long for people to realize programming a brand new type of script was not easy and, added to the poor browser support, the word was out that DHTML was dead before it even had the chance to get going.

Some argued that DHTML needed time to grow, to prove itself. To be fair, DHTML is not classed as gracefully degrading technology, so it is important to ascertain if the majority of your audience can support it. That won't be much of an issue with the modern browsers, but you may still have users using the older versions.

Time to Get Dynamic

You must be wondering how all this style changing works. It is quite simple. Every element is provided with a new style property and this has all the possible CSS style declarations inside. These properties are simply assigned a new value. Let's say we have a <div> that has id="main" defined. This would have these stylings:

div#main {color: #000000; border-left: 1px solid red; }

If we want to change how this looks, we first would need to go through the DOM to access the element. Because different models are supported by different browsers, normally you would need to do a bit of code branching -in three ways- to ensure the DHTML works across all the browsers. We're using the Level 1 DOM here. Next, the style property is accessed, and then a new value is given to the property we want to be modified. Let's change the color of the text:

document.getElementById('main').style.color = '#ff0000';

When either an event handler or a function executes this code line, the text changes to red in that div wherever it appears on the page.

If we want to change a compound property value (a property with two words separated with a dash, such as border-left), the dash is removed and the first letter of the second word is capitalized.

document.getElementById('main').style.borderLeft = '2px dashed red';

If we want to change an element's position, we would need access to the left and to top, the positioning properties. If the div was defined like this:

div#nav {position: absolute; top: 20px; left: 120px; }

We could use this to change the position with

document.getElementById('nav').style.left = 300;

What we have done here is give the property a numerical value rather than the strings we've been using. When a number is used, the browser automatically assumes its pixels and this is what allows you to carry out computations on the value, such as adding 20 to the current value. We could also use element.style.left = '300px' to set the value.

Netscape 4 DHTML

Netscape 4.7 was a bit dodgy where DHTML was concerned. It offered no support for changing the color or font for text using DHTML. In fact, all it could be used for was changing the visibility and the left and top positioning of an element. The only way to change properties was to give the element a position style declaration.

Accessing the style declarations for an element was also a little bit different using this browser. This is why we're looking at it, even though it is massively out of date – there is always a chance you will come across this code style with older JavaScript code, so you should have some familiarity.

The style property has been left out, so to change the position of the dive with a 'main' ID, you would need this:

document.layers['main'].left = 200;

Scripting Frames

These are special cases in JavaScript and each scripting frame will behave exactly like the individual document it is. This means if you want to modify something in a different frame, then work with a frame tree to get control of the current frame.

Getting Set Up

By now you know a frame is a technique in HTML, one that lets you divide a page into several contained windows. Each of these windows has its own HTML file. All of the pages are shown together, but none of them share a connection, so if you execute a function in one window, it doesn't affect any other one. What you need to do is use a part of the DOM to gain control of each of the frames; this DOM section will assume the window level place.

First, all of your frames must have a name attribute. This, likely, is already installed in each one because it is vital for cross-frame linking but double-check to make sure. Something like this will do:

```
<frame src="navigation.html" name="nav">
<frame src="maincontent.html" name="content">
```

The Frame Tree

A frame tree is created when a frameset is loaded in the main window. The window, which is called top by JavaScript, has some frames beneath it and if these frames have to contain nested framesets, the tree gets another level.

Let's say you have a page with two frames on it:

nav   content

The frame tree would look like this:

         top

nav   content

Simple, yes? The object called top has two elements – the names of nav and content were the name values supplied to those elements. All you need to understand is the relative position of one frame to the others.

Traversing the Tree

To modify something in another frame, first, you must travel the tree from the current frame to the frame you want to modify. To do this, you need keywords.

Each frame has a parent frame, which is the frame above that one in the hierarchy. The frame at the very top is also a parent frame and to access it, or any other parent, all you do is type:

parent

Some of the frames also have children frames, which, as you would expect, are those frames beneath them. In the example above, the top has two children, one called nav and one called content. Gaining access to a child frame is a simple case of writing

Self.childName

Obviously replacing childName with the actual name.

Here's a more complex example:

one

nav   two

three

The tree would look like this:

top

nav   content

one   two   three

If we wanted to traverse from three to nav, we would do it like this:

parent.parent.nav

and from three to top:

self.content.three

The last way to address a frame is to start at the very top and drill down until you reach the desired frame. This is a good shortcut if you are a long way down a complex tree and you need to access a frame further up. All you do is start at the top and work down:

top.content.two

Let's look at a real example now that you know the syntax. Let's say we are in frame one. We need to get to nav to execute a function in it. The frame tree is traversed to the right place and the code is executed as if we were in the same document. You could consider the frames bit of the code below as being equivalent to the window. Using 6 as an arbitrary parameter, a function call could look like:

parent.parent.nav.functionName(6);

And you do much the same to gain access to variables and anything else

parent.parent.nav.document.var = "Hooray";

Cookies

You know what a cookie is, don't you? I'm not talking about the delicious chocolate chip kind, it's about tiny text files stored on your computer by your browser. These cookies contain information related to websites you visit and, with JavaScript, you can write to a cookie and then remove data whenever a user comes back to your website.

Why We Need Cookies

Cookies are a vital part of building webpages because the HTTP protocol that moves webpages around the internet is classed as state-less. This means no web server can remember details about users, and that makes all of us anonymous. If you go back to a website after you've already visited, you would be treated as though you were a new user.

That might be fine for some websites, but it's a pain when you go back to a website requiring a login – you'll have to do it every single time. The server won't remember you, or your login details, your settings; nothing! That is why cookies came about – to give web servers a bit of memory.

Cookie Structure

A cookie is nothing more than a text file, a simple one at that. You can find them in your browser cache, or in a folder on your computer called Temporary Internet Files. Each cookie will have at least one entry and each of those entries consists of:

- Name-Value pair – this stores the data you specify you want to be saved
- Expiry date – the entry will expire and be deleted after this date
- Web domain and path – the webpage information associated with the entry

JavaScript can be used to read and/or write new entries into an existing cookie file. When you create a new entry, it is called "writing a cookie", but this is somewhat misleading. A cookie is a text file which stores the entries and it is the entry that has the data in it. Every web domain name can have a cookie file associated with it and every cookie can hold several entries.

When a file is requested from a server you previously used, the data inside the relevant cookie is sent on to the webserver along with the request. By doing this, any server-side requests like those written in PHP or Perl will be able to read the cookie and work out if permission should be granted to access the web page.

Of course, it's no secret cookies can and have been used for malicious purposes in the past and still are, and normally by advertising companies tracking your online behavior.

These days, the modern browsers have decent measures built-in to block cookies from websites – that leaves it down to a website user what information they disclose and to what websites.

Going back to what is in an entry; name-value pair is like a variable declaration. When you need information, you put in a request for a value associated with a specified name.

The Expiry date isn't very friendly as the format used to express it is UTC. That said, a suitable date can be generated through various methods. If the Expiry date is not set, when the browser is closed the cookie is deleted. Lastly, the domain and path must be part of the domain your website belongs to. For example, if you had a website called SimpleSimon.com, you could set the cookie as active on www.simpleSimon.com or on SimpleSimon.com – this covers all of the subdomains you might have set up. What you could not do is set the cookies as active on www.google.com as this would not be legal. With the path, cookies can be restricted so they are valid only for specific directories. Normally, you would want it set to be available on all pages in your domain so this is generally set as /, which is the root directory.

Setting, Reading and Erasing Cookies

The document contains a JavaScript object called document.cookie and this is what we use to read cookie data and retrieve it. It is a repository that contains strings, although you mustn't confuse it with being an array because it isn't. New entries can easily be created, you can read a name-value pair that already exists or you can delete or erase an entry, all through JavaScript. Creating a cookie would look something like this:

document.cookie =

   "testvalue1=Yes; expires=Wed, 03 Apr 2019 05:28:21 UTC; path=/";

The entire entry is one single string, in quotes, and with semicolons used to segment it. First comes the name-pair value, followed by expiry date in the right format, and then the path and domain information. This is a fixed syntax so don't go messing around with it – the order it is in is the order it needs to be in.

If you wanted to test the contents of a cookie, you would write a short script like this:

alert(document.cookie);

Let's add another entry, this time with a different name, like this:

document.cookie =

   "testvalue2=Nah; expires=Wed, 03 Apr 201905:28:21 UTC; path=/";

If you were to check the contents of the cookie now, you would note the first value is still there, and only because we used a different name. Had we used the same name, it would have overwritten the initial value rather than adding another entry.

Erasing cookies is simple; set a new value and change the expiry date to one before today, like this:

document.cookie =

  "testvalue2=Whatever; expires=Wed, 27 Feb 2019 05:28:21 UTC; path=/";

You could also supply an expiry date of -1 to the entry and it would be removed with immediate effect.

Convenient Scripts

Let's look at some cookies using some very convenient scripts. These will make the process relatively painless, especially when it comes to reading a cookie's values, which is the easiest. Let' see the functions:

function createCookie(name, value, days)

{

  if (days) {

   var date = new Date();

   date.setTime(date.getTime()+(days*24*60*60*1000));

   var expires = "; expires="+date.toGMTString();

   }

  else var expires = "";

  document.cookie = name+"="+value+expires+"; path=/";

}

function readCookie(name)

{

  var ca = document.cookie.split(';');

  var nameEQ = name + "=";

```
for(var i=0; i < ca.length; i++) {

    var c = ca[i];

    while (c.charAt(0)==' ') c = c.substring(1, c.length); //delete spaces

    if (c.indexOf(nameEQ) == 0) return c.substring(nameEQ.length, c.length);

    }

    return null;

}


function eraseCookie(name)

{

    createCookie(name, "", -1);

}
```

These are nice scripts with good clean code and they don't need much by way of an explanation – not by now, anyway. We used a function to create a cookie and this function takes three arguments – the name-pair value, expiry date, and for how long in days the cookie should be retained. This final argument is turned into a date – the value in hours is added to the current time before it is annexed into the code line where the cookie is actually created.

The second one, reading the cookie, is a difficult function. First, the cookie string is split at every single occurrence of the semicolon used to separate the segments. This creates a new array and each of the indexes in the array has an entry pair. A loop is used to go through these to find the 'name=' string and when this is found, everything else that makes up the index is read. This will be the value of the name passed to the function earlier.

The last one is easy – just recreate the cookie and set with an expiry date of -1.

Part 6: UX

UX, or User Experience, is a fundamental component of any website, especially one that has to meet an ever-growing and ever-changing demand from users. We take it for granted that a website will do what we want and offer the best experience possible, but have you ever stopped to wonder what it's all about? As a web developer and designer, it is important to understand everything about the UX design process – the what, the when, and the how.

Why is UX Design So Important?

UX design has one major objective – to create an enjoyable, seamless, frictionless experience for the web user. A good UX designer will increase customer satisfaction by providing a website that is easy to use, trouble-free to access and navigate, and provide an experience they will enjoy. User expectations and demands are on the rise, which means UX designers must be on the ball and have an eye for detail to take them through a web interface while developers must have what it takes to create the very best in features and functionality.

An example: a single second in delay from a page response is the equivalent of a 16% drop in customer satisfaction. One single second; that's all it takes. The headline on the article or the website is responsible for more than 80% of all conversions. Get it wrong and your website is a loser straight away.

UX design is without a doubt, vital for a great website, but still few users understand it. Sure, we've all had a bad experience on a website, so we know what it feels like, but do we really put any thought into why we had such a poor experience?

The term, UX design, refers to the methods and approaches that ensure a website is customized to its target audience. If it doesn't appeal, a website is soon forgotten. Every website must be:

- Easily navigated
- Easy to use
- Have some unique advantage or benefit

Without these and some decent selling point, it doesn't take long for a website to fail.

UX designers are the people who invent the ideas about how to make the website more usable and put those ideas into practice. It is up to them to ensure all the content is relevant, up-to-date and valuable – if not, users don't have a reason to visit.

From the perspective of a designer, UX is more important than aesthetics. You may have a fantastic looking website, but what good is it if your users can't find their way around it?

UX is even more important for the more in-depth websites because the users need to navigate their way around quickly. The last thing they want to see is a chaotic, untidy website that makes no sense and is unnavigable.

Take the eCommerce websites for example. Not only do they look inviting and are easy to navigate, but they also provide potential customers with an easy way to make and complete a purchase as quickly as possible.

UX In The Design Process

The biggest question is, how do you even start to construct the best UX approach to your own online platform? Consider this – what do you want your visitors to think, how do you want them to feel when they land on your website? Think about each separate component of your website and all the content on it.

Once you have figured out the emotion that each component will provoke, then you can test how effective they are. It is also important to consider whether the right emotion was provoked, whether it was strong, what benefits it provided, and whether that experience could be used universally.

What UX Isn't and What it Cannot Do

Not all UX approaches are right for every type of customer. We're all different, we all react to things differently, and while one design element may work for one group of people, it won't work for another. That means don't force an approach that may not be suitable onto an unwilling audience, focus instead on creating for specific encounters and encouraging specific types of action.

You also cannot recreate a UX approach that worked wonderfully on another website because every website offers a unique user experience. If you cannot cater to your own benefits, skills, products and so on, you cannot reasonably expect new visitors to stay.

Equally, it is not possible to work out what value a website has used. You can look at the analytics and data, such as page visits, bounce rates, and conversion stats. You can generate estimates and ask your users for help, but there is, right now, no one tool to process user encounters directly.

UX and usability have become entwined over the years, but they are not the same thing. UX-based approaches are meant to consider a user's feelings, like how they feel about a resource or a service, whereas usability is about how quickly they learn to use your website.

If you want the very best UX you can possibly provide, then understand your user's desires and how you can fulfill them with the least amount of effort. Simple yet sophisticated is the real key.

UX Skills

UX design is more in demand now than ever before and it is a must for all UX designers to develop a diverse range of skills, and there are 10 that are absolutely essential.

If you are genuinely interested in UX design, you don't want to be a jack-of-all-trades. You can't just learn one; there are several UK skills you need to learn if you want to experience real success. If you have no clue what you need to know and what skills you need, cast your eye over these; the 10 must-haves all UX designers need:

UX Research

One of the most important things you need is to step up the game in terms of UX research. Mobile apps and websites require a lot of creativity and the decisions taken by UX designers are not fabricated. UX designers spend a great deal of time thinking, studying, and researching to get things absolutely spot on.

Collaboration

There's an old saying, "no man is an island" and that goes for UX designers too. If you don't know how to design, code, manage your projects, or understand what goes into products and marketing them, you need to collaborate to help you reach that pinnacle of success. The research will take you some way down the road but teamwork is where it's at; this is your opportunity to work in other areas, to put what you learn into practice alongside folks with different skills that perfectly complement yours.

Wireframing and UI Prototyping

If you want people to take you seriously as a UX designer, wireframing and prototyping are two imperative skills to learn. Prototyping is one of the best ways to learn and understand what the key functions of your design are before it goes to the developers to be built. Prototyping tools are in abundance and you should make good use of them.

UX Writing

Whoever thought writing was not involved has clearly never got into UX design properly. Coding is a great skill you should never dismiss, but writing is a real talent, one that takes less time to build up and create some fantastic experiences for the user. Pick up your tablet or your phone, examine one of the apps. Look at any website. What do you see? That's right, plenty of words, perfectly crafted to provide users with everything they need. And all that has been written by someone. You probably never noticed it before and that's the result of some excellent UX writing – it shouldn't be noticeable. Some of the best examples can be found with Apple, Dropbox, and MailChimp.

Visual Communication

If you don't understand visual communication, you will not get far with UX design. Visual communication is the heart of it, and all humans are, at the end of the day, visual animals. Brush up on your skills to create the best assets, presentations, icons, and prototypes that are fully interactive and use mockups.

User Empathy

Can you put yourself in the shoes of your users? If affirmative, then you are on the road to understanding what they want and what they don't want. When you appreciate that, you are opening the way to being equipped to find a solution that works. Empathy is one of the most important skills in UX design; if you detach yourself from your users, you cannot possibly design for their needs and their feelings. Without understanding your audience, all you do is create the worst possible experience for them. At the end of the day, your users are the most significant people in your life – pander to their every need.

Interaction Design

You can draw up a fantastic design that looks great, but do you know how your users are going to interact with it? There is a lot of crossover between interaction design and UX; the former is focused on the way users interact with products and services, and this is why using interactive wireframes is a great way to iterate interactions. There are plenty of UX courses to help you and guide you in the right direction.

Coding

Most UX designers can do more than one thing, and these days, we live in a world where tech designers are becoming few and far between. Is a designer-developer the answer? Coding plays a huge part and, according to a report issued recently, at least one-third of current designers also had full training as engineers, so the lines between designers and developers are fast becoming blurry. It's never a bad idea to keep your coding skills up to date!

Analytics

You don't just create a website or an app, shove it out there for the world to see, and leave it. You want to test it, you want to know if your hard work is paying off and whether your design is working. That's where analytics comes in and that means you need to have some understanding of numbers, ratios, and percentages. Lots of UX designers have a morbid fear of numbers, but those numbers could be the biggest help you will ever have. Use the analytical information to help you in your design.

Communication Skills

To sum up, while the core design and research skills are essential, so too are the business skills of time management and project management. Nevertheless, the one thing that can help any UX designer stand out from the crowd is communication skills. Think about public speakers and those who do public presentations. Being able to put your message across to your audience confidently and at the right time is invaluable as long as you use the feedback in a positive way.

UX is a difficult part of web development, and more often than not, it is a job that is 'farmed' out to specialized designers. There's nothing wrong with having a go, and provided you have these skills under your belt, you are on the veracious road.

Conclusion

Thank you once again for downloading my guide. I hope now you have a better understanding of the JavaScript language and what you can do with it. It is one of the easiest and most versatile of the programming languages and is a fundamental requirement if you want to be involved in web design and development.

We explained what JavaScript was and how to write it, covered functions, objects, statements, and much more. Then we moved to jQuery, again learning what it can do and how to use it, as well as how it works with AJAX.

We discussed how to build a website using jQuery and AJAX, a responsive one at that, working easily on mobile and desktop displays before looking at how JavaScript is used for scripting. Last, very briefly, we looked at a few ways you can use JavaScript to improve UX or user experience on a web app.

From here, you can take your learning further. There are plenty of advanced tutorials on the internet, courses you can take and books you can read. Take your time to learn JavaScript. It is an important language for those who want to get into web development and you need to know it inside out.

Thanks again; please consider leaving a review for me at Amazon if you enjoyed this book.

References

https://developer.mozilla.org

https://medium.com

https://thenewstack.io

https://hashnode.com/

https://fullstackengine.net

https://levelup.gitconnected.com

https://snipcart.com/

https://www.w3schools.com

https://css-tricks.com

https://www.bitdegree.org/

https://www.learningjquery.com

https://blog.cloudboost.io

https://hackr.io

https://learn.jquery.com/

https://www.thinkful.com

https://webdesign.tutsplus.com

https://www.tutorialrepublic.com

https://www.codementor.io

https://blog.teamtreehouse.com

https://dzone.com

https://www.tecmint.com

https://www.yourhtmlsource.com

https://www.justinmind.com

https://www.designyourway.net

www.ingramcontent.com/pod-product-compliance
Lightning Source LLC
LaVergne TN
LVHW082125070326
832902LV00041B/3039